The Democracy of Objects

New Metaphysics

Series Editors: Graham Harman and Bruno Latour

The world is due for a resurgence of original speculative metaphysics. The New Metaphysics series aims to provide a safe house for such thinking amidst the demoralizing caution and prudence of professional academic philosophy. We do not aim to bridge the analytic-continental divide, since we are equally impatient with nail-filing analytic critique and the continental reverence for dusty textual monuments. We favor instead the spirit of the intellectual gambler, and wish to discover and promote authors who meet this description. Like an emergent recording company, what we seek are traces of a new metaphysical 'sound' from any nation of the world. The editors are open to translations of neglected metaphysical classics, and will consider secondary works of especial force and daring. But our main interest is to stimulate the birth of disturbing masterpieces of twenty-first century philosophy.

Levi R. Bryant
The Democracy of Objects

OPEN HUMANITIES PRESS

An imprint of MPublishing – University of Michigan Library, Ann Arbor, 2011

First edition published by Open Humanities Press 2011
Freely available online at http://hdl.handle.net/2027/spo.9750134.0001.001

Design by Katherine Gillieson
Cover Illustration by Tammy Lu

All figures are in the public domain.

ISBN-10 1-60785-204-7
ISBN-13 978-1-60785-204-9

Open Humanities Press is an international, scholar-led open access publishing collective
whose mission is to make leading works of contemporary critical thought freely available
worldwide. Books published under the Open Humanities Press imprint at MPublishing are
produced through a unique partnership between OHP's editorial board and the University
of Michigan Library, which provides a library-based managing and production support
infrastructure to facilitate scholars to publish leading research in book form.

MPublishing
www.publishing.umich.edu

◯
OPEN HUMANITIES PRESS
www.openhumanitiespress.org

Contents

For my daughter Elizabeth,

so that you might always

remain curious and

remember that it is not

all about us.

Acknowledgements

Can I claim authorship of the book that follows? In the typical and
frustrating manner of a philosopher—if such I am—I can only answer
that this depends on what authorship is. Certainly, I spent months typing
words and editing various drafts of *The Democracy of Objects*. Yet if there
is some truth to the ontology that I here develop, then every object is
also a crowd of objects. Moreover, the circumstances under which this
book came to be written, coupled with the *way* in which this book was
written, render this point especially true. This book was already on its
way to coming into being before I even conceived of it as a result of my
encounter with the literary and media theorist Melanie Doherty. I met
Doherty around eight years ago under unusual circumstances when I was
at the height of my Lacanian period, singing endless odes to the signifier
and fully enmeshed within the linguistic and rhetorical turn. A deep
and productive friendship ensued that continues to this day. Doherty
continuously challenged my focus on the signifier and the semiotic,
conceding that these things play a role, but also drawing my attention to
the role the non-semiotic and material plays in the formation of social
relations. Like the reincarnation of Alice that she is, she sent me down the
rabbit hole of thinkers such as Latour, Ong, Kittler, Haraway, McLuhan,
Marx, and a host of others, while also underscoring the singularity of
mathematics, science, neurology, and biology. While I remain a resolute
Lacanian—how couldn't I, having suffered through all the seminars,
having gone through analysis, and having practiced for a time myself?—I

gradually found that I could no longer maintain my Lacanianism in the form I had initially articulated it, and had to set forth to develop a new ontology (for me), capable of taking into account the points that Doherty was making. I had to find a way to silence her endless protestations of "but! but! but!", but have since found that she is an equal opportunity critical thinker who finds opportunities to ask "but!" in response to my newly developed ontology. Badiou speaks of events and the truth-procedures that follow from them, while Deleuze speaks of encounters and the invention they invoke. Doherty has been an event, encounter, truth-procedure, and source of endless invention in my thought. She deserves as much credit for the authorship of this book as I do. I ardently hope she begins to write soon so that I might have the opportunity to protest "but!" in relation to her thought.

Then there was my encounter with Graham Harman nearly three years ago. I first approached Harman to be a third editor for *The Speculative Turn* as a consequence of the diligent help he provided in pulling the collection together and putting Nick Srnicek and me in contact with various presses. At the time I knew very little about Harman's ontology, having read scant little of his work (he did earn his Ph.D., after all, from a rival school!), and finding him generally rather suspect; no doubt as a result of projective identification. Over the next couple of weeks, a very friendly yet intense email discussion erupted between the two of us, with me arguing from a Deleuzian relational-monist perspective and Harman arguing from the standpoint of his object-oriented philosophy, defending both the existence of substances and their autonomy from relations. I came out of the tail end of that debate transformed, finding that I needed to rework the entirety of my thought within a framework that made room for substances independent of relations. Every page of the book that follows is inspired by Harman's work, such that it is impossible to cite all the ways in which he has influenced my thinking.

A number of the concepts and lines of argument developed in the *The Democracy of Objects* were initially developed on my blog *Larval Subjects* and I owe a deep debt of gratitude to those who amused themselves by participating in those discussions. Adrian Ivakhiv, whose own ontological instincts and ecological sympathies are so close to my own, yet simultaneously so alien, constantly challenged me from a process-relational perspective, driving me to better hone my arguments and concepts. The same is true of Christopher Vitale's engagement, which forced me to better articulate my claims. Ian Bogost's unit-operational ontology has been a deep influence in my thought as well. Joseph C. Goodson has often understood object-oriented ontology better than myself and has constantly given me insights into this burgeoning ontology that I hadn't yet seen. Adam Kotsko, Craig McFarlane, and Anthony Paul Smith have all provided helpful, if sometimes painful, criticism that has motivated my thought to evolve. Paul Bains, for over a decade, has drawn my attention to traditions and thinkers in the history of philosophy, introducing me, in particular, to autopoietic theory and Peircian semiotics. Alex Reid and Nathan Gale have provided me with endless inspiration from the domain of rhetoric and composition studies. Moreover, Michael, from *Archive Fire*, has kept me honest from the domain of ethnography. Steven Shaviro has been a constant source of illumination for me and has challenged my own thought in his debates over relations and events with Graham Harman. I aspire to be as magnanimous as he some day. Jeremy Trombley has provided similar inspiration from the direction of ethnography. Similarly, the loquacious Pete Wolfendale has forced me to refine arguments and concepts within a framework that is alien to me, hopefully rendering my claims sharper than they would have otherwise been. Finally, I would be remiss were I not to mention the profound inspiration I've drawn from the devilish novelist Frances Madeson and the sublime poet Jacob Russell. Perhaps some day I'll rise to the levels of their art, but for the moment I plod along in the world of the concept. Would this book be what it is—however short it may fall of rising to the contributions of time and thought they've put into discussion—had I not encountered these voices? Given the fact that this object was composed in this milieu, it is difficult for me to see how they are not also authors, with me functioning as a sort of stenographer.

Jon Cogburn, Timothy Morton, and Michael Flower provided invaluable editorial and philosophical critiques of earlier versions of this book. Not only did Michael Flower engage in the monotonous task of editing this text, but he also created the majority of the diagrams. Jon Cogburn, a friend from nearly two decades ago but whom I've only recently had the privilege of getting to know again, provided cogent critique and editorial comments from a philosophical orientation very foreign to my own background. I am tremendously fortunate to have his friendship and eagerly look forward to developments in his own thought in the years to come. I have only had the pleasure of knowing Timothy Morton's friendship this year, but despite the short time of our encounter, he generously provided extremely helpful editorial advice and has been a deep influence on the concepts developed in the text that follows. Carlton Clark and Timothy Richardson both endured long and disjointed conversations with me revolving around the main claims of this book, providing excellent suggestions to improve my arguments and conversations. April Jacobs also provided helpful editorial advice.

Andrew Cutrofello, who supervised my dissertation which later became *Difference and Givenness*, taught me how to read philosophy creatively so as to produce new philosophy out of the material of the history of philosophy. He also instilled me with a spirit of rigor and careful argumentation. His influence and the lessons he imparted to me continue throughout the pages of this book. Finally, I would like to thank my partner Angela and my daughter, both of whom were patient with me as I wrote this book, and supportive of the project.

Books are born out of a crowd of voices, taking on a unity where the traces of these voices often disappear. I am both humbled and tremendously grateful for all those voices that assisted me in the composition of this text.

Introduction
Towards a Finally Subjectless Object

> ...[T]he effect of the empirical method in metaphysics is
> seriously and persistently to treat finite minds as one among
> many forms of finite existence, having no privilege above
> them except such as it derives from its greater perfection
> and development. Should inquiry prove that the cognitive
> relation is unique, improbable as such a result might seem,
> it would have to be accepted faithfully and harmonised
> with the remainder of the scheme. But prima facie there
> is no warrant for the assumption, still less for the dogma
> that, because all experience implies a mind, that which
> is experienced owes its being and its qualities to mind.
> Minds are but the most gifted members known to us in
> a democracy of things. In respect of being or reality all
> existences are on an equal footing. They vary in eminence;
> as in a democracy, where talent has an open career, the most
> gifted rise to influence and authority.
>
> — Samuel Alexander[1]

Ordinarily, upon hearing the word "object", the first thing we think is
"subject". Our second thought, perhaps, is that objects are fixed, stable and
unchanging, and therefore to be contrasted with events and processes. The

object, we are told, is that which is opposed to a subject, and the question of the relation between the subject and the object is a question of how the subject is to relate to or *represent* the object. As such, the question of the object becomes a question of whether or not we adequately represent the object. Do we, the question runs, touch the object in its *reality* in our representations, or, rather, do our representations always "distort" the object such that there is no warrant in the claim that our representations actually represent a reality that is out there. It would thus seem that the moment we pose the question of objects we are no longer occupied with the question of objects, but rather with the question of the relationship between the subject and the object. And, of course, all sorts of insurmountable problems here emerge because we are after all—or allegedly—subjects, and, as subjects, cannot get outside of our own minds to determine whether our representations map on to any sort of external reality.

The basic schema both of anti-realisms and of what I will call epistemological realisms (for reasons that will become apparent in a moment) is that of a division between the world of nature and the world of the subject and culture. The debate then becomes one over the status of representation.

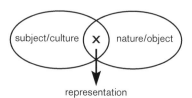

Within the schema of representation, object is treated as a pole opposed to subject. The entire debate between realism and anti-realism arises as a result of how these two circles overlap. While the overlap between these two domains seems to establish or guarantee their relation, this overlap also contains something of an antinomy or fundamental ambiguity. Because the representation lies in the intersection between the two domains, there's a deep ambiguity as to whether or not representation actually hooks on to the world as it really is. Epistemological realists seek a correspondence or adequation between subject and object, representations and states-of-affairs. They wish to distinguish between true representations and mere imaginings, arguing that true representations mirror the world as is, reflecting a world as it is regardless of whether any represents it. In short, epistemological realists argue that true representations represent a world that is in no way dependent on being represented by the subject or culture to exist as it does. Often epistemological realisms are closely connected with a project of Enlightenment critique, seeking to abolish superstition and obscurantism by discovering the true nature of the world and giving us the resources for distinguishing what is epistemologically justified and what is not.

Anti-realisms, by contrast, note that our relationship to the world still falls within the domain belonging to the subject, mind, and culture:

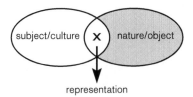

representation

Here the darkened space within the right-hand circle indicates that the domain of nature and the object has been foreclosed, that it's been blocked out, and that we are to restrict inquiry to what is given in the subject and culture circle. While the anti-realist generally does not deny that a world independent of subject, mind, and culture exists—i.e., he's not a Berkeleyian subjective idealist or a Hegelian absolute idealist—the anti-realist nonetheless argues that because representation falls entirely within the domain of the subject and culture we are unable to determine whether representations are merely our constructions, such that they do not reflect reality as it is at all, or whether these representations are true representations of reality as it is and would be regardless of whether it were represented. However, while the anti-realist argument generally bases itself on the indeterminability of whether representation is construction or a true representation of reality, it often slips into the thesis that representation *is* a construction and that reality is very likely entirely different from how we represent it. For the anti-realist, truth thus becomes inter-subjective agreement, consensus, or shared representation, rather than a correspondence between representation and reality. Indeed, the very concept of reality is transformed into reality *for-us* or the manner in which we experience and represent the world. Like epistemological realisms, anti-realisms are often closely connected to a project of critique. In this regard, they might seek to demonstrate the limits of what we can know, or alternatively they might attempt to show how "pictures" of the world are socially constructed such that they vary according to history, culture, language, or economic class. In this way, the anti-realist is able to debunk universalist pretensions behind many "world-pictures" that function to guarantee privilege.

As a consequence of the two world schema, the question of the object, of what substances *are*, is subtly transformed into the question of how and whether we *know* objects. The question of objects becomes the question of a particular relation between humans and objects. This, in turn, becomes a question of whether or not our representations map onto reality. Such a question, revolving around epistemology, has been the obsession of philosophy since at least Descartes. Where prior philosophy engaged in vigorous debates as to the true nature of substance, with or around Descartes the primary question of philosophy became that of how subjects relate to or represent objects. Nor were the stakes of these debates about knowledge small. At issue was not the arid question of when and how we know, but rather the *legitimacy* of knowledge as a foundation for *power*. If questions of knowledge became so heated during the Renaissance and Enlightenment period in Western philosophy, then this is because Europe was simultaneously witnessing the birth of capitalism, the erosion of traditional authority in the form of monarchies and the Church, the Reformation, the rise of democracy, and the rise of the new sciences. Questions of knowledge were *political* questions, simultaneously targeting arguments from authority that served as a support or foundation for the monarchies and the Church—the two of which were deeply intertwined –and laying the groundwork for participatory democracy through a demonstration that all humans have the capacity to know (Descartes and perhaps Locke) or that knowledge is not possible at all, but consists of merely sentiment, custom, or opinion (Hume).

In any event, the two options that opened Modernity—Descartes and Hume—led to much the same consequences at the level of the political: that individual humans are entitled to define their own form of life and participate in the formation of the State because either a) all humans are capable of knowing and therefore are not in need of special authorities or revelation to govern them, or b) that because absolute knowledge is unobtainable for humans, any authority claiming to ground his or her authority on the basis of knowledge is an illegitimate huckster bent on controlling and manipulating the populace. In short, behind this debate was the issue of egalitarianism or the right of all persons to participate in governance. In one form or another this debate and these two options continue down to our own time and are every bit as heated and political as when the shift to epistemology first arose. On the one hand we have the pro-science crowd that vigorously argues that science gives us *the* true representation of reality. It is not difficult to detect, lurking in the background, a protracted battle against the role that superstition and religion play in the political sphere. Society, at all costs, must be protected from the superstitious and religious irrationalities that threaten to plunge us back into the Dark Ages. Here *The God Delusion* by Richard Dawkins comes to mind.[2] On the other hand, there are the social constructivists and anti-realists vigorously arguing that our conceptions of society, the human, race, gender, and even reality are constructed. Their worry seems to be that any positive claim to knowledge risks becoming an exclusionary and oppressive force of domination, and they arrive at this conclusion not without good reason or historical precedent.

As always, the battles that swirl around epistemology are ultimately questions of ethics and politics. As Bacon noted, knowledge is power. And knowledge is not simply power in the sense that it allows us to control or master the world around us, but rather knowledge is also power in the sense that it determines who is authorized to speak, who is authorized to govern, and is the power to determine what place persons and other entities should, by right, occupy within the social order. No, questions of knowledge are not innocent questions. Rather, they are questions intimately related to life, governance, and freedom. A person's epistemology very much reflects their idea of what the social order ought to be, even if this is not immediately apparent in the arid speculations of epistemology.

Yet in all of the heated debates surrounding epistemology that have cast nearly every discipline in turmoil, we nonetheless seem to miss the point that the question of the object is not an epistemological question, not a question of how we *know* the object, but a question of what objects *are*. The *being* of objects is an issue distinct from the question of our *knowledge* of objects. Here, of course, it seems obvious that in order to discuss the being of objects we must first *know* objects. And if this is the case, it follows as a matter of course that epistemology or questions of knowledge must precede ontology. However, I hope to show in what follows that questions of ontology are both irreducible to questions of epistemology and that questions of ontology must precede questions of epistemology or questions of our *access* to objects. What an object *is* cannot be reduced to our *access* to objects. And as we will see in what follows, that access is highly limited. Nonetheless, while our access to objects is highly limited, we can still say a great deal about the being of objects.

However, despite the limitations of access, we must avoid, at all costs, the thesis that objects *are* what our access to objects *gives* us. As Graham Harman has argued, objects are not the given. Not at all. As such, this book defends a robust realism. Yet, and this is crucial to everything that follows, the realism defended here is not an *epistemological* realism, but an *ontological* realism. *Epistemological* realism argues that our representations and language are accurate mirrors of the world as it actually is, regardless of whether or not we exist. It seeks to distinguish between true representations and phantasms. *Ontological* realism, by contrast, is not a thesis about our *knowledge* of objects, but about the being of objects themselves, whether or not we exist to represent them. It is the thesis that the world is composed of objects, that these objects are varied and include entities as diverse as mind, language, cultural and social entities, and objects independent of humans such as galaxies, stones, quarks, tardigrades and so on. Above all, ontological realisms refuse to treat objects as constructions of humans. While it is true, I will argue, that all objects translate one another, the objects that are translated are irreducible to their translations. As we will see, ontological realism thoroughly refutes epistemological realism or what ordinarily goes by the pejorative title of "naïve realism". Initially it might sound as if the distinction between ontological and epistemological realism is a difference that makes no difference but, as I hope to show, this distinction has far ranging consequences for how we pose a number of questions and theorize a variety of phenomena.

One of the problematic consequences that follows from the hegemony that epistemology currently enjoys in philosophy is that it condemns philosophy to a thoroughly anthropocentric reference. Because the ontological question of substance is elided into the epistemological question of our *knowledge* of substance, all discussions of substance necessarily contain a human reference. The subtext or fine print surrounding our discussions of substance always contain reference to an implicit "for-us". This is true even of the anti-humanist structuralists and post-structuralists who purport to dispense with the subject in favor of various impersonal and anonymous social forces like language and structure that exceed the intentions of individuals. Here we still remain in the orbit of an anthropocentric universe insofar as society and culture are human phenomena, and all of being is subordinated to these forces. Being is thereby reduced to what being is for us.

By contrast, this book strives to think a *subjectless* object, or an object that is for-*itself* rather than an object that is an opposing pole before or in front of a subject. Put differently, this essay attempts to think an object for-itself that isn't an object for the gaze of a subject, representation, or a cultural discourse. This, in short, is what the democracy of objects means. The democracy of objects is not a *political* thesis to the effect that all objects ought to be treated equally or that all objects ought to participate in human affairs. The democracy of objects is the *ontological* thesis that all objects, as Ian Bogost has so nicely put it, equally exist while they do not exist equally. The claim that all objects equally exist is the claim that no object can be treated as constructed by another object. The claim that objects do not exist equally is the claim that objects contribute to collectives or assemblages to a greater and lesser degree. In short, no object such as the subject or culture is the ground of all others. As such, *The Democracy of Objects* attempts to think the being of objects unshackled from the gaze of humans in their being for-themselves.

Such a democracy, however, does not entail the *exclusion* of the human. Rather, what we get is a redrawing of distinctions and a decentering of the human. The point is not that we should think objects rather than humans. Such a formulation is based on the premise that humans constitute some special category that is *other* than objects, that objects are a pole opposed to humans, and therefore the formulation is based on the premise that objects are correlates or poles *opposing* or standing-before humans. No, within the framework of onticology—my name for the ontology that follows—there is only one type of being: objects. As a consequence, humans are not excluded, but are rather objects *among* the various types of objects that exist or populate the world, each with their own specific powers and capacities.

It is here that we encounter the redrawing of distinctions proposed by object-oriented philosophy and onticology. In his *Laws of Form*, George Spencer-Brown argued that in order to indicate anything we must first draw a distinction. Distinction, as it were, precedes indication. To indicate something is to interact with, represent, or point at something in the world (indication takes a variety of forms). Thus, for example, when I say the sun is shining, I have indicated a state-of-affairs, yet this indication is based on a prior distinction between, perhaps, darkness and light, gray days and sunny days, and so on. According to Spencer-Brown, every distinction contains a marked and an unmarked space.

marked | unmarked

The right-angle is what Spencer-Brown refers to as the mark of distinction. The marked space opens what can be indicated, whereas the unmarked space is everything else that is excluded. Thus, for example, I can draw a circle on a piece of paper (distinction), and can now indicate what is in that circle. Two key points follow from Spencer-Brown's calculus of distinctions. First, the unmarked space of a distinction is invisible to the person employing the distinction. While it is true that, in many instances, the boundary of a distinction can be crossed and the unmarked space can be indicated, in the use of a distinction the unmarked space of the distinction becomes a blind-spot for the system deploying the distinction. That which exists in the unmarked space of the distinction might as well not exist *for the system* using the distinction.

However, the unmarked space of the distinction is not the only blind-spot generated by the distinction. In addition to the unmarked space of a distinction, the distinction *itself* is a blind-spot. In the use of a distinction, the distinction itself becomes invisible insofar as one passes "through" the distinction to make indications. The situation here is analogous to watching a bright red cardinal on a tree through one's window. Here the window becomes invisible and all our attention is drawn to the cardinal. One can either use their distinctions or observe their distinctions, but never use their distinctions *and* observe their distinctions. By virtue of the withdrawal of distinctions from view in the course of using them, distinctions thus create a reality effect where properties of the indicated seem to belong to the indicated itself rather than being effects of the distinction. As a consequence, we do not realize that other distinctions are possible. The result is thus that we end up surreptitiously unifying the world under a particular set of distinctions, failing to recognize that very different sorts of indications are possible.

Within the marked space of its distinctions, much contemporary philosophy and theory places the subject or culture. As a consequence, objects fall into the unmarked space and come to be treated as what is other than the subject.

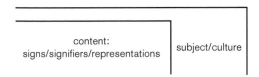

Here one need only think of Fichte for a formalization of this logic. Within any distinction there can also be sub-distinctions that render their own indications possible. In the case of the culturalist schema, the subject/culture distinction contains a sub-distinction marking content. The catch is that in treating the object as what is opposed to the subject or what is other than the subject, this frame of thought treats the object in terms of the subject. The object is here not an object, not an autonomous substance that exists in its own right, but rather *a representation*. As a consequence of this, all other entities in the world are treated only as *vehicles* for human contents, meanings, signs, or projections. By analogy, we can compare the culturalist structure of distinction with cinema. Here the object would be the smooth cinema screen, the projector would be the subject or culture, and the images would be contents or representations. Within this schema, the screen is treated as contributing little or nothing and all inquiry is focused on representations or contents. To be sure, the screen exists, but it is merely a vehicle for human and cultural representations.

Onticology and object-oriented philosophy, by contrast, propose to place *objects* in the marked space of distinction.

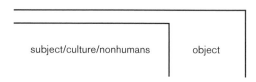

It will be noted that when objects are placed in the marked space of distinction, the sub-distinction does not contract what can be indicated, but rather expands what can be indicated. *Here subjects and culture are not excluded, but rather are treated as particular types of objects.* Additionally, it now becomes possible to indicate nonhuman objects without treating them as vehicles for human contents. As a consequence, this operation is not a simple *inversion* of the culturalist schema. It is not a call to pay attention to objects rather than subjects or to treat subjects as what are opposed to objects, rather than treating objects as being opposed to subjects. Rather, just as objects were reduced to representations when the subject or culture occupied the marked space of distinction, just as objects were effectively transformed into the subject and content, the placement of objects in the marked space of distinction within the framework of ontology transforms the subject into one object among many others, undermining its privileged, central, or foundational place within philosophy and ontology. Subjects are objects *among* objects, rather than constant points of reference related to all other objects. As a consequence, we get the beginnings of what anti-humanism and post-humanism *ought* to be, insofar as these theoretical orientations are no longer the thesis that the world is constructed through anonymous and impersonal social forces as opposed to an individual subject. Rather, we get a variety of nonhuman actors unleashed in the world as autonomous actors in their own right, irreducible to representations and freed from any constant reference to the human where they are reduced to our representations.

Thus, rather than thinking being in terms of two incommensurable worlds, nature and culture, we instead get various *collectives* of objects. As Latour has compellingly argued, within the Modernist schema that drives both epistemological realism and epistemological anti-realism, the world is bifurcated into two distinct domains: culture and nature.[3] The domain of the subject and culture is treated as the world of freedom, meaning, signs, representations, language, power, and so on. The domain of nature is treated as being composed of matter governed by mechanistic causality. Implicit within forms of theory and philosophy that work with this bifurcated model is the axiom that the two worlds are to be kept entirely separate, such that there is to be no inmixing of their distinct properties. Thus, for example, a good deal of cultural theory only refers to objects as vehicles for signs or representations, ignoring any non-semiotic or non-representational differences nonhuman objects might contribute to collectives. Society is only to have social properties, and never any sorts of qualities that pertain to the nonhuman world.

It is my view that the culturalist and modernist form of distinction is disastrous for social and political analysis and sound epistemology. Insofar as the form of distinction implicit in the culturalist mode of distinction indicates content and relegates nonhuman objects to the unmarked space of the distinction, all sorts of factors become invisible that are pertinent to why collectives involving humans take the form they do. Signifiers, meanings, signs, discourses, norms, and narratives are made to do all the heavy lifting to explain why social organization takes the form it does. While there can be no doubt that all of these agencies play a significant role in the formation of collectives involving humans, this mode of distinction leads us to ignore the role of the nonhuman and asignifying in the form of technologies, weather patterns, resources, diseases, animals, natural disasters, the presence or absence of roads, the availability of water, animals, microbes, the presence or absence of electricity and high speed internet connections, modes of transportation, and so on. All of these things and many more besides play a crucial role in bringing humans together in particular ways and do so through contributing differences that while coming to be imbricated with signifying agencies, nonetheless are asignifying. An activist political theory that places all its apples in the basket of content is doomed to frustration insofar as it will continuously wonder why its critiques of ideology fail to produce their desired or intended social change. Moreover, in an age where we are faced with the looming threat of monumental climate change, it is irresponsible to draw our distinctions in such a way as to exclude nonhuman actors.

On the epistemological front, the subject/object distinction has the curious effect of leading the epistemologist to focus on propositions and representations alone, largely ignoring the role that practices and nonhuman actors play in knowledge-production. As a consequence, the central question becomes that of how and whether propositions correspond to reality. In the meantime, we ignore the laboratory setting, engagement with matters and instruments, and so on. It is as if experiment and the entities that populate the laboratory are treated as mere means to the end of knowledge such that they can be safely ignored as contributing nothing to propositional content, thereby playing no crucial role in the production of knowledge. Yet by ignoring the site, practices, and procedures by which knowledge is produced, the question of how propositions represent reality becomes thoroughly obscure because we are left without the means of discerning the birth of propositions and the common place where the world of the human and nonhuman meets.

In shifting from a dual ontology based on the nature/culture split to collectives, onticology and object-oriented philosophy place all entities on equal ontological footing. Rather than two distinct ontological domains, the domain of the subject and the domain of the object, we instead get a single plane of being populated by a variety of different types of objects including humans and societies:

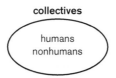

The concept of collectives does not approach being in terms of two separate domains, but rather as a single plane in which, to use Karen Barad's apt term, objects are entangled with one another.[4] In this regard, society and nature do not form two separate and entirely distinct domains that must never cross. Rather, collectives involving humans are always entangled with all sorts of nonhumans without which such collectives could not exist. To be sure, such collectives are populated by signs, signifiers, meanings, norms and a host of other sundry entities, but they are also populated by all sorts of asignifying entities such as animals, crops, weather events, geographies, rivers, microbes, technologies, and so on. Onticology and object-oriented ontology draw our attention to these entanglements by placing the human and nonhuman on equal footing.

However, it would be a mistake to suppose that collectives necessarily involve humans. There are collectives that involve humans and other collectives of objects that have nothing to do with humans:

In short, not everything is related to the human, nor, as I will argue in what follows, is everything related to everything else. While we might be particularly interested in collectives involving humans because we happen to be human, from the standpoint of ontology we must avoid treating all collectives as involving the human.

From the foregoing it can be gathered that the ontology I am proposing is rather peculiar. Rather than treating objects as entities opposed to a subject, I treat all entities, including subjects, as objects. Moreover, in order to overcome the dual world hypothesis of Modernity, I argue that it is necessary to staunchly defend the autonomy of objects or substances, refusing any reduction of objects to their relations, whether these relations be relations to humans or other objects. In my view, the root of the Modernist schema arises from relationism. If we are to escape the *aporia* that beset the Modernist schema this, above all, requires us to overcome relationism or the thesis that objects are constituted by their relations. Accordingly, following the ground-breaking work of Graham Harman's object-oriented philosophy, I argue that objects are withdrawn from all relation. The consequences of this strange thesis are, I believe, profound. On the one hand, in arguing that objects are withdrawn from their relations, we are able to preserve the autonomy and irreducibility of substance, thereby sidestepping the endless, and at this point rather stale, debate between the epistemological realists and anti-realists. On the other hand, where the anti-realists have obsessively focused on a single gap between humans and objects, endlessly revolving around the manner in which objects are inaccessible to representation, object-oriented philosophy allows us to *pluralize* this gap, treating it not as a unique or privileged peculiarity of humans, but as true of all relations between objects whether they involve humans or not. In short, the difference between humans and other objects is not a difference in kind, but a difference in degree. Put differently, all objects translate one another. Translation is not unique to how the mind relates to the world. And as a consequence of this, no object has direct access to any other object.

Onticology and object-oriented philosophy thus find themselves in a strange position with respect to speculative realism. Speculative realism is a loosely affiliated philosophical movement that arose out of a Goldsmith's College conference organized by Alberto Toscano in 2007. While the participants at this event—Ray Brassier, Iain Hamilton Grant, Graham Harman, and Quentin Meillassoux—share vastly different philosophical positions, they are all united in defending a variant of realism and in rejecting anti-realism or what they call "correlationism". With the other speculative realists, onticology and object-oriented philosophy defend a realist ontology that refuses to treat objects as constructions or mere correlates of mind, subject, culture, or language. However, with the *anti-*

realists, onticology and object-oriented philosophy argue that objects have no direct access to one another and that each object translates other objects with which it enters into non-relational relations. Object-oriented philosophy and onticology thus reject the epistemological realism of other realist philosophies, taking leave of the project of policing representations and demystifying critique. The difference is that where the anti-realists focus on a single gap between humans and objects, object-oriented philosophy and onticology treat this gap as a ubiquitous feature of all beings. One of the great strengths of object-oriented philosophy and onticology is thus, I believe, that it can integrate a number of the findings of anti-realist philosophy, and continental social and political theory, without falling into the deadlocks that currently plague anti-realist strains of thought.

For those not familiar with the basic claims of object-oriented philosophy and onticology, a list of object-oriented heroes might prove helpful for gaining orientation within onticology. Among the heroes of onticology are Graham Harman, Bruno Latour, Isabelle Stengers, Timothy Morton, Ian Bogost, Niklas Luhmann, Jane Bennett, Manuel DeLanda, Marshall McLuhan, Friedrich Kittler, Karen Barad, John Protevi, Walter Ong, Deleuze and Guattari, developmental systems theorists such as Richard Lewontin and Susan Oyama, Alfred North Whitehead, Donna Haraway, Roy Bhaskar, Katherine Hayles, and a host of others. Some of these thinkers appear more than others in the pages that follow, and others appear scarcely or not at all, but all have deeply influenced my thought. The thread that runs throughout the work of these thinkers is a profound decentering of the human and the subject that nonetheless makes room for the human, representation, and content, and an accompanying attentiveness to all sorts of nonhuman objects or actors coupled with a refusal to reduce these agencies to vehicles of content and signs. In developing my argument, I have proceeded as a bricoleur, freely drawing from a variety of disciplines and thinkers whose works are not necessarily consistent with one another. Of the bricoleur, Lévi-Strauss writes that,

> [t]he 'bricoleur' is adept at performing a large number
> of diverse tasks; but, unlike the engineer, he does not
> subordinate each of them to the availability of raw materials

and tools conceived and procured for the purpose of the
project. His universe of instruments is closed and the rules
of his game are always to make do with 'whatever is at hand',
that is to say with a set of tools and materials which is always
finite and is also heterogeneous because what it contains bears
no relation to the current project, or indeed to any particular
project, but is the contingent result of all the occasions there
have been to renew or enrich the stock or to maintain it with
the remains of previous constructions or destructions. The
set of the 'bricoleur's' means cannot therefore be defined in
terms of a project (which would presuppose, besides, that,
as in the case of the engineer, there were, at least in theory,
as many sets of tools and materials or 'instrumental sets' as
there are different kinds of projects). It is to be defined only
by its potential use or, putting this another way and in the
language of the 'bricoleur' himself, because the elements are
collected and retained on the principle that 'they may always
come in handy'. Such elements are specialized up to a point,
sufficiently for the 'bricoleur' not to need the equipment and
knowledge of all trades and professions, but not enough for
each of them to have one definite and determinate use. They
each represent a set of actual and possible relations; they
are 'operators' but they can be used for any operations of
the same type.[5]

For readers startled by some of the thinkers and lines of thought I forge
together in the pages that follow, it is worthwhile to recall that this is the
work of a bricoleur and that it very much reflects the idiosyncrasies of my
own intellectual background and development. For example, Lacan makes
a number of appearances in the pages that follow and this reflects my time
in a previous incarnation as a practicing psychoanalyst. As I argue in what
follows, every object is a crowd and this is above all true of books. Where
the materials out of which a book is constructed might themselves be
heterogeneous, what is important is not whether these other materials are
in themselves consistent with one another, but rather whether the product
formed from these parts manages to attain some degree of consistency in

the formation of a new object. Readers, for example, might be surprised to discover Harman's object-oriented ontology, the constructivism of Niklas Luhmann's autopoietic social theory, Deleuze and Guattari's ontology of the virtual, and the psychoanalytic theory of Jacques Lacan rubbing elbows with one another. Standing alone, these various theories are opposed on a number of fronts. However, the work of a bricoleur consists in forging together heterogeneous materials so as to produce something capable of standing on its own. I hope that I've done so, but I make no claim that this is the only way that object-oriented ontology can be formulated, nor am I particularly interested in policing others with a theory of reality.

It is unlikely that object-oriented ontologists are going to persuade epistemological realists or anti-realists that they have found a way of surmounting the epistemological problems that arise out of the two-world model of being any time soon. Quoting Max Planck, Marshall and Eric McLuhan write, "A new scientific truth does not triumph by convincing its opponents and making them see the light, but rather because its opponents die, and a new generation grows up that is familiar with it".[6] This appears to be how it is in philosophy as well. New innovations in philosophy do not so much refute their opponents as simply cease being preoccupied by certain questions and problems. In many respects, object-oriented ontology, following the advice of Richard Rorty, simply tries to step out of the debate altogether. Object-oriented ontologists have grown weary of a debate that has gone on for over two centuries, believe that the possible variations of these positions have exhausted themselves, and want to move on to talking about other things. If this is not good enough for the epistemology police, we are more than happy to confess our guilt and embrace our alleged lack of rigor and continue in harboring our illusions that we can speak of a reality independent of humans. However, such a move of simply moving on is not unheard of in philosophy. No one has yet refuted the solipsist, nor the Berkeleyian subjective idealist, yet neither solipsism nor the extremes of Berkeleyian idealism have ever been central and ongoing debates in philosophy. Philosophers largely just ignore these positions or use them as cautionary examples to be avoided. Why not the same in the endless debates over access?

Nonetheless, in the pages that follow I do try to formulate arguments that epistemically ground the ontological realism that I defend. The first chapter outlines the grounds for ontological realism, drawing heavily on the transcendental realism developed by Roy Bhaskar. The basic thrust of this argument is transcendental in character and argues that the world must be structured in a particular way for experimental activity to be intelligible and possible. Bhaskar's articulation of these transcendental, ontological conditions also provides me with the means of outlining the basic structure of objects, the relation between substance and qualities, the independence of objects from their relations, and the withdrawn structure of objects. Here I also uncover the root assumption that leads to the endless debates of anti-realism and epistemological realism.

Having outlined the basic structure of objects, the second chapter explores Aristotle's concept of substance, carefully distinguishing it from that which is simple or indivisible, and outlining the relationship between substance and qualities. Here a problem emerges. On the one hand, substance is necessarily distinct from its qualities in that qualities can change, yet substance persists. On the other hand, the subtraction of all qualities from a substance seems to lead us to a bare substratum or a completely featureless substance that would therefore be identical to all other substances or objects. Additionally, while substance is the very being of an object, its individuality or singularity, substances only ever manifest themselves through their qualities. With respect to this third problem, I argue that the very being of substance consists in simultaneously withdrawing and in self-othering. The structure of substance is such that it others itself in its qualities. However, if such an account of substance is to be successful, it is necessary to provide an account of withdrawn substance that is structured without being qualitative. How are we to think such a non-qualitative structure?

Having encountered the problem of non-qualitative structure, the third chapter turns to Deleuze's ontology and the distinction between the virtual and the actual. There I critique Deleuze's tendency to treat the virtual as something other than the individual, arguing that the individual precedes the virtual such that virtuality is always the virtuality of a substance. I refer to this as "virtual proper being" and treat it as the powers or capacities of an entity. Deleuze's concept of the virtual provides us with the means of thinking substance as structured without being qualitative. I refer to the qualities produced out of virtual structure as "local manifestations" and treat them as events, actions, or activities on the part of objects.

If objects are withdrawn from one another, then how do they relate? This is the problem of what Harman refers to as "vicarious causation". How do objects relate to one another when they are necessarily independent of all their relations? Chapter four picks up with this question and turns to the autopoietic theory of Niklas Luhmann to provide an account of interactions between withdrawn objects. There I argue that all objects are operationally closed such that they constitute their own relation and openness to their environment. Relations between objects are accounted for by the manner in which objects transform perturbations from other objects into information or events that select system-states. These information-events or events that select system-states are, in their turn, among the agencies that preside over the production of local manifestations in objects.

Chapter five turns to questions of constraint, relations between parts and wholes, and time and entropy. If objects are withdrawn from one another, how is it that they can constrain one another? Drawing on the resources of developmental systems theory in biology, I attempt to provide an account of how an object can simultaneously construct its environment and be constrained by its environment, leading local manifestations to take particular forms. The section on mereology develops an account of relations between larger-scale objects and smaller-scale objects, defending the autonomy of larger-scale objects from the smaller-scale objects out of which they are built and the autonomy of the smaller-scale objects that compose the larger-scale object. Here I argue that a number of problems that have haunted contemporary social and political theory arise from a failure to be properly attentive to these strange mereological relations. The chapter closes with a discussion of temporalized structure, the relation of objects to time and space, and how objects stave off entropy or destruction across time.

Finally, chapter six outlines the four theses of flat ontology advocated by onticology. The first of these theses is that all objects are withdrawn, such that there are no objects characterized by full presence or actuality. Withdrawal is not an accidental feature of objects arising from *our* lack of direct access to them, but is a constitutive feature of all objects regardless of whether they relate to other objects. To develop this thesis I draw on Lacan's graphs of sexuation, treating them not as accounts of sex, but rather as two very different ontological discourses: ontologies of immanence and withdrawal and ontologies of presence and transcendence. The second thesis of flat ontology is that the world does not exist. Here I argue that there is no "super-object", Whole, or totality that would gather all objects together in a harmonious unity. The third thesis is that humans occupy no privileged place within being and that between the human/object relation and any other object/object relation there is only a difference in degree, not kind. Finally, the fourth thesis is that objects of all sorts and at all scales are on equal ontological footing, such that subjects, groups, fictions, technologies, institutions, etc., are every bit as real as quarks, planets, trees, and tardigrades. The fourth thesis of flat ontology invites us to think in terms of collectives and entanglements between a variety of different types of actors, at a variety of different temporal and spatial scales, rather than focusing exclusively on the gap between humans and objects.

In the pages that follow I have, above all, pursued three aims. First, I have sought to provide an ontological framework capable of providing a synthesis of two very different research programs. Within cultural studies there is a sharp divide between those forms of inquiry that focus on signification and those forms of inquiry that focus on the material in the form of technologies, media, and material conditions. Likewise, the broader and dominant tendency of the humanities has been to focus on content, excluding the material. I have sought an ontological framework capable of integrating these diverse tendencies. However, second, such an integration requires an avoidance of reductivism. To the same degree that natural entities ought not be reduced to cultural constructions, social, semiotic, and cultural entities ought not be reduced to natural entities. This requires us to shift from thinking in terms of reduction or grounding one entity in another, to thinking in terms of entanglements. Entanglements allow us to maintain the irreducibility, heterogeneity, and autonomy of various types of entities while investigating how they influence one another. Finally, third, I have above all sought to write a book that is both accessible to a wide audience and that can be put to work by others in a wide variety of disciplines and practices, generating new questions and projects. I hope I have been somewhat successful in accomplishing these aims.

Chapter 1
Grounds For a Realist Ontology

Things-in-themselves? But they're fine, thank you very much. And how are you? You complain about things that have not been honored by your vision? You feel that these things are lacking the illumination of your consciousness? But if you missed the galloping freedom of the zebras in the savannah this morning, then so much the worse for you; the zebras will not be sorry that you were not there, and in any case you would have tamed, killed, photographed, or studied them. Things in themselves lack nothing, just as Africa did not lack whites before their arrival.

— Bruno Latour[7]

1.1. The Death of Ontology and the Rise of Correlationism

Our historical moment is characterized by a general distrust, even disdain, for the category of objects, ontology, and above all any variant of *realism*. Moreover, it is characterized by a primacy of epistemology over ontology. While it is indeed true that Heidegger, in *Being and Time*, attempted to resurrect ontology, this only took place through a profound transformation of the very meaning of ontology.[8] Ontology would no longer be the investigation of being *qua* being in all its variety and diversity regardless of whether humans exist, but rather would instead become an interrogation of *Dasein's* or *human* being's *access* to being. Ontology would become an investigation of being-*for*-Dasein, rather than an investigation of being *as such*. In conjunction with this transformation of ontology from an investigation of being *as such* into an investigation of being-*for*-humans, we have also everywhere witnessed a push to dissolve objects or primary substances in the acid of experience, intentionality, power, language, normativity, signs, events, relations, or processes. To defend the existence of objects is, within the framework of this line of thought, the height of naïveté for objects are held to be nothing more than surface-effects of something more fundamental such as the signifier, signs, power or activities of the mind. With Hume, for example, it is argued that objects are really nothing more than bundles of impressions or sensations linked together by associations and habits in the mind. Here there is no deeper fact of objects existing beyond these impressions and habits. Likewise, Lacan will tell us that "the universe is the flower of rhetoric"[9], treating the beings that populate the world as an effect of the signifier.

We can thus discern a shift in how ontology is understood and accompanying this shift the deployment of a universal acid that has come to dissolve the being of objects. The new ontology argues that we can only ever speak of being as it is for us. Depending on the philosophy in question, this "us" can be minds, lived bodies, language, signs, power, social structures, and so on. There are dozens of variations. The key point here is that it is argued that being can only be thought in terms of what Graham Harman has called our *access* to being.[10] As such, ontology becomes not an interrogation of being *as such*, but rather an interrogation of our *access* to being. The answer to the question, "what is being?" now, everywhere and always, carries a footnote, colophon, or bit of fine print such that the question must be read as "what is being *for us*?"

And if the question of ontology now becomes the question, "what is being *for us*?" it follows that there can be no question of what being might be *as such*, for we have resolved to treat being only in terms of our access to being such that what being might be apart from *our* access to being now becomes an entirely meaningless question. This for two reasons: First, were we capable of knowing being apart from our access to being, it is argued, it would follow that we therefore have access to this being, thereby converting this being alleged to be beyond its givenness to us back into being-for-us. Second, to know something, the argument runs, we must have access to that thing. Yet being beyond our access to it is precisely a form of being to which we have no access. Therefore it follows that claims about such a being are, strictly speaking, meaningless. I hope to show later why there is good reason to doubt the soundness of both of these arguments, but for the moment it is enough simply to tarry with them to understand their logic, for these arguments constitute the basic schema of nearly every reigning philosophical position today.

If, then, these arguments are granted, it follows that there can be no question of what being might be like *apart* from our access to being. For the condition under which it would be possible to speak of being apart from our access to being would require access to that being, yet we do not have such access. Consequently, it follows that philosophy must abandon the question of whether being as it is *given* to us is like being as it is in-itself because we are unable to "get out of ourselves" to compare being as it manifests itself to us with being as it is in-itself apart from us. The best we can hope for, the most we can know, is being as it manifests itself to *us*, and philosophy shifts from being a discourse concerned with the being of beings, with what substance, as Meillassoux has put it, constitutes true substance (objects, God, nature, particles, processes, and so on?)[11], to being a discourse about the mechanisms through which beings are manifested to us (mind, language, normativity, signs, power, for example). Ontology becomes *transcendental anthropology* and the world becomes a mirror in which we don't recognize our own reflection.

Philosophy, of whatever stripe, thus comes to be characterized by what Meillassoux has aptly named *correlationism*. As Meillassoux puts it, "[b]y 'correlation' we mean the idea according to which we only ever have access to the correlation between thinking and being, and never either term considered apart from the other".[12] While I have reason to disagree with Meillassoux's proposal for escaping the correlationist circle (and with his ontology), I believe that his concept of correlationism nicely summarizes the *episteme*, in the Foucauldian sense, that governs contemporary philosophy. When, in *The Order of Things*[13] and *The Archeology of Knowledge*[14], Foucault introduces the concept of *epistemes*, he intends *epistemes* not as determinate positions in some discipline that might be opposed to another position, but rather as a set of *statements* functioning as the *historical* a priori of a particular discursive space. An *episteme* would be precisely that set of *statements* that allow opposed theories of, for example, language, to be *opposed*. It is the common framework these opposed positions share that allows them to enter into antagonistic relations with one another. The claim that correlationism constitutes the *episteme* of contemporary philosophy is thus not a claim about any *specific* philosophical position, but rather about the common framework regulating philosophical discourse in our contemporary moment. This *episteme* is shared by thinkers as diverse and opposed, for example, as the early Wittgenstein of the *Tractatus*, the Merleau-Ponty of *The Phenomenology of Perception*, and the Derrida of *Of Grammatology*. Despite the vast differences and disagreements among these positions, their thought and disagreements nonetheless unfold within the horizon of the unspoken premise of a necessary correlation between being and thought. The object of these disputes is not whether correlationism is true, but rather how the primordial or most fundamental correlation is to be articulated.

With correlationism we thus discover the root of contemporary theory's suspicion of both objects and realism. Realism must necessarily be anathema to all variants of correlationism by virtue of the fact that it claims knowledge of beings *independent* of the correlation between thinking and being. All realisms are committed to the thesis that it is possible to know something of beings independent of their being-for-thought, yet this is precisely what is precluded by the correlationist gesture. Here it is important to be precise. Correlationism is not the thesis of *subjective* idealisms whereby *esse est percipi* or where to be is to be perceived. Subjective and absolute idealism are only two variations of correlationism. The correlationist need not be committed to the thesis that there is *no* being apart from thought. Indeed, most correlationists are committed to the thesis that there is something other than thought. Kant, for example, held that in addition to phenomena (beings for-us) things-in-themselves exist. The correlationist merely argues that we have no access to these beings that are apart from thought and can therefore only speak of being as it is for-us. And here we find the categorical dividing line between realisms and anti-realisms or correlationisms: for the anti-realist or correlationist, claims about beings are never claims about beings-in-themselves or beings apart from us, but are always and only claims about beings as they manifest themselves to *us*. For the realist, by contrast, claims about objects *really are* claims about *objects* and not objects as they are *for-us* or only in relation to us.

As a consequence, it becomes clear that, for the correlationist, objects take on the status of *fictions*. Because objects can no longer be equated with things-in-themselves, because objects are only ever objects for-us and never things as they are independent of us, objects become *phenomena* or are reduced to actual or possible manifestations to us. Philosophy now shifts from being a debate about the nature of things-in-themselves or substance, to a debate about the *mechanisms* by which *phenomena* are produced or structured. Is it mind that structures phenomena? Language? Power? Intentionality? Embodied experience? Such are but a handful of the options that have been entertained by contemporary theory.

At the heart of correlationism it is thus clear that there is a profound *anthropocentrism*, for where it is held that being can never be thought in its existence apart from thought, it becomes clear that any claims about being ultimately harbor the implicit colophon that claims about being are claims about being for *humans*. Moreover, despite declarations of anti-humanism on the part of both Heidegger and the structuralists and post-structuralists, it is clear that these anti-humanisms bring us no closer to realism. For, to put it crudely, what the anti-humanisms object to is not the correlationist thesis of a necessary relation between being and thought such that the two can never be thought apart from one another, but rather the manner in which humanisms situate the primordial correlation in the *minds* of *individual knowers*. Thus, for example, structuralist and post-structuralist anti-humanisms emphasize the autonomy and independence of language and social relations. Here the argument runs that it is not sovereign subjects that are calling the shots, but rather language and/or social relations. What the structuralist and post-structuralist anti-humanists wish to examine is the manner in which language and social relations are determinative of the actions of individuals and how, if Althusser is to be followed, the individual itself is an effect of these more primordial agencies. It now follows that these impersonal and anonymous agencies are the condition for manifestation, not individual human minds. World, the story goes, is not a construction of the mind of human individuals or transcendental subjectivity, but of impersonal and anonymous social structures.

However, while anti-humanisms rescue philosophy from its focus on individual minds, allowing us to discern the sway of far more impersonal and anonymous patterns and structures at work in the heart of thought and social relations, it by no means follows that anti-humanism has escaped *anthropocentrism*. For social relations, economic relations, and language are nonetheless human phenomena, even where the human is discursively constructed, and it therefore follows that we remain within the orbit of anthropocentrism; for just as we began humanistically with the premise that we cannot know what being might be independent of our thinking of being, we now conclude that our claims about being are claims about being in relation to or correlation with language, power, or social relations. The question of what the world might be like apart from humans is, for both the humanists and the anti-humanists, entirely foreclosed.

1.2. Breaking the Correlationist Circle

With correlationism, the question of ontology is no longer, "what is being *qua* being?" but rather, "what is being *qua* Dasein?" or, "what is being *qua* language?" or, "what is being *qua* power?" or, "what is being *qua* history?" or, "what is being *qua* the lived body?" and many other avatars besides. While disputes among these various formulations of the correlation are heated, we are nonetheless faced with a series of anthropomorphic determinations such that being is always to be thought in relation to some aspect of the human. Protagoras, in one form or another, rules the day. What we thus get is not a *democracy* of objects or actants where all objects are on equal ontological footing and the philosopher can be just as interested in questions of how, to evoke Harman's favorite example, cotton relates to fire as she is in questions of how humans relate to mangoes, but instead a *monarchy* of the human in relation to all other beings where some instance of the human is treated as that which overdetermines all other beings and where the primary order of the day is always to determine how individual minds relate to other objects or how the social and cultural relates to being. If, as Žižek contends, metaphysics, in the pejorative sense of ontotheology, consists in elevating a part to the ground of the whole, then the anthropocentrism of correlationism is metaphysical through and through despite its protestations to the contrary or its characterizations of itself as a critique of metaphysics.[15] Correlationism is ontotheology with the human in the place of God.

Our question is two-fold: on the one hand, what are the philosophical premises that led correlationism to become such a persuasive position in contemporary philosophy? On the other hand, is there a way to twist free from the correlationist deadlock so as to convincingly defend a genuinely post-humanist, realist ontology? A post-humanist, realist ontology is not an *anti-human* ontology, but is rather, as we will later see, an ontology where humans are no longer monarchs of being but are instead *among* beings, *entangled* in beings, and *implicated* in other beings. In this section, I will address the second of these questions through a foray into the early thought of the philosopher of science Roy Bhaskar. This discussion will also set the stage for my later discussion of the ontology of objects. Ironically, it turns out that the way out of correlationism is to be found through *transcendental* argumentation. But here I am getting ahead of myself.

Before outlining Bhaskar's defense of ontological realism, it is first necessary to express a note of caution. In his early work, and especially *A Realist Theory of Science* on which I will lean heavily here, Bhaskar is primarily interested in the ontology of *science*. Within the context of the present book, this poses special dangers as readers might arrive at the mistaken impression that I am arguing that the objects of the natural sciences are exhaustive of being *as such*. In short, one might conclude that I advocate the thesis that being and the objects of the natural world are *synonymous*. As I develop Bhaskar's argument for a realist theory of science, my aim is not to defend *naturalism* as the one true ontology, but rather to unfold the argument by which he arrives at a realist ontology. And here I am only interested in the *ontological* dimension of his argument. As Bhaskar writes,

> Any adequate philosophy of science must find a way of
> grappling with this central paradox of science: that men in

their social activity produce knowledge which is a social
product much like any other, which is no more independent
of its production and the men who produce it than motor
cars, armchairs or books, which has its own craftsmen,
technicians, publicists, standards and skills and which is no
less subject to change than any other commodity. This is one
side of 'knowledge'. The other is that knowledge is '*of*' things
which are not produced by men at all: the specific gravity of
mercury, the process of electrolysis, the mechanism of light
propagation. None of these 'objects of knowledge' depend on
human activity. If men ceased to exist sound would continue
to travel and heavy bodies fall to the earth in exactly the same
way, though ex hypothesi there would be no one to know it.[16]

Bhaskar refers to these two dimensions of knowledge as the transitive
and the intransitive respectively. The transitive refers to the dimension of
the social in the production of knowledge, such as inherited discourses,
scientific training, institutions, and so on. By contrast, the intransitive
refers to the domain of being that would exist regardless of whether or not
humans know of them. We can thus say that Bhaskar, in his philosophy of
science, wishes to reconcile something like the insights of Kuhn's *Structure
of Scientific Revolution*[17] or Foucault's *Order of Things* (the transitive or
social dimension of knowledge production), with a realist ontology of
science (the intransitive dimension). In the present context, my focus is
on Bhaskar's arguments on behalf of realist ontology and therefore the
intransitive, though readers should not conclude from this that the social
dimension through which knowledge is produced is ignored.

As subsequent chapters of this book will hopefully demonstrate, the
domain of real being advocated by onticology is far broader than the
domain of beings belonging to the *natural* world. Put differently, *natural*
beings constitute a *subset* of the category of *real* beings. In addition to
natural beings, onticology also counts technologies, symbolic entities,
fictional entities, groups, nations, works of art, possible beings, artificial
entities, and many other entities besides as belonging to the domain of real
being. Bhaskar's arguments for the reality of natural entities thus functions

as a launching point for ontology, but is by no means exhaustive of the domain of real beings.

Consequently, second, the ontology defended in these pages will expand significantly on the ontology Bhaskar proposes in *A Realist Theory of Science*, going, I believe, well beyond what he proposes in his own ontology. Thus, while I am deeply indebted to the ontology Bhaskar proposes in *A Realist Theory of Science*, it should not be assumed that the ontology presupposed by onticology is identical to the ontology proposed by Bhaskar's transcendental realism. In what follows, there will be many points of overlap between these ontologies, and many points of divergence as well. My aim in this book is not to provide a commentary on Bhaskar's ontology, nor to remain true to his ontology, but rather to develop a post-humanist, realist theory of being capable of breaking with correlationism, that is nonetheless capable of integrating the most important and significant findings of the correlationists.

Bhaskar's defense of ontological realism begins with a very simple transcendental question: "...what must the world be like for science to be possible?"[18] In asking what the world must be like for science to be possible, Bhaskar is asking a *transcendental* question and deploying a transcendental mode of argumentation. The question here is not, "how do we have access to the world?" or, "how do we know the world?" but rather what must be *presupposed* about the nature of the world in order for our scientific practices to be possible. As Deleuze reminds us, the transcendental is not to be confused with the *transcendent*.[19] The transcendent refers to that which is above or beyond something else. For example, God, if it exists, is perhaps transcendent to the world. The transcendental, by contrast, refers to that which is a *condition* for some other practice, form of cognition, or activity.

Thus, for example, perhaps speech requires *language* as its *transcendental* condition. *If* this is the case, then it would be because the condition under which it is possible for two people to communicate requires the existence of a shared *code* in the form of *language*. The conditions under which it is possible for *me* to *speak* to *you* would here lie in both of us sharing the same language, whether language be something minimal like gestures or something very complex like chains of signifiers capable of self-reflexively commenting on themselves. By contrast, the *referent* of speech would, perhaps, be *transcendent* to both language and speech. If the referent of speech is transcendent to speech, then this is because 1) we can speak about fictional entities that have no physical referent or, 2) we can speak of entities in their absence, and 3) we can speak of speech itself, transforming speech into an object. Too often questions of the transcendental have been confused with questions of the transcendent. The point, however, is that transcendental questions are questions about what renders a particular practice or activity *possible*. Transcendental questions are questions of what a particular practice *requires* to take place and refer to what is immanent to these practices.

Additionally it should be noted that transcendental questions are not *foundationalist* in character. Transcendental questions do not seek an absolutely secure and unassailable foundation for knowledge or practice, but merely ask, "given such and such a practice, what must be the case in order for this practice to be possible?" As such, transcendental inquiry sidesteps the epistemological project inaugurated by Descartes and so compellingly critiqued by Hume, by disavowing the project of seeking for an absolute foundation for knowledge.

Yet already, with Bhaskar's question, we sense that the air or atmosphere is very different. Bhaskar does not ask what the *mind* must be like for science to be possible, but rather what the *world* must be like for science to be possible. In framing the question of science in this way, Bhaskar shifts the transcendental question from the domain of *epistemology* to the domain of *ontology*. The world itself must be a particular way for science to be possible, not the mind. And if Bhaskar's deployment of transcendental argument is ironic as a defense of realism, it is for precisely this reason. For beginning with Kant, who first explicitly invented the transcendental model of argument, all subsequent models of transcendental argument have either traced the conditions of certain forms of practice back to mind or some variant of the social. Yet with Bhaskar we here have a thorough inversion of this mode of argumentation. The question is no longer, "what must the mind be like for X to be possible?" nor, "what must the social be like for X to be possible?" but rather, "what must the *world* be like for X to be possible?" And in this way Bhaskar already shifts transcendental philosophy out of its constraint to some form of transcendental idealism or anti-realism, and shifts it to the framework of transcendental realism. For in asking what the world must be like for science to be possible, we begin with the premise of a world apart from and independent of human beings.

Thus, elsewhere, in a gloss on the nature of transcendental argumentation, Bhaskar will write,

> If philosophy is to be possible (and I want to contend
> that it is in practice indispensable) then it must follow
> the Kantian road. But in doing so it must both avoid any
> commitment to the content of specific theories and recognize
> the conditional nature of all its results. Moreover, it must
> reject two presuppositions which were central to Kant's own
> philosophical project, viz. that in any inquiry of the form
> 'what must be the case for ϕ to be possible?' the conclusion,
> X, would be a fact about us and that ϕ must invariably stand
> for some universal operation of mind. That is to say, it must
> reject the idealist and individualist cast into which Kant
> pressed his own inquiries.[20]

To this I would add that we must avoid the conclusion that any answer to the question, "what must be the case for ϕ to be possible?" must refer to society, language, or power. In effect, Bhaskar thus proposes a de-suturation of transcendental modes of argumentation from mind and the social. To suture is to tie, and in this respect all correlationism is a suture. The mark of any and every correlationism is a suture of being to the human in some form or another. Thus, a de-suturing would amount to an untying and systematic separation of the domains of being and thought, thereby undermining the reign of Protagoras in the modern era. Yet, nonetheless, as promising as this strategy of de-suturation sounds, we require compelling reasons to follow Bhaskar in this de-suturation of being and thought, or in this move directly from mind to world.

Bhaskar argues that the condition under which science is possible is the existence of what he calls "intransitive objects" which are real structures that exist independently of our minds and that are often "out of phase" with actual patterns of events.[21] As Bhaskar articulates it,

> ...the intransitive objects of knowledge are in general
> invariant to our knowledge of them: they are the real things
> and structures, mechanisms and processes, events and
> possibilities of the world; and for the most part they are quite
> independent of us. They are not unknowable, because as a
> matter of fact quite a bit is known about them... But neither
> are they in any way dependent upon our knowledge, let alone
> perception, of them.[22]

The claim that intransitive objects are invariant to our *knowledge* of them is not equivalent to the claim that intransitive objects are *invariant*. Rather, the point is that these objects would do what they do regardless of whether anyone knew about them or perceived them. The claim that intransitive objects can be "out of phase" with actual patterns of events is the claim that these intransitive objects can act or be dormant, thereby not producing certain events that they would produce in other settings or contexts.

So far we know *what* Bhaskar claims are the transcendental conditions of scientific practice, but we do not know *why* Bhaskar claims these are the transcendental conditions of science. Indeed, as it stands, it sounds as if he is dogmatically affirming the existence of mind-independent objects without providing any grounds as to why these objects must be presupposed by scientific practice. Here everything turns on Bhaskar's thesis that intransitive objects can be "out of phase" with actual patterns of events and the nature of *experiment* in scientific practice. "The intelligibility of experimental activity presupposes not just the intransitivity but the structured character of the objects investigated under experimental conditions".[23] But why is this so? According to Bhaskar,

> ...an experiment is necessary precisely to the extent that the
> pattern of events forthcoming under experimental conditions
> would not be forthcoming without it. Thus in an experiment
> we are a causal agent of the sequence of events, but not of
> the causal law which the sequence of events, because it has
> been produced under experimental conditions, enables us
> to identify.[24]

To understand Bhaskar's point, it is necessary to compare his thesis here to that advocated by sense-data empiricism. "A causal law is analysed in empiricist ontology as a constant conjunction of events perceived (or perceptions)".[25] Borne out of foundationalist aspirations, the empiricist attempts to eradicate all unfounded ontological presuppositions by resolving to tarry with what is *given* in sensations *alone*. For example, for the empiricist there is no deeper fact independent of the sensations. I now regard a clementine with relish. This clementine just *is*, for the sense-data empiricist, the sheen of orange and roundness I see before me, the fragrant citrus scent that fills my nostrils, the refreshing coolness I feel as I now touch it, and so on. What we call a clementine, for the empiricist, is a bundle of sensations that my mind has unified together through the operations of association. If, according to the empiricist, there is more to the clementine than these sensations afford me, if it has independent existence in its own right, then I can know nothing about it for I only ever have access to the object through these sensations. Therefore the empiricist, practicing a sort of critical vigilance, decides to cut the real independent object out of the discussion altogether as an unjustified metaphysical residue, restricting philosophical discussion to what is *given* in sensation *alone*.

When the empiricist arrives at discussions of causality, she thus has no recourse but to discuss claims about causality as claims about constant conjunctions of events or impressions. For the empiricist, a causal claim is no more nor less than a constant conjunction of sensations in experience. Above all, causal claims are not claims about *powers* that reside in objects, precisely because we have no access to these hidden powers. As Hume puts it, "[t]he bread which I formerly eat, nourished me; that is, a body of such sensible qualities, was, at that time, endowed with such secret powers: But does it follow, that other bread must also nourish me at another time, and that like sensible qualities must always be attended with like secret powers?"[26] What we are given is not the powers of the object—in this case bread—but rather a constant connection of sensations: the visual appearance of the bread followed by the sensations of our painful hunger being satiated. The causal relation is nothing but the mental association of these sensations in the order of time.

We are now in a position to better appreciate Bhaskar's point. Were the empiricist thesis correct, there would be no point to the activity of experiment, for causal knowledge would be nothing but constant conjunctions of events presented in sensations. For the empiricist experiment must be unintelligible precisely because the idea of *hidden* or *disguised* powers of objects is banished by the empiricist reduction that resolves to treat being only in terms of what is present or given in sensations. Accordingly, elsewhere, in a moment of humor, Bhaskar will write that

> ...the Humean account depends upon a misidentification of causal laws with their empirical grounds. Notice that as human activity is in general necessary for constant conjunctions, if one identifies causal laws with them then one is logically committed to the absurdity that human beings, in their experimental activity, cause and even change the laws of nature![27]

This absurdity would follow from the claim that causal relations are nothing more than constant conjunctions of events or sensation, forbidding any hidden powers in objects, thereby leaving the only site for the emergence of new sensations in the experimenter.

1.3. The Onto-Transcendental Grounds of Experimental Activity

Bhaskar thus concludes that the transcendental conditions under which experimental activity is intelligible are *ontological* in character. In order for experimental activity to be intelligible, it is the *world*, not our minds, that must be a certain way. And the world must be this way regardless of whether any science takes place or whether any sentient beings exist to engage in something approximating science. Above all it is necessary that 1) objects be intransitive to our knowledge, perception, or discourse about objects, and that 2) it be possible for objects to be out of phase with actual events. I will address the second of these points first.

If we must draw an *ontological* distinction between objects and the events they generate to understand the intelligibility of scientific practice, then this is precisely because objects do not *ordinarily* or *regularly* produce constant conjunctions of events. Constant conjunctions of events are the *exception* rather than the rule, and it is for this reason that we engage in experimental practice. In this connection, Bhaskar draws a distinction between *open* and *closed* systems. Closed systems are systems where constant conjunctions of events obtain. Open systems are, by contrast, systems where the powers of objects are either not acting or are rather disguised or hidden by virtue of the intervention of other causes. Open systems are the norm rather than the exception. And within open systems or entanglements of objects, the powers of discrete objects are often veiled or inactive. It is here that we encounter the rationale behind experimental activity. As Bhaskar puts it,

> Now once it is granted that mechanisms and structures may be said to be real, we can provide an interpretation of the independence of causal laws from patterns of events, and a fortiori of the rationale of experimental activity. For the real basis of this independence lies in the independence of the generative mechanisms of nature from the events they generate. Such mechanisms endure even when not acting; and act in their normal way even when the consequents of the law-like statements they ground are, owing to the operation of intervening mechanisms or countervailing causes, unrealized. It is the role of the experimental scientist to exclude such interventions, which are usual; and to trigger the mechanism so that it is active. The activity of the mechanism may then be studied without interference [...]. It is only under closed conditions that there will be a one-to-one relationship between the causal law and the sequence of events.[28]

We thus have an ontological distinction between objects or generative mechanisms on the one hand, and events, on the other. If experimental activity is necessary, then this is because generative mechanisms can be dormant, inactive, or veiled by the agency of other objects or generative mechanisms. Nonetheless, it is generative mechanisms or objects that are responsible for the production of events. As Bhaskar will remark further on, "[t]he world consists of things, not events. Most things are complex objects, in virtue of which they possess an ensemble of tendencies, liabilities and powers. It is by reference to the exercise of their tendencies, liabilities and powers that the phenomena of the world are explained".[29]

Because things, objects, or generative mechanisms can be out of phase with events, experimental activity is required to produce closed systems so that the relation between generative mechanisms and events might be discovered. To illustrate this point, Bhaskar provides a diagram distinguishing between the domains of the real, the actual, and the empirical:[30]

	Domain of Real	Domain of Actual	Domain of Empirical
Mechanisms	X		
Events	X	X	
Experiences	X	X	X

The domain of the empirical reduces events to experiences and excludes mechanisms altogether. As we saw in the case of Hume's empiricism, only sensations are given. In the domain of the actual, some events *may* be experiencable, yet there can be many events that we are yet to experience and even other events that are beyond the possibility of any experience. Moreover, events or actualities can be out of phase with mechanisms, objects, or things. Finally, the domain of mechanisms or the real is inclusive of both mechanisms, events, and experiences *without* the requirement that these categories overlap or always occur together. Thus there can be the presence of mechanisms without the presence of events or experiences, and there can be the presence of events without anyone about to experience them or anyone even capable of experiencing them. Zebras run across the savannah just fine without the aid of our gaze.

Bhaskar drives his point home rather dramatically by claiming the condition under which experimental practice is intelligible lies in the possibility of "a world without men".[31] Initially this thesis sounds paradoxical in that it is humans and perhaps other sentient beings that conduct experiments. However, Bhaskar's point lies elsewhere. He is not making the absurd claim that experiment requires no humans or sentient beings to conduct experiments—it does—but rather that because constant conjunctions of events ordinarily require humans or some other sentient being to produce them, because constant conjunctions of events are not the rule but the exception, and because generative mechanisms or objects are ordinarily out of phase with events or actualities, the intelligibility of our experimental activity is premised on the possibility of a world without humans where objects reside in the world unrealized and unwitnessed, and without producing certain actualities such as those we find in the experimental setting.

Consequently, Bhaskar's thesis is radically opposed to something like Lacan's claim that the universe is the flower of rhetoric. Such a thesis is misguided on two grounds: first, this thesis conflates propositions *about* the world with the world itself. Yet the world requires no propositions about the world to be the world. Second, and more importantly, this thesis renders experimental activity completely incoherent because science does not *begin* with true propositions, but seeks to create closed systems (where possible) so as to trigger generative mechanisms and thereby produce or uncover constant conjunctions of events. Were the world the totality of true *propositions* or constructed by language, this activity would be most peculiar indeed as there would be no *unknown* generative mechanisms to uncover in the experimental setting. In other words, the intelligibility of experimental practice is premised on the *ontological* supposition of generative mechanisms or objects *independent* of that activity.

And it is for this reason also that the condition for the intelligibility of experimental activity is the existence of objects that are intransitive or independent of mind and perception. For if objects were dependent on mind, perception, or culture, then there would be nothing to discover in the closed systems produced in the experimental setting. Consequently, not only are intransitive objects the premise of experimental activity, but the generative mechanisms discovered in experimental activity are also treated as operative in open systems once they are discovered, despite the fact that they operate in open systems in a fashion where the events they are *capable* of producing go unrealized because the mechanism is either dormant or countervailed by other generative mechanisms.

Bhaskar thus argues that claims about generative mechanisms are *transfactual*. Experimental activity does not show that constant conjunctions of events must always be operative in open systems, but rather that where these generative mechanisms exist without producing actualities or events, they are nonetheless operative in these open systems. Bhaskar thus argues that generative mechanisms must be understood as *tendencies* or *powers*. "[T]endencies are potentialities which may be exercised or as it were 'in play' without being realized or manifest in any particular outcome".[32] Needless to say, a tendency or power is a real feature of objects themselves, a feature of the *being* of objects, and not the being of objects *for-us*. Moreover, the distinction between generative mechanisms or objects with their tendencies or powers and events or actualities is an *ontological* distinction, not a distinction pertaining to our knowledge. Events are real beings or occurrences produced by generative mechanisms, and generative mechanisms are real entities with the power to produce these events. Thus the transcendental conditions Bhaskar uncovers for the intelligibility of experimental practice are thoroughly ontological and realist in character. They are features of the world itself and not the mind that regards the world.

Already we can sense just how far we are from Kant and Hume, both of whom have influenced contemporary theory so deeply, albeit in an often subterranean fashion. Where both Kant and Hume call for an investigation of mind when raising questions of knowledge, Bhaskar calls for a philosophical investigation of the *world*. For Bhaskar, it is ontology that is first philosophy, not epistemology. More importantly, where both Kant and Hume treat claims about causality as claims about constant conjunctions of events, Bhaskar vigorously rejects the thesis that claims about causality are claims about constant conjunctions of events on the grounds that constant conjunctions of events are the exception rather than the rule, and instead argues that claims about causality are claims about generative mechanisms that may or may not produce certain events depending on their entanglements with other objects.

Additionally, it will be noted that the ontology proposed by Bhaskar is immune to the charge of being a *naïve* realism. The charge of naïve realism is a favorite lazy rejoinder of anti-realist and correlationist styles of argument whenever encountering a defense of realism. Now, naïve realism is the thesis that the world is exactly as we perceive or experience it. It is, in short, the thesis that the qualities we perceive in an object truly belong to the object itself regardless of whether anyone perceives that object. However, it is clear that nothing could be further from Bhaskar's position. In distinguishing between generative mechanisms or objects and events or actualities, in noting the manner in which objects behave differently in open and closed systems, Bhaskar underlines the manner in which objects are withdrawn from any qualities they might happen to manifest. Put otherwise, a key feature of Bhaskar's argument is that objects or generative mechanisms cannot be equated with or reduced to their qualities. I shall have much more to say about this later when I deal with exo-relations or relations between generative mechanisms or objects, but for the moment it is sufficient to note that the ontology proposed by Bhaskar is anathema to any variant of naïve realism.

1.4. Objections and Replies

No doubt a number of objections will have arisen in the mind of the reader sympathetic to the correlationist line of argument. In particular, three lines of argument can be anticipated: First, that the realist ontology and transcendental line of argument proposed by Bhaskar purports to know objects *a priori* before knowing them; second, that it is impossible to imagine a world without men because we still imagine ourselves as being present to this world in our absence to this world; and third, in a closely related vein, that it is impossible to think anything without, as it were, including ourselves in the picture of what is to be thought. I will address each of these objections in their turn.

The first of these arguments is the easiest to dispatch. What this argument purports is that realist ontology claims to know before we know. Through this line of attack it hopes to establish the primacy of epistemology over ontology, or that epistemology is, in fact, first philosophy. For, the argument runs, how can ontology make claims about the being of being without first knowing these beings? As Bhaskar formulates this line of argument, "ontology is dependent upon epistemology since what we can know to exist is merely a part of what we can know".[33] I suspect that this line of argument, more than any other, motivates the subordination of ontology to epistemology and the treatment of ontology as "onto-epistemology". This seems to follow as obvious: to speak of being, we must *know* being and therefore an inquiry into knowledge or epistemology must precede any discussion of being. Heidegger, for example, argues that before we can even formulate the question of the meaning of being (it's noteworthy that he formulates this question as a question of *meaning* rather than a question of what being *is*) we must first investigate Dasein's ontic-ontological pre-comprehension of being.[34] Nothing could be more obvious.

However, as Bhaskar argues,

> this defense trades upon a tacit conflation of philosophical and scientific ontologies. For if 'what we can know to exist' refers to a possible content of a scientific theory then that it is merely a part of what we can know is an uninteresting truism. But a philosophical ontology is developed by reflection upon what must be the case for science to be possible; and this is independent of any actual scientific knowledge. Moreover, it is not true, even from the point of view of the immanent logic of a science, that what we can know to exist is just a part of what we can know. For a law may exist and be known to exist without our knowing the law. Much scientific research has in fact the same logical character as detection. In a piece of criminal detection, the detective knows that a crime has been committed and some facts about it but he does not know, or at least cannot yet prove, the identity of the criminal.[35]

Ontology does not tell us *what* objects exist, but *that* objects exist, that they are generative mechanisms, that they cannot be identified with events, actualities, or qualities, and that they behave differently in open and closed systems. These are ontological premises necessary to render our experimental activity intelligible. It is the job of actual inquiry to discover *what* objects exist. However, if inquiry is to be intelligible then it must begin with the premise that there are objects that act independently of this inquiry.

A second line of argument holds that it is impossible to intelligibly think a world without men because, in the very act of thinking such a world, we are picturing ourselves as present to this world. The thesis here is that every picturing of the world includes ourselves in that picture. However, as Quentin Meillassoux has convincingly argued, such a line of argument leads to the conclusion that the thought of our own death is unintelligible or that we are necessarily immortal. For if it is true that we cannot think the world without thinking our presence to the world, then it follows that even the thought of our own death requires the presence of our thinking, thereby undermining the possibility of dying. As Meillassoux formulates this line of argument, "I can only think of myself as existing, and as existing the way I exist; thus, I cannot but exist, and always exist as I exist now".[36]

Such is the argument of absolute idealists that 1) denies the existence of an in-itself apart from thought, and 2) argues that the correlation between being and thought is absolute or reality itself, i.e. that there is *nothing* apart from correlation (Berkeley and Hegel, though in very different ways). In response to this line of argument, Meillassoux cites the agnostic—the correlationist that concedes the *possible* existence of the in-itself apart from thought while maintaining the index of all thought to phenomena or being-for-us—pointing out that,

> In order to counter the latter [the strong or absolute correlationist], the agnostic has no choice: she must maintain that my capacity-to-be-wholly-other in death (whether dazzled by God, or annihilated) is just as thinkable as my persisting in my self-identity. The 'reason' for this is that I think myself as devoid of any reason for being and remaining as I am, and it is the thinkability of this unreason—of this facticity—which implies that the other three theses—those of the two realists and the idealist—are all equally possible. For even if I cannot think of myself, for example, as annihilated, neither can I think of any cause that would rule out this eventuality.[37]

While I do not follow Meillassoux in his inference from the contingency of *our* being to the contingency of being *as such* (I await a clearer formulation of this argument), I do believe his argument here hits the mark. If it is conceded that our annihilation is, *in principle*, thinkable, then we are also conceding that a world without humans is thinkable. For to think our annihilation just is to think a world where we are absent. Yet if this is the case, then the correlationist argument that it is impossible to think a form of being apart from thought is severely challenged.

Here it must be emphasized that Meillassoux's argument does not rest on establishing that we *are* annihilated with death or that we know that death entails the extinction of our being. As unlikely as it is given what we have come to know about the relationship between mind and brain, it *could* be that we persist after death. All that is required for Meillassoux's argument is that our extinction or annihilation be *thinkable* as a possibility. And if it is thinkable as a possibility—a point that seems amply supported by people's anxieties about death—then it also follows that it is possible to think a world without humans.

A final, and closely related line of argument, revolves around the reflexivity of thought. Here the idea is that it is impossible to think anything without simultaneously thinking that I am thinking it. Like the second objection, this objection revolves around the thesis that the thinker is always included in the picture of what she thinks. Thus, for example, as I think about making myself a cup of coffee, it is held that I must *also* be aware of thinking that I am thinking about making myself a cup of coffee. All thought, therefore, must include the thought of the thought in the activity of the thinking. As such, all thought must necessarily be reflexive or must simultaneously be aware of the object that it thinks *and* the fact that it is thinking this thought. And if this is the case, then it follows that the thinker must be included in the thought of any being other than thought, and that therefore it is impossible to escape the correlation between thought and being.

As Meillassoux amusingly puts it in his Goldsmith's talk, thought turns out to be like a bit of dual adhesive tape one attempts to remove from one's finger.[38] This talk was the occasion of a conference organized by Alberto Toscano, where Ray Brassier, Iain Hamilton Grant, Graham Harman, and Meillassoux each gave talks. It was here that the term "speculative realism" was used for the first time. In his talk, Meillassoux illustrated the correlationist argument through analogy to a dual adhesive bit of tape stuck to a person's finger. Each time she attempts to remove the tape it ends up sticking to another finger, such that the tape is inescapable. Likewise, if thought indeed has this character of reflexivity as a characteristic that *always* accompanies thought, then it follows that correlation or thought is inescapable. Such is the import of Descartes' famous analysis of the wax in the second meditation. As Descartes writes,

> What, I ask, am I who seem to perceive this wax so distinctly?
> Do I not know myself not only much more truly and
> with greater certainty, but also much more distinctly and
> evidently? For if I judge that the wax exists from the fact that
> I see it, certainly from this same fact that I see the wax it
> follows much more evidently that I myself exist. For it could
> happen that what I see is not truly wax. It could happen that
> I have no eyes with which to see anything. But it is utterly
> impossible that, while I see or think I see [...], I who think am
> not something. Likewise, if I judge that the wax exists from
> the fact that I touch it, the same outcome will again obtain,
> namely that I exist.[39]

Descartes' innocent little thesis here has been the source of much mischief in subsequent philosophy and is one of the root premises of correlationist thought. Whether we are speaking of Kant's transcendental unity of apperception which is treated as something that must accompany all thought[40], or Hegel's dialectical gymnastics where it is shown that the thinker is always included in the thought[41], the root of these claims traces back to Descartes' thesis that all thought is necessarily reflexive. It is this, for example, that will ultimately allow Hegel to assert the identity of substance and subject in *The Phenomenology of Spirit*.

However, is this seemingly obvious thesis truly so obvious? Meillassoux believes that this is a powerful argument that must be addressed. I'm not so sure. Is it self-evident that any thought must include the thinker or that the thinker is thinking the thought? While I certainly concede the thesis that in many instances we are *capable* of self-reflexively thinking the thought that we are thinking a thought, I am much more circumspect about the claim that all thought is *necessarily* reflexive. Were this the case, then it would seem that thought is impossible, for we would fall into an infinite regress. Thus, as I sit here thinking that I would like to make myself a cup of coffee, I would, if the reflexivity thesis were true, have to think that I am thinking that I would like to make myself a cup of coffee. But since it is asserted that all thought is reflexive, I would additionally have to think that I am thinking that I am thinking that I would like to make a cup of coffee, and so on to infinity. Yet if this were what truly takes place in the activity of thought, thought would be paralyzed. As Bhaskar puts it, "[i]t is possible for A to think ε and be aware of thinking ε without thinking about thinking ε; and unless this were so no-one could ever intelligently think".[42] What we need here is something like Sartre's "pre-reflexive *cogito*" which thinks something without simultaneously thinking itself.[43] Yet if such a *cogito* is possible, and indeed it appears *necessary*, then we have a thinking that doesn't simultaneously posit itself but which is completely absorbed in what we are thinking.

1.5. Origins of Correlationism: Actualism and the Epistemic Fallacy

In 1.2 I raised the question of what philosophical premises render correlationism such an appealing and persuasive hypothesis. We are now in a position to answer this question. In *A Realist Theory of Science*, Bhaskar identifies "actualism" as the root premise that ultimately leads to correlationism. As articulated by Bhaskar,

> 'actualism' [...] refer[s] to the doctrine of the actuality of causal laws; that is, to the idea that laws are relations between events or states of affairs (which are thought to constitute the objects of actual or possible experiences). Behind this idea of course lies the notion that only the actual (identified as the determinate object of the empirical) is real.[44]

Here it should be noted that actualism does not treat the actual as events that take place in the world regardless of whether or not anyone is about to witness them, but rather identifies the actual with what is given in sensations or impressions. Moreover, this hypothesis is not restricted to empiricists such as Hume, but is also carried over by Kant and his descendents. Consequently, it is necessary to distinguish between classical empiricists, such as Hume, and empiricist ontology. Classical empiricists hold that knowledge arises from sensation alone. Empiricist ontology holds that only the actual, construed as what is given in atomistic sensations, is real; or, at any rate, is all that we can speak of.

Kant does not question Hume's thesis that our knowledge is restricted to what is given in impressions or sensations, but rather embraces it wholesale. And because Kant carries over the actualist thesis of empiricist ontology, he is committed to the thesis that causal claims are claims about constant conjunctions of events given in sensation rather than about powers residing in objects or generative mechanisms that may go unactualized. Kant's innovation, therefore, does not reside in rejecting Hume's doctrine of impressions, but in recognizing that psychological operations of the mind such as the principles of association are insufficient to account for the necessity we attribute to causal relations. Sensation, Kant contends, requires supplementation by the mind, for relations are not themselves directly given in impressions. Consequently, Kant will argue that our judgments of necessity arise not from sensations or associations, but rather from the application of a priori categories of the understanding such as cause and effect to the manifold of sensations.

Yet Kant and his heirs are only led to the conclusion that sensation requires supplementation by categories of mind (or culture, language, norms, or power) as a result of presupposing the actualist hypothesis of empiricist ontology. For where knowledge is restricted to the actual, and the actual is equated with sensation or impressions, relations among objects become thoroughly mysterious as these relations are not directly given in the actual. As Harman has persuasively argued, what we get is a secularized form of occasionalism.[45] The occasionalist argues that all events are radically independent of one another. For the occasionalist there is no direct link between objects. In traditional occasionalisms, God is called upon to link objects to one another. Thus, when the paper burns it is not the flame that causes the paper to burn, but rather the intervention of God that brings the paper and the flame into relation with one another.

If, with Hume and Kant, we get a secularized form of occasionalism, then this is because the thesis that events, in the form of sense impressions, are absolutely independent of one another and without relation. As such, mind, rather than God, brings about the relation between events. For Kant, this linkage takes place through the a priori categories of the understanding and the a priori forms of intuition in the form of space, while for Hume this linkage is effected through the operations of association. The problem is that it is unclear how mind acquires this mysterious power to link that which is without linkage and why mind *alone* should have this privileged capacity. There is no more reason to think that mind should have this power than events themselves. However, this problem only emerges where the real is equated with the actual and the actual is treated as composed of atomistic sensations. Where claims about cause and effect relations are no longer treated as claims about constant conjunctions of events given in experience, but about generative mechanisms that may or may not produce certain events, the problem disappears. Causal claims are not claims about our experience of objects, but about objects themselves. And wherever we encounter arguments to the effect that sensations require supplementation by some other agency such as principles of association, categories of the understanding, language, signs, norms, and so on, we can be sure that actualism is lurking in the shadows and that the *ontological* conditions for the intelligibility of experimentation have been ignored.

Yet how comes it that we fall into this sort of actualism? Bhaskar contends that actualism originates in what he calls the "epistemic fallacy". As Bhaskar articulates it,

> This consists in the view that statements about being can be reduced to or analyzed in terms of statements about knowledge; i.e. that ontological questions can always be transposed into epistemological terms. The idea that being can always be analysed in terms of our knowledge of being, that it is sufficient for philosophy to 'treat only of the network, and not what the network describes', results in the systematic dissolution of the idea of a world (which I shall here metaphorically characterize as an ontological realm) independent of but investigated by science.[46]

Earlier Bhaskar remarks that, "[t]hese presumptions can [...] only be explained in terms of the need felt by philosophers for certain foundations of knowledge".[47]

Here it is necessary to clarify what the epistemic fallacy is and is not about. A critique of the epistemic fallacy and how it operates in philosophy does not amount to the claim that *epistemology* or questions of the nature of inquiry and knowledge are a fallacy. What the epistemic fallacy identifies is the fallacy of reducing ontological questions to epistemological questions, or conflating questions of *how* we know with questions of what beings *are*. In short, the epistemic fallacy occurs wherever being is reduced to our *access* to being. Thus, for example, wherever beings are reduced to our impressions or sensations of being, wherever being is reduced to our talk about being, wherever being is reduced to discourses about being, wherever being is reduced to signs through which being is manifest, the epistemic fallacy has been committed.

We have seen why this is so, for our experimental practice is only intelligible based on a series of ontological premises and these *ontological* premises cannot be reduced to our access to being. They are ontological in the robust sense. These ontological premises refer not to what is present or actual *to* us. Indeed, they refer, as we will see, to beings that are radically withdrawn from any presence or actuality. And as such, they are genuinely ontological premises, not epistemological premises pertaining to what is *given*.

In recognizing that the epistemic fallacy emerges from foundationalist aspirations on the part of philosophers, Bhaskar hits the mark. It is the desire for a secure and certain foundation for knowledge that leads philosophy to adopt the actualist stance and fall into the epistemic fallacy. These decisions, in turn, ultimately lead to correlationism. In raising the question, "how do we know?" and seeking an argument that would thoroughly defeat the skeptic or sophist, the philosopher concludes that only what is *present* or *given* can defend against the incursions of the skeptic. But what is present or given turns out either to be mind or sensations. Therefore the philosopher finds himself in the position of restricting all being to what is given as actual in sensations. From here a whole cascade of

problematic consequences follow that increasingly lead to the dissolution of
the world as a genuine ontological category.

However, once these foundationalist aspirations are abandoned, the
nature of the problem changes significantly and we no longer find ourselves
tied to the actualist premise that generates all of these issues. And indeed,
these aspirations *should* be abandoned, for foundationalism is premised
on the possibility of absolute presence, absolute proximity, the absence of
all absence, and we have now discovered that it is being *itself* that is split
between generative mechanisms or objects and the actual. Difference,
deferral, absence, and so on are not idiosyncrasies of *our* being preventing
us from ever reaching being, but are, rather, ontological characteristics of
being *as such*. Moreover, this split at the heart of all beings is not simply
characteristic of those objects that we would seek to know, but are also
characteristics of the peculiar object that we are. We ourselves are split.
If, then, this split is a general ontological feature of the world, then the
dream of presence required for any form of foundationalism is a priori
impossible. We are then left with two paths: to persist in the correlationist
thesis that would reduce ontological questions to epistemological questions
and which is itself implicitly premised on the ontotheological assumption
of actualism, or to investigate the split in being in a post-humanist, realist
fashion that is genuinely ontological. It is the second of these two paths that
I here attempt.

1.6. On the Alleged Primacy of Perception

In response to the preceding line of argument, one might argue that
nonetheless we must *identify* objects in order to know the being of objects,
and that the identification of an object requires some reference to a
perceptual convention. To be an object is to possess a boundary or to be
distinguished from other things, and in order to distinguish one object
from another we must refer to perception. This, then, would be the first
step in the argument, asserting the primacy of epistemology over ontology.
The next step would then consist in pointing out that different creatures
perceive or divide up the world in different ways. Thus, for example, while
I very clearly see a tree, it is unlikely that the amoeba encounters this

tree *as* a tree. Likewise, flowing water encounters no difference between a frog jumping into its currents, a rock obstructing its path, or a gust of wind impacting it. The point, then, is not only that we must refer back to epistemology or perceptual conventions to distinguish objects, but that *also*, while there is something *other* than perception (Berkeleyian subjective idealism is mistaken), there is no reason to suggest that being-in-itself is composed of objects or that this something is anything like *our* perception of the world.

This line of argument underlines just why it is so important to distinguish between arguments advanced on *ontological grounds* and arguments advanced on *epistemological grounds*. Why is this distinction so important? The reigning assumption in philosophy since the 17th century is that questions of epistemology must precede questions of ontology. The idea here is that we must first know an object before we can begin talking about the being of objects. This hearkens back to common readings of Meno's paradox in Plato. In the *Meno*, Socrates asks, "how can we inquire into the nature of virtue without first knowing virtue?" And if this constitutes a paradox, then this is precisely because if we already know virtue, then we have no reason to inquire into the nature of virtue.

The question of perception is not a question about the *being* of objects, but a question about our *access* to the being of objects. The point of the question is two-fold: first, the claim is that in order to talk about the being of objects we must first have access to objects. Second, the claim is that perhaps our access to objects has nothing to do with what *reality itself* is like. This is the point of the amoeba and the tree. The amoeba doesn't encounter the tree *as* a tree, and thus we should be skeptical of the idea that entities like trees are independent or real entities at all. The thesis is thus that the being of an object arises not from the *object's own* independent structure, but rather from the distinctions the being perceiving it makes. This is the correlationist gesture *par excellence*. To be sure, the correlationist may concede that there is *something other* than the amoeba, but he wishes to argue that there's no reason to suppose that this something is *anything like* how the amoeba experiences it because the nature of the being that the amoeba perceives is a function of the *amoeba's* distinctions, not of the being of this other-being itself.

Let us now return to the difference between arguments that are ontologically driven and arguments that are epistemologically driven. The first point to note with respect to the correlationist's argument is that it seems to ignore the fact that this argument already *concedes the existence* of at least *one object.* What object is that? Certainly not the existence of the tree. Rather, the correlationist concedes the existence of the *amoeba.* In order for the amoeba to grasp anything *as* anything at all, it must exist as an entity, substance, or object. In short, the correlationist's argument can only get off the ground through the presupposition of at least one entity. And this is a central reason that arguments about how *observers* constitute objects are unconvincing: these arguments always forget that the observer *is* an *object.*

Let us return to the example of the water encountering a rock, frog, or gust of wind. Here the argument was made that these entities aren't distinct for the water but produce all the same qualitative effects. In chapter four we will see why this is the case, but for the moment, rather than speaking about the water, let's instead speak of the relation between a frog and the amoeba. When we discuss the relation between the amoeba and the frog, we encounter exactly the same problem as the relation between the water and stones, frogs, and wind: the frog does not distinguish amoebas. The amoeba does not encounter the frog *as* a frog, nor does the frog encounter the amoeba *as* an amoeba. From the standpoint of the frog's experience, the amoeba is *indistinguishable* from *air* or *water.* The frog is every bit as *indifferent* to the existence of the amoeba *as* an amoeba, as the water is indifferent to the existence of a rock or frog or the wind as a rock, frog, or wind. There is no real difference here. It might as well *not* exist. However, here's the rub: does the fact of the amoeba's non-existence within the frog's *Umwelt* have anything to do with the *amoeba's* existence? To claim that it does is to be led to the peculiar conclusion that it is the *entity's* distinctions that make *other* entities what they *are.*

Here, then, we arrive at the difference between epistemologically-driven arguments and ontologically-driven arguments. Epistemologically-driven arguments will always pitch questions of what beings *are* in terms of our *access* to these entities. Rather than asking what beings must be by right, we instead ask what conventions *we use* to distinguish entities. However, as can be clearly seen, this changes the issue or question. Rather than treating the question as a question of what beings are, the correlationist instead transforms the question into a question of how we know what things are. And because the correlationist has transformed the question from the issue of what must belong to entities by right in order to be entities, regardless of whether anyone else knows these entities, to the question of how we know entities, the correlationist finds himself confronted with the question of givenness or access. Having transposed a properly ontological question into an epistemological question, and having thereby arrived at the problem of givenness (the reference to perception) or access, the correlationist now notices that *different entities* or observers *perceive* the world *differently*, i.e., that the world is *given* in different ways to different observers. The amoeba doesn't encounter the tree as a tree. A person who is colorblind cannot see the color purple, and so on.

Based on this line of argumentation, we can now see why Bhaskar refers to the epistemic fallacy as a *fallacy*. The epistemic fallacy does not lie in raising questions of epistemology. That would be absurd. Of course we should raise epistemic questions. The epistemic fallacy consists in the thesis that properly ontological questions can be fully transposed into epistemological questions. Because the correlationist has transformed questions of what beings are into questions of our access to beings, and because questions of access necessarily trace back to questions of givenness, givenness now comes to legislate what exists and what does not exist. The correlationist is therefore compelled to argue that the tree does not exist or that frogs and rocks don't exist. If this move is problematic, then this is because it always finds itself trapped in a self-referential paradox: to wit, it concedes the existence of at least one entity, and then uses the manner in which that entity observes the rest of the world through its own distinctions to erase the existence of other entities. Every argument of this sort, driven by how we cognize or perceive the world, will run afoul of this sort of problem.

The point here is that questions of ontology cannot, in any manner, shape, or form, be reduced to questions of epistemology. Put otherwise, claims about the being of beings cannot be transposed into claims about our access to beings. Wherever claims about the being of beings are transposed into questions about our access to beings, we end up with givenness legislating what exists and what doesn't exist based on what is given or accessible, and we thereby find ourselves trapped in a self-defeating self-referential paradox where we simultaneously concede the existence of objects while denying their existence.

As a consequence, claims about the being of entities are arrived at in an entirely different manner than the epistemological question of access. We do not begin with our access to beings, but instead ask what the world must be like for certain practices to be possible. The object-oriented ontologist is not claiming that we have access to beings, that they are given, or that our perception is identical to the way the world is, but that the existence of substance is a necessary premise for a whole slew of our practices to be intelligible. In other words, the onticological thesis is that the world must be a particular way for certain practices and activities like perception, experimentation, discourse, and so on, to be possible and that the world would be this way regardless of whether we perceived, experimented, or discoursed about it.

Perhaps the best way to defeat the correlationist is to shift the terms of the debate. It is almost always the case that the correlationist proceeds through a discussion of how *humans* perceive and discourse about the world. Rather than beginning with humans, however, why not instead begin with the amoeba? Does the correlationist really wish to claim that the amoeba constitutes *his* being? This conclusion follows directly from the correlationist argument about how the amoeba encounters the tree. If he doesn't wish to arrive at this conclusion, then why? There are only two possible conclusions here, both of which lead to the collapse of the correlationist's argument. The first possible conclusion would be that it is not possible for the amoeba to constitute the correlationist's being because humans are somehow special in the order of being by virtue of being the only beings capable of constituting other beings from the primordial flux of "other-being". The second possible argument is that the amoeba doesn't constitute the correlationist's being through perceiving the correlationist because the correlationist is a substance or independent being in his own right and how something perceives another being has nothing to do with that being's status as a substance.

Now, one might expect the realist to reject the first possibility on the grounds that it is anthropocentric. However, while this is true, this is not my argument. If we follow the correlationist in the first counter-argument (which really is the disavowed, yet fully embraced, implicit premise of all correlationisms), we have to note that the correlationist has conceded the existence of at least *one* object, namely, the correlationist himself. From here it is but a short step to asking why humans or the correlationist should have this privileged status within the order of being. Moreover, it's quite remarkable that any being should be able to perform this feat like Atlas holding the world on his shoulders, carving up a structureless world, a pre-individual flux, into discrete packets or units. If we grant the second argument, then, of course, we've conceded the existence of withdrawn substances that have their own being regardless of how other substances perceive them. Those who advise us to observe the observer somehow seem to miss the point that the very act of observing the observer or observing how other observers observe presupposes the existence of an observer that is doing the observing of other observers. Far from undermining the thesis that substances or objects exist, in other words, this move presupposes the existence of at least one substance or object. And as a consequence, this move is incapable of consistently maintaining the thesis that the world is a product of how observers perceive other objects.

Chapter 2
The Paradox of Substance

> When the materiality of the glove, the rat, the pollen, the
> bottle cap, and the stick start to shimmer and spark, it was
> in part because of the contingent tableau that they formed
> with each other, with the street, with the weather that
> morning, with me. For had the sun not glinted on the black
> glove, I might not have seen the rat; had the rat not been
> there, I might not have noted the bottle cap, and so on.
> But they were all there just as they were, and so I caught a
> glimpse of an energetic vitality inside each of these things,
> things that I generally conceived as inert. In this assemblage,
> objects appeared as things, that is, as vivid entities not
> entirely reducible to the contexts in which (human) subjects
> set them, never entirely exhausted by their semiotics.
>
> — Jane Bennett[48]

2.1. Introduction

From Roy Bhaskar's early work we have learned that, if experimental
practice is to be intelligible, the *world* must be a particular way. First,
objects must be capable of behaving differently in open and closed systems.
For this reason, the being or substance of generative mechanisms cannot
be identified with its actualized qualities, but must be located elsewhere.

It is only in closed systems, Bhaskar contends, that constant conjunctions of events in cause and effect relations obtain. In open systems, by contrast, objects can remain dormant, producing no events at all, or the intervention of countervailing causes can either a) hide events produced by objects, or b) produce events different from those that the generative mechanism or object would produce in a closed system by virtue of how entanglements of objects are woven together. Consequently, second, objects or generative mechanisms must be distinguished from events or actualities. Objects or generative mechanisms are defined not by their qualities or events, but rather by their *powers* or capacities. An object cannot be without its powers or capacities, but it can be without its qualities or events. Finally, third, if it is possible to form closed systems where constant conjunctions of events *can* obtain, then it also follows that objects or generative mechanisms must be *independent* of their *relations*.

While I readily concede that objects *can* enter into relations—how else would open systems be possible?—it does not follow from this that objects *are* their relations. In short, if it is to be possible to form closed systems in which constant conjunctions of events occasionally obtain as they sometimes do in experimental settings, then it follows that relations cannot ontologically be *internal* to their terms or the objects that they relate. In other words, objects are not *constituted* by their relations to the rest of the world. While relations to other objects often play a key role in the precipitation of events or qualities in objects, we must here recall that objects are not identical to their qualities but are rather the ground of qualities. Accordingly we must distinguish between objects and their relations, or rather the structure of objects and the relations into which objects enter. I call the former "endo-relations" (or, following Graham Harman, "domestic relations"), and the latter "exo-relations" (or, as Harman calls them, "foreign relations"[49]). Endo-relations constitute the internal structure of objects independent of all other objects, while exo-relations are relations that objects enter into with other objects. Were objects constituted by their exo-relations or relations to other objects, the being would be frozen and nothing would be capable of movement or change. It is only where relations are external to objects that such change can be thought.

Insofar as what Bhaskar calls generative mechanisms are the ground of events or qualities, they deserve the archaic, Aristotelian name of *substance*. Because substances have the power to produce events, I shall refer to them as *difference engines*, for the production of an event is the production of differences in the world. Because difference engines or substances are not identical to the events or qualities they produce, while nonetheless substances, however briefly, endure, the substantial dimension of objects deserves the title of *virtual proper being*. And because events or qualities occur only under particular conditions and in a variety of ways, I will refer to events produced by difference engines as *local manifestations*. Local manifestations are *manifestations* because they are *actualizations* that occur in the world.

To this list of the properties of substances we can add a fourth: local manifestations are not to be confused with manifestations *to* or *for* a subject, but are rather events that take place in the world regardless of whether or not any subjects or sentient beings exist to witness them. Consequently, local manifestation is not equivalent to the empirical or what is experienced by a subject. Experience is a subset of local manifestation, but the set comprised of local manifestations is infinitely larger than the set consisting of experience. In this respect, the category of local manifestation shares some affinity to Badiou's conception of appearance as appearing without a subject to which appearance appears or is given.[50]

If, by contrast, local manifestations or events are *local*, then this is because the qualities or events of objects are variable depending on internal dynamisms in the object or difference engine and the exo-relations into which the object enters. Consequently, we must not say that an object *has* its qualities or that qualities *inhere* in an object, nor above all that objects *are* their qualities, but rather in a locution that cannot but appear grotesque and bizarre, we must say that qualities are something an object *does*. The concept of local manifestation is here designed to capture the context dependency—whether that context be internal or external—of the events an object produces in its manifestations.

Finally, insofar as substances are not identical to events or their qualities—nor, moreover, their exo-relations to other objects—I refer to difference engines as *split-objects*. The characterization of difference engines as split-objects refers not to a physical split such as the idea that objects can always be broken in half or divided, but rather to the split between the virtual proper being of objects or their powers and their local manifestations or qualities. Here the point to be borne in mind is that objects are always in *excess* of any of their local manifestations, harboring hidden volcanic powers irreducible to any of their manifestations in the world. In this respect, the concept of split-object captures my version of what Graham Harman has referred to as the "withdrawal" of objects. As Harman puts it, "[t]here are objects [...] withdrawn absolutely from all relation, but there is also a ubiquitous ether of qualities through which these objects interact".[51]

Harman defends the withdrawal of objects in a much more radical sense than I do here; however, there are strong points of overlap between our positions. Within the framework of onticology, the claim that objects are withdrawn from other objects is the claim that 1) substances are independent of or are not constituted by their relations to other objects, and 2) that objects are not identical to any qualities they happen to locally manifest. The substantiality of objects is never to be equated with the qualities they produce. Thus, as Harman goes on to remark,

> If there are objects, then they must exist in some sort of vacuum-like state, since no relation fully deploys them. The recent philosophical tendency is to celebrate holistic interrelations endlessly, and to decry the notion of anything that could exist in isolation from all else. Yet this is precisely what an object does. An object may drift into events and unleash its forces there, but no such event is capable of putting the object fully into play. Its neighboring objects will always react to some of its features while remaining blind to the rest. The objects in an event are somehow always elsewhere, in a site divorced from all relations.[52]

Onticology finds much to admire in this passage. Like Harman's object-oriented philosophy, onticology argues that objects or substances are withdrawn from or independent of their relations to other substances. Like Harman's object-oriented philosophy, onticology rejects the thesis of holistic interrelations where objects or substances are understood to be *constituted* by their relations to other substances. Finally, like Harman's object-oriented philosophy, onticology holds that no relation ever deploys all of the forces contained within an object. The point where onticology and Harman's object-oriented ontology diverge is on the issue of whether the independence of objects or substances entails that objects never touch or encounter one another, or that objects, by virtue of their withdrawal, must be *vacuums*. Were this the case, it seems that it would be impossible for any object to ever unleash the forces of another object. Given that objects often do unleash forces in other objects, it thus appears that objects must somehow be capable of perturbing one another, while the virtual proper being of an object forever remains in excess of this encounter and is nonetheless closed.

In this chapter, my aim is to articulate the structure of substance and the relationship between virtual proper being and local manifestation in the production of qualities. However, before proceeding to this task it is first necessary to articulate some features of the concept of substance and respond to what Kenneth Burke has called "the paradox of substance". If Burke's discussion of the paradox of substance in *The Grammar of Motives* is here relevant, then this is because what Burke treats as a *paradox*, and therefore critique of substance, unwittingly provides us with a fundamental clue as to the ontological structure of substance and why it is necessarily characterized by withdrawal.

2.2. Aristotle, Substance, and Qualities

It is often said that Aristotle has an analogical conception of being, holding that being is said in many senses. However, as is so often the case in the history of philosophy, the issue is more complicated than this; for while Aristotle does indeed argue that, for example, we use the term "being" differently when referring to secondary substances (qualities) and primary substances (individual things or objects), Aristotle also argues that the primary meaning of being is that of individual things. As Aristotle puts it in book Z of the *Metaphysics*,

> There are several senses in which a thing may be said to be
> [...], for in one sense it means what a thing is or a 'this', and

in another sense it means that a thing is of a certain quality
or quantity or has some such predicate asserted of it. While
'being' has all these senses, obviously that which is primarily
is the 'what', which indicates the substance of a thing [...].
And all other things are said to be because they are, some
of them, quantities of that which *is* in this primary sense,
others qualities of it, others affections of it, and others some
determination of it. And so one might raise the question
whether 'to walk' and 'to be healthy' and 'to sit' signify in each
case something that is, and similarly in any other case of this
sort; for none of them is either self-subsistent or capable of
being separated from substance, but rather, if anything, it is
that which walks or is seated or is healthy that is an existent
thing. Now these are seen to be more real because there is
something definite which underlies them; and this is the
substance or individual, which is implied in such a predicate;
for 'good' or 'sitting' are not used without this. Clearly
then it is in virtue of this category that each of the others
is. Therefore that which is primarily and *is* simply (not is
something) must be substance.[53]

To be, for Aristotle, is to be a substance or a thing. All other senses of
being, Aristotle argues, ultimately refer back to substance for ultimately
all these other forms of being reside in substances or are made possible
by substances. It is this Aristotelian orientation to the being of being as
substance or individual thing that onticology, and object-oriented ontology
more broadly construed, defends. The question, then, is what precisely is a
substance? It is this question that this book seeks to answer.

Elsewhere, in the *Categories*, Aristotle gives us an important clue as to
the nature of substance. There Aristotle writes that, "[a] *substance*—that
which is called a substance most strictly, primarily, and most of all—is that
which is neither said of a subject nor in a subject, e.g., the individual man
or the individual horse".[54] In short, *a substance is that which is not predicated
of anything else*, and which therefore enjoys *independent* or *autonomous*
existence. Color, for example, is always predicated *of* a substance. Put
differently, color must always reside *in* something else. The color red is

never a substance in its own right, but is always in a ball or a strawberry or lipstick. Qualities reside in substances, they are predicated of substances, whereas substances are not predicated of anything.

Thus Aristotle will remark that, "of the primary substances one is no more a substance than another: the individual man is no more a substance than the individual ox".[55] In short, there is an equality of objects, a democracy of objects, in the precise sense that all substances are equally substances. This does not entail that substances are equal to one another, that there are no differences among substances, and that there are not substances more or less powerful than other substances, but rather that all substances are equally substances. When I discuss the concept of flat ontology we will see that this thesis of "equal being" has profound consequences for critical theory and how we practice critical theory. In particular, it entails that we cannot treat one kind of being as the ground of all other beings.

Likewise, when I discuss mereology later, we will see that the thesis that 1) a substance is not itself predicated of anything else, and the thesis 2) that no substance is more or less a substance than any other gives rise to a host of delicate and fascinating problems pertaining to relations between parts and wholes. If objects or substances are not predicated of anything else, then it follows that substances cannot be treated as identical with their *parts*. Were objects identical to their parts, then this would entail that objects are predicates of their parts. This, in turn, would undermine the autonomy or independence of objects. Consequently, while substances certainly cannot exist without their parts, substantiality must be something *other* than the parts of which an object is composed. Here we encounter one of the ways in which the realism advocated by onticology is anathema to every form of classical *materialism*. The sorts of classical materialism defended by thinkers such as Democritus, Epicurus, and Lucretius hold that objects ultimately *are* their parts in the form of atoms and that these atoms, in their turn, are the only true substances. Onticology, by contrast, argues that scale and whether or not something is an aggregate is irrelevant to whether or not something is a substance. As Harman nicely articulates it, "[n]o privilege is granted to objects over and against mere aggregates, as though atoms were real and baseball leagues only derivative, or individual

soldiers real and armies only derivative".[56] "Instead", Harman goes on
to remark, "we have a universe made up of objects wrapped in objects
wrapped in objects wrapped in objects" such that, "[e]very object is both a
substance and a complex of relations".[57]

Mereologically this entails that we must develop an ontology capable
of maintaining the autonomy or independence of substances from one
another such that parts are understood as themselves being substances
independent of the whole to which they belong—i.e., they are not merely
predicates of the wholes to which they belong—and wholes are treated
as independent of their parts. A key feature of each and every object—in
fact, a defining feature—is its autonomy. Regardless of whether an object
is simple or compound—and onticology strongly suspects that all objects
are compound—each object is nonetheless autonomous. As we will see,
these seemingly arid ontological issues of the relation between parts and
wholes are of surprising importance for a host of issues in social and
political theory. Here it is also important to note that "size doesn't matter".
Insofar as no substance is neither more nor less a substance than another
substance, it follows, as Harman points out, that atoms are no more nor less
substances than molecules, aardvarks or baseball teams.

Insofar as substances are not predicated of anything else, it follows
that substances are not *in* anything else in the sense that qualities are
in substances. As Aristotle puts it, "[i]t is a characteristic common to
every substance not to be in a subject. For a primary substance is neither
said of a subject nor in a subject".[58] Substances are not something *in* an
individual thing, but are rather what individual things *are*. Consequently,
all substances have the characteristic of sets whereby sets do not include
themselves as a member of themselves. Thus, while all substances are
"multiplicities" insofar as they contain parts that are themselves objects—
though in a very different way, we shall see, than Badiou proposes in
Being and Event—the substantiality of a substance is not itself a *part* of the
substance. Substantiality, rather, *is* the substance.

Insofar as substances cannot be identified with their parts or the objects
which compose them, it follows that substances are always numerically *one*.
As Aristotle puts it, "[s]ubstance, it seems, does not admit of a more or a
less".[59] A substance is always *a* substance. As a consequence, a substance

is neither more nor less than itself, nor is a substance ever any more than *one*. In the first instance, a substance is neither more nor less than itself in the sense that when a person gains weight or loses an arm they are still *this* substance. In the second instance, if a substance is always one then this is because, while a substance might be compounded of many parts or other objects, *qua* substance the substance is still one substance. Once again, it is clear that this determination of substance raises a number of delicate mereological issues revolving around problems of the one and the many.

Finally, it is a peculiar characteristic of substances that they are *non-dialectical*. As Aristotle remarks, "[a]nother characteristic of substances is that there is nothing contrary to them".[60] Beginning with Hegel, dialectic takes on two meanings that are distinct but often conflated with one another. First, and especially in a Marxist context, dialectic can be taken to refer to thinking that is specifically *relational* in character. Marx, for example, shows how *commodities* can only exist in certain social formations characterized by wage labor and capitalism. Later, in our discussion of regimes of attraction and exo-relations we will see how some notion of dialectic in this relational sense can be retained with respect to local manifestations. Second, dialectic can be taken to mean a thinking of relation in terms of contraries and contradictions that are sublated in ever greater wholes or totalities. While onticology readily recognizes the existence of antagonisms, it sees no reason to see antagonisms as the equivalent to contraries or contradictions.

Substances are not defined by contraries or opposites, but simply are what they are. This, of course, is not to suggest that substances do not come into being or that they cannot pass out of being, only that they do not admit of opposed or contrary terms. An individual cane toad does not have an opposite. Rather, *if* there is contrariety, it exists only in the domain of qualities. Later, when discussing local manifestation and virtual proper being we will see that there is reason to doubt that contrariety is a genuine *ontological* category. Insofar as substances are not *constituted* by their relations, insofar as relations are not internal to their terms, it follows that substances cannot be dialectical in either the relational sense or the sense of contrariety. Contrariety, if it exists, exists at the level of qualities, not substances. It is only through an erasure of substances, through a reduction of substances to their qualities, through the gesture of *actualism* as discussed in the last chapter, that it can be supposed that substance *is* dialectical.

This leads Aristotle to formulate another definition of substance that has wide-ranging ontological consequences. We have already seen that substance is that which is not predicated of anything else. In addition to this, Aristotle remarks that "[i]t seems most distinctive of substance that what is numerically one and the same is able to receive contraries".[61] Aristotle goes on to illustrate this point with an example: "[A]n individual man—one and the same—becomes pale at one time and dark at another, and hot and cold, and bad and good".[62] In short, a substance is that which is capable of actualizing a variety of different qualities while remaining one and the same substance. Later in the *Categories* Aristotle will remark that qualities are "that in virtue of which things are said to be qualified somehow".[63] Here we find confirmation of the onticological thesis that substances are not identical to their qualities for, insofar as substances are able to take on different qualities while remaining the same substance, it follows that objects must be distinct from their qualities.

However, here we must take care. For, in claiming that substances are distinct from their qualities, we do not mean to imply that they are *numerically* distinct from one another, as if the qualities were one *entity* and the substance another entity. Speaking of the difference between real distinctions, numerical distinctions, and formal distinctions, Deleuze writes,

> We can conceive that names or propositions do not have the same sense even while they designate exactly the same thing (as in the case of the celebrated examples: morning star- evening star, Israel - Jacob, *plan - blanc*). The distinction between these senses is indeed a real distinction [*distinctio realis*], but there is nothing numerical—much less ontological—about it: it is a formal, qualitative or semiological distinction.[64]

While I do not wish to follow Deleuze in his thesis that the difference between numerical distinction and formal distinction is merely a *semiological* distinction that refers to nothing ontological, Deleuze nonetheless draws attention to a difference between two very important forms that real distinctions take. On the one hand, two things are *numerically distinct* when they exist *independently* of one another. As we have seen, all substances are numerically distinct insofar as they are independent of one another. On the other hand, two things are *formally distinct* if they really are distinct from one another, but they cannot exist independently of one another.

In the case of the relation between substances and their qualities, there is a real distinction insofar as substances are never identical to their qualities. However, the distinction between substances and their qualities is not a *numerical* distinction but a *formal* distinction. Here, however, I hasten to add that the formal distinction between substances and their qualities is not *symmetrical* but rather *asymmetrical*. As we saw in the last chapter, substances can exist unactualized or without producing any events. As a consequence, substances are not dependent on their qualities, but can exist without any qualities at all (in a form yet to be specified). The contrary, however, is not true. Where substances can exist without their qualities or without producing any events, qualities can never exist without substances in which to exist. Finally, to this we must add that the distinction between substance and quality is not a distinction between what is real and what is not real. Both substances and qualities are entirely real. The point is merely that substances can never be reduced to any of their local manifestations or actualized qualities.

2.3. The Paradox of Substance

As we saw in the last chapter, the *ontological* category of substance is indispensable to rendering our account of experimental practice intelligible. The practice of experiment is premised on the existence of generative mechanisms, difference engines, or substances that act in open systems, that they can be out of phase with the events they are capable of producing, and that they are separable from their relations to other substances. Nonetheless, it is clear that the concept of substance has fallen into disrepute within philosophy, often being equated with a metaphysical ghost or fiction with no warrant whatsoever.

One of the roots of the disdain with which the concept of substance is today received can be found in Locke's *An Essay Concerning Human Understanding*. There Locke writes that,

> if any one will examine himself concerning his *Notion of pure Substance in general*, he will find he has no other *Idea* of it at all, but only a Supposition of he knows not what support of such Qualities, which are capable of producing simple *Ideas* in us; which Qualities are commonly called Accidents. If any one should be asked, what is the subject wherein Colour or Weight inheres, he would have nothing to say, but the solid extended parts: And if he were demanded, what is it, that that Solidity and Extension inhere in, he would not be in a much better case, than the *Indian* before mentioned; who, saying that the World was supported by a great Elephant, was asked, what the Elephant rested on; to which his answer was, a great Tortoise: But being again pressed to know what gave support to the broad-back'd Tortoise, replied, something, he knew not what. And thus here, as in all other cases, where we use words without having clear and distinct *Ideas*, we talk like Children... The *Idea* then we have, to which we give the general name Substance, being nothing, but the supposed, but unknown support of those Qualities, we find existing, which we imagine cannot subsist, *sine re substante*, without something to support them, we call that Support *Substantia*; which, according to the true import of the Word, is in plain *English, standing under*, or *upholding*.[65]

Locke's criticism of the concept of substance spins on the manner in which substance and qualities are split. Within the Aristotelian framework, substance is the ground of qualities, yet we never encounter substance as *such*, but rather only ever encounter the *qualities* of substance. From this observation, two problems emerge for Locke: first, what *warrant* is there for supposing the existence of substance at all? If substance is never encountered at all, if all we ever encounter are qualities, how is substance any different from a reference to Zeus to explain lightning? Second, if substance differs fundamentally from its qualities, what could it possibly be? If substance is stripped of all its qualities aren't we left with a *bare substratum*, leading to the bizarre and absurd conclusion that all substances are ultimately identical?

Elsewhere, in *The Grammar of Motives*, Kenneth Burke, in a discussion of Locke, will call this "the paradox of substance". There Burke writes that, "the word 'substance,' used to designate what a thing *is*, derives from a word designating something that a thing *is not*. That is, though used to designate something *within* the thing, *intrinsic* to it, the word etymologically refers to something *outside* the thing, *extrinsic* to it".[66] Burke's point is that substance is supposed to be that which is intrinsic to an object, that which makes an object what it is, but that oddly substance ends up being *external* to the object. If substance, according to Burke, turns out to be external to the object, then this is because we only ever encounter the *qualities* of the object, and never the *substance* of the object. If, then, the object is equated with its qualities, then substance turns out to be strangely *other* than the object.

Locke's critique of substance precipitates something of a crisis that reverberates all the way down to contemporary philosophy today. As Meillassoux remarks, in prior philosophy "one of the questions that divided rival philosophers most decisively was, 'Who grasps the true nature of substance? He who thinks the Idea, the individual, the atom, God? Which God?'"[67] However, with Locke's critique of substance, this entire debate is thrown into crisis as there no longer seems to be any epistemic warrant for the ontological concept of substance. However, while the *ontological* concept of substance seems to be banished to the world of occult and unwarranted suppositions with no place in philosophy, *individual things* nonetheless persist in the world of our *experience*. Having banished the *ontological* concept of substance—viz., substances as they exist in their own right, independent of any cognition—philosophy thus finds itself confronted with the question of how to account for individual things without recourse to mind-independent substances inaccessible to experience. Hume, for example, will argue that substance is not a feature of the *world*—or, at least, any world that we can *know*—but rather arises from the operations of *mind*. Having experienced the combination of many similar sensations occurring together in the past, the mind comes to associate these impressions or sensations with one another. In this respect, the object itself, for Hume, is not a substance, but rather the sense that one encounters a substance when encountering an object is instead an *effect* of how the mind associates impressions and ideas together in a unity. In this way, Hume responds to Locke's challenge by making no reference to "occult entities" independent of what is *given* in sensation.

We encounter a similar move from world to mind in Kant's *Critique of Pure Reason*. As Kant observes,

> in experience, to be sure, perceptions come together only contingently, so that no necessity of their connection is or can become evident in the perceptions themselves, since apprehension is only a juxtaposition of the manifold of empirical intuition, but no representation of the necessity of the combined existence of the appearances that it juxtaposes in space and time is to be encountered in it. But since experience is a cognition of objects through perception, consequently the relation in the existence of the manifold is to be represented in it not as it is juxtaposed in time but as it is objectively in time, yet since time itself cannot be perceived, the determination of the existence of objects in time can only come about through their combination in time in general, hence only through *a priori* connecting concepts. Now since these always carry necessity along with them, experience is thus possible only through a representation of the necessary connection of the perceptions.[68]

For Kant, the realm of empirical intuition (sensation) is a sort of confused chaos and therefore cannot, contra Hume, provide us with any ordered or structured experience. "[O]ur entire sensibility is nothing but the confused representation of things, which contains solely that which pertains to them in themselves but only under a heap of marks and partial representations that we can never consciously separate from one another".[69] Or, as Kant will write when discussing the first analogy, "[o]ur *apprehension* of the manifold of appearance is always successive, and is therefore always changing. We can therefore never determine from this alone whether this manifold, as objects of experience, is simultaneous or successive".[70]

It will be noted that Kant fully carries over the premise of Locke's critique of substance, leaving this critique itself unquestioned. Beginning with the premise that we have no access to substances but only qualities *as they are experienced*, and with the thesis that the "manifold of intuition" or empirical sensation is unformatted, Kant has no other recourse than to claim that the substantiality of substances is not an *ontological* feature of *objects themselves*, but rather issues from our mind. To be sure, Kant endorses the thesis that things-in-themselves exist, but maintains that we have no access to these objects and therefore no means of determining whether, like the objects of our experience, things-in-themselves are autonomous, individual unities, or whether the things-in-themselves are, in reality, really a *thing*-in-itself, a primordial unity or One, that is then subsequently formatted or "cut up" by our minds. Since the substantiality of substance must issue from somewhere, and since we cannot appeal to being itself to ground substance, Kant contends that substance is instead an *a priori* category of mind that is imposed on the chaotic manifold of intuition giving it structure or formatting it.

What we have here is what Harman has referred to as the "overmining" of substances. Where undermining dissolves objects in a something that is purported to be more fundamental such as atoms, water (Thales), the One, the pre-individual, and so on, overmining dissolves objects in something that is treated as being more immediate. Of overmining, Harman writes, "it is said that [objects] are too deep. On this view the object is a useless hypothesis, a '*je ne sais quoi*' in the bad sense".[71] In the case of Hume, substances are overmined in favor of impressions or sensations that are then bundled together by associations of the mind, while in the case of Kant, substances are overmined in favor of the manifold of intuition (sensations), along with the pure a priori forms of space and time and the a priori categories of the *mind*. In both instances, objects or substances are treated as *effects* of something more immediate or accessible (empirical experience and mind).

It would be difficult to overestimate the impact of Locke's critique of substance and Hume's and Kant's proposed solution to the paradox of substance on the subsequent history of philosophy and theory. For while direct reference to Locke, Hume, and Kant in subsequent philosophy and theory will often be absent, we nonetheless encounter Locke's critique of substance as an *implicit* presupposition, and Hume's and Kant's *style* of solving this problem throughout contemporary philosophy and theory. Wherever, for example, we are told that it is language that structures reality, we are encountering a variant of Kant's response to Locke. While, to be sure, the content of the critique and the proposed solution differs, the form of the critique remains the same. Here the premises that 1) the ontological category of substance should be banished because we have no direct access to substance, and 2) that the manifold of intuition is a chaotic rhapsody of sensation have been fully embraced and Kant's mind and *a priori* categories have been replaced by society and language.

Ironically, however, Kant's reasoning is based on an *amphiboly*, though of an *ontological* rather than a transcendental sort. In the *Critique of Pure Reason* Kant tells us that a transcendental amphiboly is, "a confusion of the pure object of the understanding with [an empirical] appearance".[72] For Kant, there is both a rationalist and an empiricist way of falling into amphibolous reasoning. Drawing on Leibniz and Locke as examples, Kant argues that "Leibniz *intellectualized* the appearances, just as Locke totally *sensitivized* the concepts of the understanding, i.e., interpreted them as nothing but empirical or abstracted concepts of reflection".[73] Kant's charge is that Leibniz is guilty of amphibolous reasoning by virtue of finding, directly in sensation, what only issues from the *a priori* concepts of the understanding. Leibniz treats sensations as if they were identical to what is found only in concepts. For example, sensations are always particular and require the presence of a thing, whereas concepts allow me to think a plurality of things with a shared characteristic in their absence. By contrast, Locke, according to Kant, falls prey to amphibolous reasoning by virtue of arguing that categories that can only be found *a priori* in the understanding, concepts that can only be generated by mind, can be abstracted from sensation or the domain of the empirical. In both cases, Kant contends, Locke and Leibniz conflate the transcendental structure of mind and the empirical dimension of sensation.

If Kant (and Locke) are guilty of amphibolous reasoning, this arises not from conflating the transcendental (as understood by Kant as a structure of the mind) and the empirical, but rather from conflating the *ontological* and the empirical. For on the one hand, Locke infers that because substances are not *given* in experience but rather only *empirical* qualities are given, we are warranted in banishing substance from our *ontology*. Likewise, Kant infers that because substance is not given in the manifold of sensation, we must reject the claim that substance pertains to things-in-themselves, but must instead see substance as a category issuing from mind. An ontological amphiboly thus consists in confusing two distinct domains of inquiry: the ontological and the epistemological. The ontological is here subordinated to the epistemological, and the epistemological is then used to determine what is and is not. The problem is that what we can and cannot know cannot be used to legitimately legislate what is and is not. The being of a thing is independent of our ability to know a thing.

However, the problem with the Humean and Kantian solution is much more serious than a mere conflation of two distinct sets of questions or domains of inquiry. Let us take the example of Kant to illustrate this point. Kant's thesis is that the manifold of intuition, being a sort of rhapsodic chaos, cannot deliver the determinations necessary for experience. Rather, this delirious manifold must be structured by a priori categories of mind. And for this reason, these a priori categories of mind cannot be drawn or abstracted from experience, but must instead spring from the mind alone. Whether these categories represent reality as it is independent of our mind is, according to Kant, forever beyond our knowledge because we cannot sneak up on ourselves from behind to see how we see reality and determine whether our experience corresponds to reality. Consequently, whenever we experience an individual thing or speak of an individual thing, this thing is the result of how our mind has formatted the chaotic manifold of intuition through the application of the a priori categories of unity, reality, substance, and existence. And here we must note that these four categories issue from *mind* not *world*.

Initially it would seem that Kant provides a clever solution to the question of why our experience is formatted in the way that it is, thereby evading Locke's critique of substance as a sort of occult concept by showing how these concepts issue a priori from the mind (to which we *do* have access). However, a moment's reflection reveals that Kant's solution is far more problematic than it first appears. Speaking in the context of Heidegger's early 1919 discussions of being where being is distinguished between "being as a whole" and "something at all", Harman observes that "no explanation is offered of why certain specific qualities should be assigned to one 'something at all' rather than another".[74] This same criticism applies equally to Kant's proposed solution to Locke's critique of substance. Kant has no way of explaining how or why a priori categories such as unity, substance, and existence get applied to one manifold of sensations rather than another. Why, for example, are the categories of substance and unity not applied to an aggregate consisting of my daughter, my parents' dog Rula, and the United Nations? Insofar as the categories are purely a priori, they themselves have no content. What is it then that leads an a priori category to be applied to one thing rather than another? The same problem emerges with those variations of the Kantian solution that would have language rather than pure a priori concepts of the understanding do this work. In both cases we are left without the means of explaining how the "something at all" is ever specified as a concrete entity. As Deleuze puts it in the context of his discussion of Bergson's critique of dialectic and the category of possibility, these categories are "like baggy clothes, [that] are much too big".[75]

The point here is not that we have incorrigible knowledge of substances and access to them in our experience, nor that the way *we* parse the world is the way the *world* is actually formatted. Rather, the point is that 1) questions of substance are *ontological* questions absolutely distinct from how we *know* substances, and 2) that questions of substance cannot be dissolved in questions of access or knowledge. As we saw in the last chapter, ontology cannot be erased by epistemology, nor can ontological questions be transformed into epistemological questions revolving around our access to beings. Wherever one attempts to erase ontological questions in this way, we end up with a variant of Harman's "something at all" problem.

Locke, Kant, Hume and much of the subsequent philosophical tradition ends up where they do precisely because they fall into what Bhaskar calls the "epistemic fallacy" and actualism, confusing questions of our access

to beings with questions of what beings are. Beginning with the actualist
thesis borne out of a desire for secure *foundations* (i.e., a desire secondary
to the demands of ontology), they restrict discourse to what is *given* in
experience. They then find that they are unable to account for the furniture
of the universe precisely because substance is that which *withdraws* from
any givenness, experience, or, indeed, actuality. As such, substance is
not something that can anywhere be found in *experience*—no one has
ever seen or experienced, I contend, a single substance—but is rather an
irreducible *ontological* premise necessary if our commerce with the world
and experimental activity is to be intelligible. The existence of substance
is not something that can be arrived at through an experience or a direct
observation, but can only be arrived at as a premise through transcendental
argumentation. When we adopt the actualist gesture of restricting
knowledge to what is directly given in experience, this way of reaching
substance is irrevocably foreclosed.

Returning then to what Burke called "the paradox of substance", we
should not so much argue that Burke is *mistaken* in his characterization of
substance, as that Burke articulates the very *essence* of substance. In short,
we should embrace Burke's characterization of substance as split between
qualities and substantiality. It is only when we begin from the standpoint
of *epistemology*, from the standpoint of what is *given* in experience, that
substance appears paradoxical. And if this is the case, then it is because
beginning with epistemology leads us to simultaneously claim that the
object we experience *is* its qualities *and* that it is something radically *other*
than its qualities. However, if we begin from the other end with *ontology*
and note that substance is such that 1) it can actualize different qualities
at different times (Aristotle), and that 2) it can fail to actualize qualities
(Bhaskar), we can now argue that the very essence or structure of substance
lies in *self-othering* and *withdrawal*. Insofar as objects or substances alienate
themselves, as it were, in qualities, they are self-othering. They generate
differences in the world. However, insofar as objects are never identical to
their qualities, insofar as they always harbor a volcanic reserve in excess of
their qualities, they perpetually withdraw from their qualities such that they
never directly manifest themselves in the world. As Harman remarks, it's

as if all objects are vacuums populating the universe. It is precisely for this reason that the being of substance is essentially *split*.

And here it should be noted that onticology and object-oriented philosophy are both *metaphysics* or *ontologies* that thoroughly escape what Derrida refers to as ontotheology and the metaphysics of presence. Far from being a signifier that denotes *presence* or the fullness of being, the very essence of substance is to withdraw from presence and to be in excess of all actuality. However, this overturning of the metaphysics of presence occurs not through a demonstration of the manner in which being always harbors deferral and difference *for us* such that presence is forever unobtainable, but rather by showing that being as such, being in itself, withdraws in this way. Let us look more closely at this split between virtual proper being and local manifestation through a concrete example.

Chapter 3
Virtual Proper Being

> What would a truly democratic encounter between truly
> equal beings look like, what would it be—can we even
> imagine it?
>
> — Timothy Morton[76]

3.1. The Mug Blues

Although we have addressed Locke's criticism of substance as an occult
entity not warranted by the givens of experience, the problem of the
bare substratum remains. If substance is not its qualities, does this not
entail that substance *as such* is without qualities and is therefore a *bare*
substratum? And if substance is a bare substratum, does this not entail that
all substances are *identical*? If this is the case, then this spells the ruin of
the concept of substance for substance is supposed to account, in part, for
the *individuality* of substance. Yet where substance is *bare*, all individuality
is erased. If this difficulty is to be avoided, we require some way of talking
about the structure or formatting of substances or split-objects without this
structure consisting of qualities. Towards this end, it would prove helpful to
investigate the being of a particular substance.

Suppose, for the sake of argument, that my blue coffee mug sitting
here on the table is a substance. When I distinguish between the virtual
proper being of an object and the actual local manifestation of an object, I

am attempting to distinguish between the object *qua* formatted structure and as an enduring unity, and the object *qua* qualities or properties. The virtual proper being of an object is its self-othering substantiality, its being as substance, or its being as a (more or less) enduring unity. Here it is important to bear in mind that the time of endurance is irrelevant to whether or not a substance is a substance. A substance can exist for the briefest moment before being destroyed, or for billions of years. It will be recalled that, according to Aristotle, no substance is any more or less a substance than any other. This holds no less for the difference between a rock and a human than it does for an object that is long-lived or instantaneous.

The virtual proper being of an object is what makes an object properly an object. It is that which constitutes an object as a difference engine or generative mechanism. However, no one nor any other thing ever encounters an object *qua* its virtual proper being, for the substance of an object is perpetually withdrawn or in excess of any of its manifestations. Rather, the virtual proper being of an object can only ever be *inferred* from its local manifestations in the world. By contrast, the local manifestation of an object is the manner in which a substance or virtual proper being is actualized in the world under determinate conditions. Here it is important to emphasize that manifestation refers not to phenomena or appearances *for a subject*, though clearly this can take place as well. When I refer to manifestation, I am *not* referring to *givenness to a subject*, but rather to actualization within a world. Objects require no subject to manifest themselves in the world. The universe could be a universe in which no sentient beings of any sort exist and manifestation would continue to take place. We are therefore fortunately relieved of playing Atlas. Consequently, appearances and phenomena, what is given, are a *subset* of manifestation, not the reverse. Manifestation is an *ontological* predicate, not an *epistemological* predicate.

It is my contention that traditional ontology was correct to distinguish between the substance and qualities of objects, but mistaken in how it thought about the nature of substance. It is correct to hold that objects cannot be reduced to their qualities because qualities *change* and *shift* while the object remains *this* substance. Traditional philosophy goes astray, however, in concluding that because substances cannot be reduced to their qualities, then substance must be the object *stripped* of all qualities or, as Locke puts it, a bare substratum. Where substance is conceived in this way, its concept becomes entirely incoherent.

My thesis is that the substantiality of objects is not a bare substratum, but rather an absolutely individual system or organization of *powers*. Powers are the capacities of an object or what it can *do*. The powers of an object are never something that is *directly* manifested in the world. And if this is so, then this is because the qualities of an object are only ever *local manifestations* of the object's power. That is, the domain of power possessed by an object is always *greater* than any local manifestation or actualization of an object. For this reason, following Manuel DeLanda, I distinguish between the *phase space* of an object and the powers of an object. A phase space is a set of points that can be occupied in a series of variations. For example, as a pendulum swings back and forth, it passes through a series of points between two maxima and a minima. Each of these points is a point in phase space. Moreover, none of these points are ever occupied all at once. Likewise, we can think qualities or properties as points an object manifests or actualizes as points in a phase space. The power of the pendulum is its ability to move through this phase space, to produce these actualizations, while each point the pendulum moves through is a local manifestation of this power of the pendulum.

Two points follow from this thesis about the relationship between substance or virtual proper being and qualities or local manifestations. First, we should not speak of qualities as something an object *possesses*, *has*, or *is*, but rather as *acts*, *verbs*, or something that an object *does*. Second, knowing an object does not consist in enumerating a list of essential qualities or properties *belonging* to an object, but rather consists in knowing the *powers* or *capacities* of an object. As we will see in the next chapter, this entails that no object is ever fully known insofar as every object necessarily has an infinite phase space while simultaneously having a finite structure of powers.

Here I return to the blue mug with which I began this section. Within the ontological framework I am proposing, it would be inaccurate to suggest that the mug *is* blue or that the mug *possesses* the quality of blue.

Rather, if we had an ontologically accurate language, we would instead say that "the mug blues" or that "the mug is bluing" or that "the mug does blue". The blueness of the mug is not a quality that the mug *has* but is something that the mug *does*. It is an *activity* on the part of the mug. Nor would it be accurate to claim, at the level of the mug's virtual proper being, that "the mug has blue power". The mug does not have *blue* power, but rather *coloring* power. If this is the case, then it is because the mug always has the power to produce a broader range of colors than the shade it produces at any given time.

The decision to think qualities of an object as acts or doings rather than as possessions, along with onticology's rejection of the thesis that the mug has blue power rather than coloring power, is motivated by two interrelated concerns. First, qualities are *acts* on the part of objects precisely because qualities *vary*. If it is inaccurate to suggest that the mug *is* blue, then this is because the mug is a variety of different colors as a function of the exo-relations with light the mug enters into. As I look at the mug under the warm light of my desktop lamp, it is now a very dark, deep, flat blue. Now I open the shade to my office window, allowing *sunlight* to stream in. The mug becomes a brilliant, bright, shiny blue. Sharing a romantic moment with my coffee mug by candlelight, the colors are deep and rich as they were under my office light, but now the blue flickers and dances in response to the shifting intensity of the candle flame. And finally, I blow out the candle and the mug becomes *black*.

Here there are a couple of points worth making. First, in pointing to the manner in which the qualities of the mug change, I am not making the claim that these qualities are *unreal* or that the mug is *truly* one shade of blue and that these other shades are *distortions* or deviations from the mug's *true* color. Rather, these qualities of the mug are entirely *real* and the mug is *all* these colors. Indeed, we can say that in principle the mug is *potentially* an infinite number of colors because there is no limit to the exo-relations into which the mug can enter. Consequently, we cannot say that we would finally get the true being of the mug by adding up all the qualities that it actualizes. The being of the mug is not the sum of its qualities, but rather qualities are unique events that a substance produces.

Second, what is true of the color of the coffee mug is also true of all its qualities or properties. For example, the spatial shape of the mug, while certainly far more enduring than the color of the mug, is no less variable, *in principle*, than the color of the mug. The mug tends to have a relatively stable spatial or extensional structure because it exists within a stable regime of attraction or set of exo-relations. Change the temperature or gravity of the mug's exo-relations and the extension or spatial shape of the mug will also change.

Here, then, we encounter one of the central ways of distinguishing between the virtual proper being of an object and its local manifestations. Where local manifestation is *geometrical*, virtual proper being is *topological*. As described by Steven Connor,

> Topology may be defined as the study of the spatial properties of an object that remain invariant under homeomorphic deformations, which is to say, broadly, actions of stretching, squeezing, or folding. [It is] not concerned with exact measurement, which is the domain of geometry [...] but rather with spatial relations, such as continuity, neighborhood, insideness and outsideness, disjunction and connection [...]. Because topology is concerned with what remains invariant as a result of transformation, it may be thought of as geometry plus time, geometry given body by motion.[77]

Where geometry treats fixed metric properties and shapes, topology, by contrast, treats of structures capable of undergoing variation through operations of stretching, squeezing, or folding while retaining its structure. Here the distinction between topology and geometry should not be understood mathematically in terms of two different ways of approaching *space*, but rather *philosophically* as two distinct aspects of substance. The topological domain refers to the domain of how the virtual powers of a substance are organized, whereas the geometrical refers to how substances are actualized in locally fixed qualities. There is no less a topology and geometry of colors in substances than there is topology and geometry of spatial qualities in objects. As a consequence we can say—and I'll have much more to say about this in section 3.5—that the virtual proper being of objects is characterized by a topological plasticity that is nonetheless absolutely individual and concrete.

The coloring power of the mug is not a Euclidean property of the mug, a geometric property of the mug—which is to say, a *fixed* property—but is rather a topology or series of variations that are a function of the exo-relations the mug enters into with other objects (different photons of light). For this reason, we must say that the mug *blues*, that it "does" blue, rather than that the mug *is* blue. The bluing of the mug is the local manifestation of the mug. Likewise, if we don't say that the mug has blue power, but rather has *coloring* power, then this is because the mug has the topological *power* to produce a whole range of colors ranging from black to brilliant blue. This *range* is the power of the mug, while every point or variation within this range is the phase space of the mug. Finally, the actualization of a point within this topology or phase space is a local manifestation of the mug. Aristotle's formal cause must be rescued from its fixed-structure Euclideanism and placed soundly within the field of topology or structures that contain the potential for a series of variations volcanically locked within substances. And this is why I refer to objects as "difference engines" or "generative mechanisms", for objects are these powers of producing differences in the world at the level of qualities or local manifestations.

Why, then, are we inclined to say that the mug *is* blue rather than that the mug blues and has coloring power? I think there are three reasons for this, one cognitive, another sociological, and a third having to do with *logoi*, local ontological situations, or regimes of attraction in which objects manifest themselves. Cognitively our thought and perception is geared towards action and therefore what interests us. As Bergson so nicely puts it,

> [m]y body [...] acts like an image which reflects others, and which, in doing so, analyzes them along lines corresponding to the different actions which it can exercise upon them. And consequently, each of the qualities perceived in the same object by my different senses symbolizes a particular direction of my activity, a particular need.[78]

In relating to other objects, there's a way in which our body reduces objects, simplifies them, as a target of its own aims, needs, and desires. As a consequence, variations in objects are ignored and the object is reduced to a geometric identity most congenial to its desired action. As we will see in the next chapter, this is not a peculiarity of human or animal nature, but rather is true of all inter-object relations, whether animate or inanimate, whether human or animal, whether living or non-living. The reduction or simplification of one object by another object is a general *ontological* feature of how objects relate to one another. In short, this sort of simplification is not an *epistemological* peculiarity of human beings.

Sociologically, philosophers, as writers and scholars, do a lot of sitting. This is also true of those times when we *pause* to reflect and wonder what objects are. Everything is *still*. Rather than *acting* on objects, we *look* at objects. Where *acting* on objects tends to produce qualitative differences in the objects, gazing at objects tends to reveal fixed properties (especially if we and the object are sitting still). As such, when we cast about for objects to contemplate, our tendency is to encounter objects in relatively *fixed circumstances*. The philosopher picks up the first item that is about or nearby, such as my blue mug. But as a result of these relatively fixed circumstances characterizing reflection, we encounter qualities not in their changes or transitions, but rather as abiding qualities *possessed* by an object. We then build this lack of *engagement* with objects and the consequent non-variation into the very foundations of our ontology without realizing it. In this connection, Gilbert Simondon suggests that a prejudice for fully constituted local manifestations or the geometric reflects the social hierarchy of Greek philosophy.[79] Likewise, in works like *Pascalian Meditations*, Pierre Bourdieu shows how what he calls "the scholastic disposition" leads us to systematically distort questions about the nature of practice.[80] The claims of Simondon and Bourdieu hold not only for ancient Greece and sociological questions of practice, but also for our contemporary historical moment and questions of ontology. Intellectual work today, no less than in ancient Greece, is dependent on a certain distribution of labor that renders academic life possible by relieving a particular segment of society largely independent of manual labor. This, in turn, leads objects to be encountered in a particular way insofar as the academic, by and large, does not encounter the volcanic potentials hidden within objects by virtue of not directly acting on objects. As a consequence, this leads to a systematic distortion of ontological questions and what constitutes an object.

Finally, third, the objects that populate our world tend to exist in fairly *stable* sets of exo-relations or regimes of attraction. For example, gravity, pressure, and temperature are fairly stable on our planet—at least in the environments where we most commonly act. This entails that there is very often very little *variation* in the qualities of the objects that make up the furniture of our daily experience. This, no doubt, is one reason that the confusion of objects with their qualities is such a persistent tendency of thought. If Aristotle was able to think the formal cause of objects in largely fixed Euclidean or geometric terms rather than in dynamic topological terms, then this is because there is often a sort of *détente* of exo-relations among objects leading to fairly stable qualities or local manifestations among objects. If I am led, for example, to think my body as possessing a rather fixed form, then this is because the *atmospheric pressure* produced by the Earth's gases pressing down upon me is fairly constant. If, by contrast, a mad scientist were to place me in a room that slowly decreased atmospheric pressure, the form or shape of my body would change in subtle ways up to the point where I would finally decompress and become a plurality of objects. Likewise, the form of my body changes in subtle ways with changes in temperature, becoming now more compact when it is very cold and somewhat swollen when it is very hot. Even the spatial form of my body is an *act* on the part of my body, something that my body *does*, not something my body *has* or *is*. This is why I refer to *logoi*, local ontological situations, or regimes of attraction rather than *logos*. These *logoi* or local ontological situations are relatively stable exo-relations among objects that tend to generate, as a consequence, enduring and stable qualities in objects.

3.2. Deleuze's Schizophrenia: Between Monism and Pluralism

No one has explored this anterior side of substance—in the transcendental, not the temporal, sense—more profoundly than Gilles Deleuze. In *Difference and Repetition*, Deleuze names this dimension of substance that is formatted or structured without possessing qualities the virtual. Here the virtual is not to be confused with virtual reality. The latter is generally treated as a simulacrum of reality, as a sort of false or computer generated reality. By contrast, the virtual is entirely real without, for all that, being actual. The term "virtuality" comes from the Latin *virtus*, which has connotations of potency and efficacy. As such, the virtual, as *virtus*, refers to powers and capacities belonging to an entity. And in order for an entity to have powers or capacities, it must actually exist. In this connection, while the virtual refers to potentiality, it would be a mistake to conflate this potentiality with the concept of a *potential object*. A potential object is an object that does not exist but which could come to exist. By contrast, the virtual is strictly a part of a real and existing object. The virtual consists of the volcanic powers coiled within an object. It is that substantiality, that structure and those singularities that endure as the object undergoes qualitative transformations at the level of local manifestations.

However, in evoking Deleuze's concept of the virtual, we must proceed with caution for two deeply opposed tendencies animate Deleuze's discussions of the virtual. On the one hand, Deleuze often speaks of the virtual in terms of an ontological monism that suggests he is committed to the thesis that there is only *one* substance that is then broken up into discrete entities through a process of actualization. Monism tends to come in one of two variants. One variant of monism has it that only a *single* substance exists and that everything that exists is a property or quality of that one substance. Spinoza's monism, for example, argues that only a single substance exists and that all entities (modes) are expressions of this one substance. Another variant of monism has it that there is only a single *type* of being, but that being is populated by numerically distinct entities of this type. Lucretius, for example, could be construed as a monist of this sort, as he holds that only atoms and their combinations exist, not two distinct ontological types such as Plato's world of the forms and the fallen world of entities or appearances.

Deleuze often appears to advocate this former sort of monism, while object-oriented ontology and onticology might appear to be committed to the latter type. Throughout Deleuze's work, we find the theme of a single substance that somehow comes to be formatted into discrete entities. By contrast, object-oriented ontology advocates the thesis that being is composed only of discrete entities or substances. DeLanda articulates this variant of Deleuze nicely when he remarks that,

> Deleuze distinguishes the progressive unfolding of a
> multiplicity through broken symmetries (differen*t*iation), from
> the progressive specification of the continuous space formed
> by multiplicities as it gives rise to our world of discontinuous
> spatial structures (differen*c*iation). Unlike a transcendent
> heaven which exists as a *separate dimension* from reality,
> Deleuze asks us to imagine a continuum of multiplicities
> which *differentiates itself* into our familiar three-dimensional
> space as well as its spatially structured contents.[81]

I will discuss Deleuze's concept of multiplicity momentarily, but for the moment it is important to note that "multiplicity" is among Deleuze's terms for the virtual. The suggestion here is that the virtual seems to consist of a *single* continuum, such that there is only *one* virtual, *one* substance, that is then partitioned into *apparently* distinct entities. And indeed, as Deleuze remarks, "all [multiplicities] coexist, but they do so at points, on the edges".[82] Moreover, Deleuze's constant references to the virtual as the *pre-individual* suggests this reading as well, for it implies a transition from an *undifferentiated* state to a differenciated individual. If the virtual is pre-individual, then it cannot be composed of discrete individual unities or substances. Here the individual would be an *effect* of the virtual, not primary being itself.

On the other hand, Deleuze speaks of the virtual as a *part* of the *real object*. Here Deleuze seems to move in the direction of the second sense of the monism, where monism entails that being is composed of a pluralism of distinct entities, all of the same type. As Deleuze remarks, "the virtual must be defined as strictly a part of the real object—as though the object had one part of itself plunged as though into an objective dimension".[83] Deleuze goes on to ask,

> How, then, can we speak simultaneously of both complete
> determination and only a part of the object? The
> determination must be a complete determination of the
> object, yet form only a part of it. Following suggestions made

by Descartes in his *Replies to Arnauld*, we must carefully
distinguish the object in so far as it is complete and the object
in so far as it is whole. What is complete is only the [virtual]
part of the object, which participates with other parts of
objects in the [Multiplicity] (other relations, other singular
points), but never constitutes an integral whole as such. What
the complete determination lacks is the whole set of relations
belonging to actual existence. An object may be *ens*, or rather
(*non*)-*ens omni modo determinatum*, without being entirely
determined or actually existing.[84]

In treating the virtual as a part of the *object* and as completely
determined (structured), Deleuze seems to suggest that the virtual—far
from constituting a pre-individual continuum that is then parceled up
into discrete entities—is, in fact, purely discrete and *individual*. Under
this reading, multiplicities or endo-relational structures would be discrete,
existing *individuals*. Here there would be no transition from the pre-
individual virtual to the individual actual, but rather the relation between
endo-structure and actuality would be a transition between unexercised
power and actualized quality *within an individual*.

It is not my aim here to provide a commentary on Deleuze's ontology
nor to remain true to his thought, but rather to determine how it is
possible for substance to be formatted without this formatting consisting
of substance's qualities. My contention is that the transcendental condition
(in the transcendental realist sense) under which it is possible for an object
to be out of phase with its qualities lies in a formatted structure that is not
itself qualitative. It is only in this way that the bare substratum problem can
be avoided and Aristotle's insight that substances are capable of carrying
contrary qualities can be vindicated. However, paraphrasing Karen Barad
in her discussion of Niels Bohr, "I propose an ontology that I believe to be
consistent with [a number of Deleuze's] views, although I make no claim
that this is what he necessarily had in mind".[85] Consequently, Deleuze's
thought is only relevant here insofar as it advances our understanding of the
split-nature of substance. In chapter 1, I take it that I have demonstrated
the ontological necessity for the existence of discrete or individual
substances. Contra Deleuze's Spinozist monism and his continuum

hypothesis with respect to the virtual, this necessity follows above all from the requirement that objects be separable from their relations to other objects if experimental activity is to be intelligible. In order for experiment to be possible, it is necessary that it be possible to form closed systems in which objects can express their powers. If objects or generative mechanisms were merely expressions of a continuum that is itself one, then it is difficult to see how this condition could ever be met. Yet given that it seems that this condition is regularly met, it seems that Deleuze's monism must clearly be mistaken.

Approaching Deleuze's thought more directly, two difficulties seem to besiege his monist continuum hypothesis. First, if the virtual is a single substance that is then partitioned into discrete entities, it is difficult to understand why the virtual ever departs from itself to become "alienated" in individuals at all. Deleuze's tendency is to speak of the actual, of the individuated, as that which contributes no differences of its own but which is merely a sort of sterile secretion of the virtual. As Deleuze puts it,

> [d]ifference is explicated, but in systems in which it tends to be cancelled; this means only that difference is essentially implicated, that its being is implication. For difference, to be explicated is to be cancelled or to dispel the inequality which constitutes it. The formula according to which 'to explicate is to identify' is a tautology. We cannot conclude from this that difference is cancelled out, or at least that it is cancelled in itself. It is cancelled in so far as it is drawn outside itself, *in* extensity and *in* the quality which fills that extensity. However, difference creates both this extensity and this quality.[86]

The terms "implication" and "explication" should be read *etymologically* here, rather than literally. "Explication" denotes not the activity of *explanation*, but rather "to unfold". Here, then, the emphasis should be placed on the term "plication", which indicates that which is folded. Consequently, the term "implication" should be read not in the sense of a possible logical inference from a given fact, but rather as denoting that which is enfolded or hidden in something else. From this we can derive the following table:

	Implication	Explication
Virtual	Potent, yet unactualized difference/ Cause of beings/Pre-Individual	Canceled Difference/Formation of Quality/Sterile Being
Actual	Condition/Cause of the Actual	Product/Individual being without causal efficacy/Completion or end of Process

Following Simondon, Deleuze arrives at this conception of being and the relationship between the virtual and the actual on the grounds that "[i]t is notable that extensity does not account for the individuations which occur within it".[87] When Deleuze refers to an extensity, he is referring to an entity with qualities situated in time and space. Returning to the example of my blue coffee mug, simply by examining my coffee mug here and now, I cannot determine how it came to have the shape it has, the color that it has, why it is sitting here on my desk, etc.

Deleuze's suggestion is thus that because extensity does not account for the individuations that occur within it (the qualities and structure that make it *this* individual), we must refer to *another* dimension, the implicit, the virtual, to account for these individuations. Furthermore, since the extensive consists of individual or individuated entities, Deleuze concludes that this supplementary dimension must be *pre-individual*. As Deleuze remarks, "[t]he individuating is not the simple individual".[88] However, in making this move, Deleuze renders the motivating grounds of individuation thoroughly mysterious. If the virtual is, as Deleuze suggests, a continuum and a whole populated by potent yet unactualized differences, and if the actual is merely a secretion or excrescence of the virtual, what is it that leads the virtual to ever ex-plicate itself, to unfold itself, or to leave itself and fall into the *sterile*, actual individual? Difference comes from the domain of the virtual, not the actual, for the actual is precisely that domain where difference is *canceled*. Here, then, we encounter a problem similar to the one that haunted Plato's theory of the forms, where we are left to wonder why the world of imperfect creatures ever comes into being and why the world of the perfect forms doesn't simply reside in tranquil and *unmoving* eternal existence.

These observations lead to a second problem. As Hallward notes in his controversial study, *Out of This World*, Deleuze's ontology essentially conceives being in terms of creativity and creating. This, according to Hallward, leads Deleuze to distinguish between the creating and the creature, the individuating and the individual, with the creature and the individual being granted a derivative status to that of the creating and individuating. As Hallward puts it,

> Almost every aspect of Deleuze's philosophy is caught up with the consequences of this initial correlation of being, creativity and thought. Roughly speaking, it implies: (a) that all existent things or processes exist in just one way, as so many distinct acts of creation or so many individual *creatings*; (b) that these creatings are themselves aspects of a limitless and consequently singular creative power, a power that is most adequately expressed in the medium of pure thought; (c) that every creating gives rise to a derivative *creature* or created thing, whose own power or creativity is limited by its material organisation, its situation, its actual capacities and relations with other creatures, and so on; (d) that the main task facing any such creature is to loosen and then dissolve these limitations in order to become a more adequate or immaterial vehicle for that virtual creating which alone individuates it.[89]

Hallward's third point here is particularly salient. In treating difference, the virtual, the implicit, as that which is responsible for individuation, and the explicate, the actual, the individual as the product of individuation, Deleuze inevitably grants the creature or the individual a derivative place within being. The individual becomes a product of being, an effect of virtual difference, but certainly cannot be treated as a motor of difference in the world. Like the trail of slime left behind in the wake of a snail or slug, the individual is merely the remainder or excrescence of a differential process of individuation that has already moved on.

What we thus get in Deleuze's thought is a sort of vertical ontology of the depths. Rather than entities or substances interacting with each other laterally or horizontally, we instead get an ontology where difference arises vertically from the depths of the virtual. As a consequence, the individual takes on a secondary status as a mere effect of the genuine processes that all occur at the level of the virtual.

In a philosophically rich review of Hallward's book, John Protevi contends that Hallward illicitly flattens the complexity of Deleuze's ontology. As Protevi remarks,

> The relations among actual, virtual and intensive form the most important issue in explicating Deleuze's ontology. I would argue that we should consider the intensive as an independent ontological register, one that mediates the virtual and actual, which are its limits. Even if one doesn't accept this and insists on a dualism of the virtual and actual, one would have to say that the intensive belongs with the actual.[90]

Protevi goes on to argue that,

> Spatio-temporal dynamisms, that is, morphogenetic processes exhibiting intensive properties, are processes of individuation, of emergence from pre-individual fields. The paradigm cases for Deleuze are embryos and weather systems. In the biological register, the "field" of individuation (the gradients of which are laden with pre-individual singularities) is the egg, while the process of individuation is embryonic morphogenesis; in the meteorological register, the field of individuation is the pre-condition (the bands of different temperature and pressure in air and water) to the formation of wind currents or storms, which are the spatio-temporal dynamisms. [...]. Any resident of Louisiana will be able to locate hurricanes for you in terms of their spatio-temporal co-ordinates. To be fair, we do have to distinguish between the location of a hurricane as embedded in a geographic co-ordinate system—its extensive properties—and the thresholds proper to its intensive properties. It's only at certain singular points in the differential relations among air and water temperature and wind currents that thunderstorms, tropical depressions, tropical storms, and hurricanes form. Nonetheless, the point is that the weather system itself is the

intensive process by which those singularities are actualized, and that this intensive process operates here, in this world.[91]

Quite right. What Protevi doesn't seem to notice, however, is that this treatment of the relationship between the virtual, the actual, and the intensive requires a significant revision of Deleuze's ontology. In his reading of Deleuze's ontology, we note that Protevi perpetually refers to discrete and actual substances or individuals that interact with one another and perturb each other in a variety of ways. Far from a monistic virtual continuum that is then cut up into discrete entities, Protevi's parsing of Deleuze's ontology requires the existence of discrete substances or entities that interact with one another and evoke virtual powers within one another through these interactions. And here, in passing, we should recall Deleuze's constant polemics against the concept of causality. As Deleuze remarks,

> It is sufficient to understand that the genesis takes place
> in time not between one actual term, however small,
> and another actual term, but between the virtual and its
> actualisation—in other words, it goes from the structure to
> its incarnation, from the conditions of a problem to the cases
> of solution, from the differential elements and their ideal
> connections to actual terms and diverse real relations which
> constitute at each moment the actuality of time.[92]

If Deleuze is so quick to reject the notion of causality, then this is because causality works laterally or horizontally, from object to object, whereas the virtual works vertically from the implicate to the explicate. It is precisely this thesis that must be rejected under Protevi's account. If Deleuze's account of time in the relation between the virtual and the actual is here embraced, it is difficult to see how the actual terms evoked in Protevi's characterization of Deleuze's thought can have the sort of causal efficacy Protevi attributes to them. Rather, under Deleuze's model of virtual time, any causal relation between actual terms can only be *apparent* or a sort of transcendental illusion. My point here is not that Protevi is mistaken in *his* account of the relation between the virtual, the actual, and the intensive, but rather that Deleuze's account of virtual time, of the time of actualization, must be abandoned if something like Protevi's account is to remain coherent. It must be possible for actual terms to causally interact with one another and for the actual to affect the virtual.

But if this is the case, then we can no longer say that the virtual is the pre-individual and the actual is the individual. The virtual is not something that produces the individual, but rather must strictly be a dimension *of* the *individual*. It is precisely the individual that precedes the virtual—transcendentally, not temporally—not the virtual that precedes the individual. If it is to be possible for substances or individuals to perturb each other, then being cannot consist of a whole or a continuum, but must instead come in discrete packets or substances. Moreover, it follows that the actual dimension of the entity cannot mark the *erasure* or *cancellation* of difference, but must instead itself be an instigator of difference in other entities and one of the mechanisms by which the volcanic, yet unactualized, powers of the virtual are released and set forth in the world. And here I note that when outstanding commentators on Deleuze such as Protevi and DeLanda set out to analyze the world, it is precisely in these terms that they speak. Far from treating the actual and substances as derivative, they instead display a profound attentiveness to the differences that individual substances make. Here the ontology of theoretical practice belies the ontology espoused when striving to describe what they're doing in their practice.

In an interview Deleuze once remarked that,

> Philosophers introduce new concepts, they explain them, but they don't tell us, not completely anyway, the problems to which those concepts are a response. Hume, for example, set out a novel concept of belief, but he doesn't tell us how and why the problem of knowledge presents itself in such a way that knowledge is seen as a particular kind of belief. The history of philosophy, rather than repeating what a philosopher says, has to say what he must have taken for granted, what he didn't say but is nonetheless present in what he did say.[93]

It is in this way, I believe, that we should approach Deleuze's deployment of the concept of the virtual. In short, what is the *problem* to which Deleuze's concept of the virtual responds? However dimly Deleuze might have discerned the problem himself, the problem to which the concept of the virtual seems to respond is that of the split in objects between withdrawn being and qualities, coupled with the problem of the bare substratum. It appears that Deleuze clearly recognized that the being of substance cannot be identified with its qualities and actualized structure. Because substance changes, because it is capable of carrying contrary qualities, substance, in its proper being, must differ from its qualities. However, if substance is to differ from its qualities, then it requires a form of structure that is formatted without being qualitative. Without this other dimension of substances, we fall into the bare substratum problem discussed in the last chapter, where substances are completely blank, completely indifferent, and therefore, absurdly, all identical to one another.

It is precisely this domain of being that the virtual names, for the virtual is structure and potency without quality. However, having dimly glimpsed this problem, Deleuze immediately falls into a set of errors that lead his account of the virtual into incoherence. Oddly, these problems seem to arise from conceding far too much to actualism. Having recognized that the domain of the actual or qualities and extensities is incapable of accounting for the individuality of the individual or the substantiality of substance, Deleuze nonetheless treats the actual as the *sole* domain of the individual or primary substance. As a consequence, he's led to characterize the domain of the virtual as the *pre*-individual, when he should instead treat the domain of the virtual as the domain of the individual, the substantial, or that which persists through change. The consequences of this decision are profound. By treating the domain of the virtual as the pre-individual and the domain of the actual as an *effect* of the virtual, Deleuze is left without an account of why the virtual actualizes itself at all (despite his impressive efforts to the contrary), and is led to treat the actual as a mere product, an excrescence, that itself has no efficacy within being. What is required, by contrast, is an account of the virtual that treats it as a dimension of primary substances or discrete individuals, where substance precedes the virtual (transcendentally, not temporally) not the reverse, and where *actual* entities are capable of interacting with one another. It is to this account of the virtual that I now turn.

3.3. Virtual Proper Being

In *Difference and Repetition*, Deleuze remarks that "[t]he virtual is opposed not to the real but to the actual. *The virtual is fully real in so far as it is virtual.* Exactly what Proust said of states of resonance must be said of the virtual: 'Real without being actual, ideal without being abstract'".[94] Within the framework of onticology, the claim that the virtual is real is the claim that the virtual is always the virtuality of *a* substance or individual being. Put differently, the claim that the virtual is real is not the claim that the virtual is a *potential being*, but rather the claim that the virtual is always the virtuality or potentiality *of a* being or substance. Here the genitive is of the utmost importance. The virtual always belongs to a substance, not the reverse. Moreover, the virtual is always the potential harbored or carried by a discrete or individual being. In this regard, we must distinguish between the two halves of any object, substance, or difference engine. On the one hand, there is the actual side of an object consisting of qualities and extensities, while on the other hand, there is the virtual side of substances, consisting of potentialities or powers. In claiming that the virtual is "ideal", Deleuze is not claiming that the virtual is mental or cognitive—though minds too have their virtual dimension—but rather that the virtual is *relational*. These relations, however, are not relations *between* entities, but constitute the endo-structure of an object, its internal topology. Finally, we can claim that it is entirely possible—if not common—for actually existing entities to remain in a state of virtuality such that they are fully real and existent in the world, fully concrete, without producing any qualities or extensities. Only on this condition can we make sense of Bhaskar's claim that it is possible for generative mechanisms, difference engines, or substances to be real while remaining dormant such that they are out of phase with their qualities or events.

How, then, are we to understand this dimension of substance that is formatted without possessing qualities? Two features in particular render Deleuze's concept of the virtual particularly well suited for theorizing this withdrawn dimension of substance. On the one hand, Deleuze is careful to emphasize that the virtual shares no *resemblance* to the actual. "Every object is double without it being the case that the two halves resemble one another".[95] If the actual is treated as embodying qualities and geometrical structure in the sense specified in section 3.1, then this captures the manner in which the virtual dimension of a substance differs from anything qualitative, thus providing us with substance that is structured or formatted without being qualitative. To illustrate this lack of resemblance between the virtual and actual halves of split objects, Deleuze gives the illuminating example of genes. "[G]enes as a system of differential relations", of which virtual multiplicities are composed, "are incarnated at once in a species and the organic parts of which it is composed".[96] Genes, as a contributor to the overall form that an actualized organism embodies form a set of differential relations and singularities that share no resemblance to that actualized organism. Genes are among the conditions for the form the organism will take, but in no way *resemble* that organism.

On the other hand, the concept of virtuality allows us to theorize the manner in which substances are always *individual* substances without requiring reference to other substances or beings. According to Deleuze, the virtual is composed of "multiplicities". I will have more to say about multiplicities momentarily, but for the moment it bears noting that according to Deleuze, "'[m]ultiplicity', which replaces the one no less than the multiple, is the true substantive, substance itself".[97] Deleuze draws the concept of multiplicity from the differential geometry of Friedrich Gauss and Bernhard Riemann. As explained by Manuel DeLanda,

> In the early nineteenth century, when Gauss began to tap into these differential resources, a curved two-dimensional surface was studied using the old Cartesian method: the surface was embedded in a three-dimensional space complete with its own fixed set of axes; then, using those axes, coordinates would be assigned to every point of the surface; finally the geometric link between points determining the form of the surface would be expressed as algebraic relations between the numbers. But Gauss realized that the calculus, focusing as it does on infinitesimal points on the surface itself (that is, operating entirely with local information), allowed the study of the surface *without any reference to a global embedding space*. Basically, Gauss developed a method to implant the

coordinate axes on the surface itself (that is, a method of
'coordinatizing' the surface) and, once points had been so
translated into numbers, to use differential (not algebraic)
equations to characterize their relations.[98]

The concept of multiplicity is of great significance not for only
mathematics, but ontology as well. For through enabling us to think the
internal structure of a space without reference to a *global embedding space*, the
concept of multiplicity also enables us to think the being of an individual
substance *independent* of its relations to other substances or its exo-relations.
It is for this reason that I refer to the virtual proper being of substance as
consisting of endo-relations, an endo-structure, or an endo-composition.
The point is not that all substances are spatial—when we discuss flat
ontology we will see that this is not the case—but rather that multiplicity
allows us to think individual substance in a purely immanent fashion
detached from any sort of global embedding space or set of exo-relations.
While substances *can* and *do* enter into relations with other substances,
their being *qua* substance is not constituted *by* these exo-relations. Exo-
relations often play a crucial role in the *qualities* a substance comes to
embody at the level of local manifestations, but the being of substance in its
substantiality is something other than these exo-relations. As an additional
consequence of this concept of multiplicity, the Kantian conception of
space and time as *containers* must here be abandoned as well in favor of a
model of space and time arising from substances.

In defining multiplicities Deleuze remarks that "the utmost importance
must be attached to the substantive form: multiplicity must not designate a
combination of the many and the one, but rather an organisation belonging
to the many as such, which has no need whatsoever of unity in order
to form a system".[99] A moment later, Deleuze goes on to explain that
multiplicities must "thus be defined as a structure".[100] If multiplicities must
be defined as a structure or a system, then this is because the elements that
compose them,

> must in effect be determined, but reciprocally, by reciprocal
> relations which allow no independence whatsoever to subsist.
> Such relations are precisely non-localisable ideal connections,

whether they characterise the multiplicity globally or proceed by the juxtaposition of neighboring regions. In all cases the multiplicity is intrinsically defined, without external reference or recourse to a uniform space in which it would be submerged.[101]

In his drive to formulate a differential ontology or account of being resting on nothing but difference without reference to identity, Deleuze's concept of multiplicity is pulled in two opposing directions. On the one hand, associating unity with identity, Deleuze wishes to deny any unity to multiplicities. On the other hand, in his discussions of multiplicities Deleuze seems ineluctably drawn to treating them as *unities*. With respect to this second tendency, we need only observe the manner in which Deleuze refers to multiplicities as structures where all the elements are reciprocally determined, such that they embody an organization. If multiplicities are structured or organized, if they are intrinsically "defined", then it seems difficult to maintain that they lack unity.

Rather, it appears that the very being of multiplicities consists in their unity. It is only on these grounds that we can refer to them as substances. In thinking multiplicities, Deleuze seems to be groping for the classical categories of totality or community. A totality is a system in which all of the parts depend on one another such that they are, as Deleuze puts it, reciprocally determined. My body, for example, is a totality. By contrast, a community is not so much a *social* entity, as a system in which all the parts simultaneously cause and affect one another. Thus, for example, every organic body is simultaneously a totality and a community insofar as its parts are both dependent on one another and constantly interact with one another. Likewise, the relation between the Earth and the moon is a community insofar as the moon's gravitation affects the Earth and the Earth's gravitation affects the moon. It is precisely this sort of structure that Deleuze seems to have in mind when he evokes the concept of multiplicity. However, while systems of this sort are certainly differentiated internally, they are nonetheless unities or substances.

In defining the being of the virtual or multiplicities, Deleuze argues that "[t]he reality of the virtual consists of the differential elements and relations along with the singular points which correspond to them. The reality of the virtual is structure".[102] If Deleuze treats the virtual or multiplicities as pre-individual and the actual as individual, then this is because he fails to adequately distinguish between the topological and the geometrical within substance. Concluding that the individuality of the individual resides in its qualities, parts, or in geometric extensity, Deleuze is forced to deny individuality to multiplicities. But as I argued in section 3.2, this thesis is untenable for a variety of reasons. Rather, while multiplicities are without qualities, they are nonetheless the structure or "form" that functions as the ground of a substance's qualitative variations.

Here, then, we might think of Harman's discussion of Xavier Zubiri in *Tool-Being*. There Harman begins by noting that "[t]he reality of a thing cannot be identified with its presence".[103] Here presence can be equated with the actuality of a substance or thing, with the properties or qualities that it embodies. In contrasting the substance of a thing with its qualities or properties, Harman's Zubiri accords closely with Bhaskar's thesis that substances can be out of phase with their events or properties. Harman goes on to remark that "[t]he reality of a thing cannot be regarded as a substance endowed with properties. Instead, the thing is always a *system*, a system that unifies all of its numerous 'notes.'"[104] In treating the substantiality of a thing as a system of notes, Harman's Zubiri displays an exceptional proximity to Deleuze's conception of virtual multiplicities as composed of differential relations and singularities. Harman goes on to remark that,

> A reality is defined as that which acts on other things by virtue of its notes. This term "note" is meant as a replacement for the word "property", which Zubiri regards as biased towards reality viewed *conceptively*, that is, from the external standpoint of a relation rather than from the thing in and of itself. To speak of a *property*, he says, is to speak of the idiosyncrasies that distinguish one thing from another; in this way, the property is an extraneous feature grafted onto some underlying substrate, and always viewed from the outside rather than from within. As opposed to properties, the notes of a thing make up even the most intimate *parts* of that thing: "matter, its structure, its chemical composition, its psychic

'faculties', etc". Instead of qualities belonging to a substance, Zubiri's notes *are* the reality of the thing itself.[105]

Like Zubiri's notes, Deleuze's singularities are the most intimate reality of a thing, defining and structuring its being. However, unlike Zubiri's notes, Deleuze's singularities do not *replace* the concept of properties or qualities, but rather are evoked as the *ground* of properties or qualities. Singularities are those potencies that generate qualities or properties as acts on the part of the object. And if Deleuze is compelled to develop the concept of singularity to account for the being of objects, then this is precisely because the properties of objects or substances are variable and changing, yet a substance still—within certain limits—remains *that* substance. What is thus required is a ground that is plastic, that can vary, while retaining its identity. It is precisely this requirement that the concept of multiplicity satisfies.

Unfortunately, Deleuze tells us very little as to just what these singularities are. We know that we need them, that substances must possess singularities, but insofar as these singularities are not themselves qualities, we don't know what they are. In *Difference and Repetition*, Deleuze defines singularities as "the point of departure for a series which extends over all the ordinary points of the system, as far as the region of another singularity which gives rise to another series which may either converge or diverge from the first".[106] Unfortunately, this definition isn't very helpful. What are the ordinary points? What are the singular points? What are the series in question? Perhaps some light is shed on this issue if we return to the concept of topology.

It will be recalled that topology is a sort of dynamic geometry that studies the invariant features of an object that remain the same under homeomorphic deformations through operations of bending, stretching, folding and so on. Thus, for example, within the framework of Euclidean geometry, a triangle and a quadrilateral are completely distinct, whereas in topology quadrilaterals and triangles are equivalent to one another. If this is the case, then it is because triangles, through operations of folding, stretching, and bending can be transformed into quadrilaterals and vice versa. To transform a triangle into a quadrilateral, simply take one of its vertices and fold it over. In this regard, singularities occupy a paradoxical place within topology. Clearly singularities must simultaneously define the series of ordinary points *and* mark the threshold at which new forms emerge. On the one hand, the singularities of a topological space cannot be, for example, the vertices of the triangle. Were this the case, then the triangle and the quadrilateral would not be structurally equivalent. Rather, the vertices of the triangle and the quadrilateral must define *ordinary points* within a topological space of singularities. And here it bears noting that the singularities of a topological space themselves never appear or manifest themselves. What manifests itself are the ordinary points, the Euclidean geometry, of each individual figure. The singularities serving as the ground of these figures can only be inferred. They are never directly given but are perpetually withdrawn. There is no shape that embodies the singularities of the topological space, nor does the corresponding geometrical space ever resemble the topological space. On the other hand, singularities define thresholds between different topological spaces. For example, if I take a strip of paper and fasten its two ends or twist it and then fasten its two ends, I am now in two new topological spaces with their own variety of possible mutations.

Now, in evoking topology in the context of onticology's ontological concerns, it is important to exercise caution. First, topology is concerned specifically and exclusively with spatial relations, whereas ontology is concerned with entities and qualities of all kinds. Second, topology is concerned with homeomorphisms or structural identities across a *variety* of *distinct* entities, whereas here I am trying to account for the substantiality of *individual* entities. Consequently, parallels between topology and multiplicities diverge in important respects. The lesson to be drawn from topology is that there are variations that are nonetheless structure- or system-preserving. As Deleuze puts it, "[e]very phenomenon refers to an inequality by which it is conditioned. Every diversity and every change refers to a difference which is its sufficient reason".[107] Phenomena here should be understood in the sense of "local manifestation", whereas inequality or difference should be understood in terms of the singularities or notes belonging to a multiplicity as the condition or ground for the production of qualities.

In *Intensive Science and Virtual Philosophy*, Manuel DeLanda proposes to treat Deleuze's singularities as attractors. With a few qualifications and conceptual modifications, this is the interpretation of Deleuze's singularities that I would like to defend. However, before proceeding to discuss attractors, it is first necessary to distinguish the position I am developing here from DeLanda's position. In *Intensive Science and Virtual Philosophy*, DeLanda argues that Deleuze's concept of multiplicities is designed to replace the old philosophical concepts of essences, and that things, substances, or objects are to be explained in terms of how they are produced, rather than in terms of their essence. As DeLanda puts it, "[i]n a Deleuzian ontology [...] a species (or any other natural kind) is not defined by its essential traits but rather by the *morphogenetic process* that gave rise to it".[108]

Clearly onticology, and object-oriented philosophy more broadly construed, rejects this thesis. In section 3.2, we already saw that DeLanda endorses the Deleuzian thesis that the virtual is composed of a monistic continuum of singularities that is then cut up into discrete entities with qualities. There I argued that this position is incoherent and that the virtual must instead be strictly conceived as a part of discrete entities such that *each* object has its *own* virtual dimension. Likewise, the thesis that an entity is *defined* by the morphogentic process by which it came to be conflates two distinct issues. While many entities must certainly come to be, it does not follow from this that the being of entities can be defined by the process by which they came to be. Were this the case, then we would reduce entities to their history. However, as every parent knows, while they were certainly the efficient cause of their child coming to be, the child has a being independent of this morphogenetic process by which it came to be. The being of a being cannot be reduced to its efficient cause, but also has its formal or structural cause.

Moreover, DeLanda seems to be at odds with his own thesis, for later, in the same text, he proposes a flat ontology that would be "one made exclusively of unique, singular individuals, differing in spatio-temporal scale but not in ontological status".[109] In formulating his ontology as a flat ontology, DeLanda's thesis seems to work against his prior claim that the being of beings is to be conceived in terms of their morphogenetic processes. For here it seems that DeLanda takes the Aristotlean route of treating individual substances as what are primary. As Aristotle puts it, "anything which is produced is produced by something [...], and from something".[110] In other words, individual substances are produced by and through other individual substances. As a consequence, individual substances necessarily precede processes of production and are the condition of production. The point, then, is not that we shouldn't examine processes of production. We should. Rather, the point is that substance ontologically precedes production.

In *Intensive Science and Virtual Philosophy*, DeLanda remarks that "[s]ingularities [...] influence the behaviour [of objects] by acting as *attractors* for [their] trajectories".[111] Here it is crucial to note that the concept of attractors is not a *teleological* concept. Attractors are not *goals* towards which a substance tends, but are rather the *potentialities* towards which a substance tends under a variety of different conditions in the actualization of its qualities. As DeLanda goes on to say, "singularities are [...] the inherent or intrinsic [...] *tendencies* of a system, the states which the system will spontaneously tend to adopt [...] as long as it is not constrained by other forces".[112] In this respect, DeLanda's attractors are extremely close to Bhaskar's generative mechanisms developed in *A Realist Theory of Science*.

However, in contrast to DeLanda—though I believe his analysis already suggests this distinction—I want to argue that attractors are not *states* of an object or substance, but rather are what in substances preside over the genesis of actualized states or local manifestations. In this respect, the attractors of a substance constitute what Harman, following Zubiri, refers to as the notes or the most intimate reality of the object. They are the generative mechanisms within an object that preside over the events or qualities of which the object is capable. However, while serving as the condition of these events or qualities, these attractors are not themselves qualitative or events. As DeLanda puts it, "attractors are *never actualized*, since no point of a trajectory [of an object] ever reaches the attractor itself".[113] As such, the attractors or singularities inhabiting the endo-structure of an object are radically withdrawn. They are that which serves as the condition for the actual dimension of an object, for the local manifestations of an object, but are never themselves found on the actual side of an object. For this reason, DeLanda contends that we must "make [...] a *sharp ontological distinction between the trajectories* as they appear in the phase portrait of a system, on the one hand, *and the vector field*, on the other".[114] The phase portrait or phase space of an object is the variety of states an object occupies at the level of its actualized qualities or properties, while the vector field consists of the attractors that preside over the genesis of these qualities. Thus, for example, the phase space of the coffee mug would be, among other things, the variety of different colors it actualizes, whereas the attractor would be that singularity that functions as the genetic conditions for all of these different colors. It is the attractor that persists throughout these variations or transformations.

The claim that objects are split-objects is the claim that they are split between their virtual proper being and their local manifestations. The virtual proper being of an object is its endo-structure, the manner in which it embodies differential relations and attractors or singularities defining a vector field or field of potentials within a substance. The local manifestation of a substance is the actualization of a point within the phase space of this vector field in the form of actualized qualities. If it is crucial to distinguish between virtual proper being and local manifestation, then this is because the qualities of an object can undergo variations while still remaining the object that it is. It is a vague recognition of this capacity within substances that leads Aristotle to distinguish between substance and its qualities. However, if we are to avoid falling into Locke's bare substratum problem while maintaining the distinction between substance and its qualities, it is necessary to articulate the way in which substance can be structured without possessing qualities. It is precisely this problem that the concept of virtual proper being resolves. Yet, above all, the distinction between virtual proper being and local manifestation teaches us that objects are *plastic*. As a function of the exo-relations objects enter into with other objects, the attractors defining the virtual space of a substance can be activated in a variety of different ways, actualizing objects in a variety of different ways at the level of local manifestations. It is for this reason that the confusion of objects with their actualization in local manifestations always spells theoretical disaster, for in doing so we foreclose the volcanic potentials harbored in the depths of objects.

3.4. The Problem With Rabbits and Hats

In *Prince of Networks,* Harman, following Latour, levels a trenchant critique against the concepts of potentiality and virtuality that are at the core of my concept of split-objects. By responding to this critique, I hope to render the concept of virtual proper being a bit more concrete and bring out some of its important consequences. In *Irreductions,* Latour remarks that "[t]he origin of potency lies in this confusion: *it is no longer possible to distinguish an actor from the allies which make it strong*".[115] As Latour goes on to remark, "[t]alk of possibilities is the illusion of actors that move while forgetting the cost of transport".[116] Perhaps one way of articulating this critique would be to say that you can't pull a rabbit out of a hat without first putting it in the hat. The problem with the concept of potentiality under this model is that it treats the rabbit as if it were *already* in the hat, without accounting for the work it takes to put the rabbit in the hat.

This seems to be precisely the sense in which Harman takes Latour's critique. As Harman argues, "[t]o speak of something existing *in potentia* implies that it is already there but simply covered or suppressed. This is what Latour denies. For him, a thing is only here once it is here, not sooner".[117] Illustrating this point, Harman remarks that "[f]or Latour a person does not stand up by drawing on an inner reservoir of potency, but through a series of mediations—nervous excitations acting on muscles, which then shift the body's weight onto a hard, unyielding floor. Numerous allies are brought into play even in the simplest movements of our bodies".[118] What Latour wishes to capture are all the *translations* an actant or object must go through in order to engage in even the simplest of motions such as standing up. In this regard, the problem with the concept of potentiality is that it treats these powers as already residing in the being of the substance, thereby leading us to ignore these myriad translations necessary for an action to take place. We say, for example, that the prince has power even when he doesn't exercise it, thereby ignoring all the *work* that goes into keeping soldiers in line, maintaining a legal system, forming stable alliances with other nobles, dealing with peasant uprisings, and so on. Or, similarly, we say that the acorn contains an oak tree within it, such that it is already there only waiting to come out.

In response to Harman-Latour's critique of potentiality, there are a couple of points worth making. First, while Harman and Latour's points about translation and work are well taken, this critique seems to miss the point that substances must be *susceptible* to these translations. Returning to Harman's remarks about standing up, I readily grant that nerves must be excited so that muscles must be activated so that feet can press against a hard floor, and so on. However, in order for nerves to be excited, nerves must be *capable* of being excited. When Harman and Latour argue that only the actual exists, are they arguing that the excited nerves are an *entirely* new entity, or are they claiming that this entity merely changes its states? If they are making the claim that the excited nerves are an entirely new entity, then they seem committed to the rather odd thesis that entities are popping into existence *ex nihilo*. As a consequence of his principle of irreduction and commitment to Whitehead's ontology, it seems that this is precisely the thesis that Latour advocates. Within the Whiteheadian framework, every actual occasion (entity) is an instantaneous entity that is fully complete in its being. As Steven Shaviro puts it,

> each occasion, taken in itself, is a *quantum*: a discrete, indivisible unit of becoming. But this also means that occasions are strictly limited in scope. Once an occasion happens, it is already over, already dead. Once it has reached its final "satisfaction", it no longer has any vital power. "An actual occasion [...] never changes", Whitehead says; "it only becomes and perishes.[119]

What we get with Whitehead is a sort of radical actualism where every change implies an entirely new entity. Yet if this is the case, it is difficult to see how we can get from one entity to another entity. Rather, it seems that entities must possess the capacity, the potentiality, to undergo change.

In this regard, another way of understanding the concept of virtual singularities or attractors is in terms of Spinoza's concept of affect. As Spinoza writes in the *Ethics*, "By [affect] I understand the affections of the body by which the body's power of activity is increased or diminished, assisted or checked".[120] What makes Spinoza's concept of affect so interesting is that it doesn't restrict affect to what is *felt*, but links the concept of affect to the *capacities* of an object. And here, if I refer to the capacities of an *object*, then this is because for Spinoza *all* entities, whether human, animal, or *inanimate* possess what Spinoza calls affects. And these affects consist of both an entity's "receptivity" to other entities and the various capacities an entity has to act. Unless we are to fall into an atomism where there is an insurmountable gulf between entities, it seems that we must attribute to objects affects in Spinoza's sense. Those nerves must have the *capacity* of being excited or stimulated.

In discussion with me surrounding these issues, Harman remarks that, "[c]ontra what Bryant implies [...] however, I don't think that the acorn already has oak-qualities. I think it has acorn-qualities".[121] However, this is precisely what I *don't* claim. To suggest that the acorn has oak-qualities would be to conflate qualities with substance. But as I argued in section 3.3, the virtual proper being of an object cannot be equated with anything *qualitative*. Virtual proper being is radically other than qualities. Moreover, it cannot be said that the acorn already contains the oak tree. What the acorn contains are acorn powers or attractors, and while these powers or attractors are entirely determinate, their actualization is a purely creative process producing new qualities and eventually a new object. In this respect, Harman and I are very close, for like Harman I advocate the thesis that the acorn does not contain oak-tree qualities, but is fully determinate at its virtual level as an acorn. The virtual dimension of objects is *concrete* without being *actual*. In this regard, Harman and Latour seem to conflate the virtual with the possible.

It is precisely this conflation of the potential with the possible that Deleuze seeks to avoid with his account of the virtual. As Deleuze cautions,

> The only danger in all this is that the virtual could be confused with the possible. The possible is opposed to the real; the process undergone by the possible is therefore a 'realisation'. By contrast, the virtual is not opposed to the real; it possesses a full reality by itself. The process it undergoes is that of actualization.[122]

Deleuze criticizes the concept of the possible for reasons similar to those Latour levels against the potential. In short, he criticizes the concept

of the possible for treating the rabbit as if it were already in the hat. As
Deleuze argues,

> Every time we pose the question in terms of the possible
> and real, we are forced to conceive of existence as a brute
> eruption, a pure act or leap which always occurs behind
> our backs and as subject to a law of all or nothing. What
> difference can there be between the existent and the non-
> existent if the non-existent is already possible, already
> included in the concept and having all the characteristics that
> the concept confers upon it as a possibility. Existence is *the
> same* as the possible but outside the concept.[123]

Between the possible oak tree and the actual oak tree there is absolutely
no difference beyond the brute fact of existence. If, then, we conflate
the potentiality of the acorn with the *possibility* of the oak-tree, we are
making the claim that the acorn already contains the oak tree, but in a
potential state.

Alternatively, "[t]he actualization of the virtual, on the contrary, always
takes place by difference, divergence or differenciation [...]. Actual terms
never resemble the singularities they incarnate".[124] In contrast to a process
of realization or a movement from the possible to the real, the process
of actualization is a *creative* process within substances that requires *work*.
Moreover, the local manifestation produced in the process of actualization
is something new and shares no resemblance to the singularities which it
actualizes. To illustrate this point, let's return to the vexed example of the
acorn. The virtuality of the acorn is *not* the oak tree, but rather is the notes
of its being. The singularities that characterize its concrete existence are
folded deep within that existence and withdrawn from the world. When the
acorn enters into exo-relations with other entities, these singularities will be
activated in a variety of ways depending on the exo-relations it entertains
with other entities. If the soil is too damp and the temperature doesn't get
warm enough, the acorn rots. If the temperature is right and there is a
requisite amount of water in the soil, the acorn begins to germinate. But
now, as the acorn germinates, it encounters other entities in the field of its
exo-relations. There are, for example, all sorts of other plants growing in

the region of the acorn with which the acorn's own roots must compete. As a consequence of this, the seedling becomes weak and anemic or strong and thriving. The region in which the acorn grows is perhaps particularly windy, with sheets of wind buffeting the plain where the seedling grows from a predominantly westerly direction. When we come across the oak tree decades later, we notice that it is bent and knotted in an easterly direction like a carefully pruned bonsai tree. It is as if the oak tree has become petrified wind.

The point here is that the singularities or attractors belonging to the acorn do not contain the oak tree in advance. Rather, the acorn negotiates a milieu of exo-relations to other entities in producing its local manifestations or qualities. The attractors that preside over this process are radically non-qualitative. Here I find myself inclined to embrace Latour's thesis that "[w]hatever resists trials is real".[125] The problem with Latour's formulation is that it is purely negative and relational. In situating the endo-structure of an entity in terms of resistance, Latour emphasizes what occurs when an entity enters into exo-relations with other entities. This confuses epistemic criteria through which *we* or other entities recognize another entity as real, with what constitutes the reality of the entity regardless of whether anyone or anything knows it. In this regard, he thinks the being of an entity from the perspective of *other* entities encountering that entity. The wind, itself composed of many entities, encounters the seedling and must move around it. The seedling resists the wind. It is by virtue of its singularities, its endo-structure, that the seedling is able to resist the wind, but these singularities aren't the *resistance*. Rather, the singularities would be there in the seedling regardless of whether or not anything interacted with them.

From these observations, a number of distinctions follow. On the one hand, we must distinguish between symmetrical and asymmetrical qualities or local manifestations. Symmetrical qualities are qualities that can repeatedly snap in and out of existence. For example, the various shades of color the coffee mug manifests are symmetrical qualities in that, barring a transformation of the endo-structure of the coffee mug, these qualities can come in and out of existence. Turn off the lights and the mug becomes black. Turn on the light and the mug returns to that particular shade of blue. Asymmetrical qualities, by contrast, are irreversible qualitative transformations that take place within an object. These are qualitative transformations that can be produced by either the object itself, or through exo-relations to other objects. Thus, for example, the bent figure of the tree is an asymmetrical quality produced by the tree's exo-relations to the wind and perhaps other plants in its vicinity it competes with for sunlight. The key point not to be missed with asymmetrical qualities is that they are irreversible. Asymmetrical transformations cut off other possibilities within the vector field of a substance's attractors.

On the other hand, we must distinguish between exo-qualities and endo-qualities. Exo-qualities are qualities that can only exist in and through a set of exo-relations to other objects. Color, for example, seems to be a quality of this sort. Color is an event that only takes place through a network of exo-relations between the molecular endo-composition of the object, particular wavelengths of light, and a particular neurological structure in an organism. Take any of these elements away and color puffs out of existence. As such, color, as an exo-quality, is a genuine creation of these three agencies being woven together. It is not the *cup* that is colored, but rather the entanglement of these agencies that produces color as an event. The cup merely has the power to contribute to the production of this exo-quality. Endo-qualities, by contrast, are qualities that really are in the object. However, endo-qualities, as local manifestations of a substance, come about in two ways. First, endo-qualities are local manifestations that can come about through the internal dynamisms of an object independent of any other objects. Here the object need not be perturbed by another object for the endo-quality to be produced. Second, endo-qualities can come about through exo-relations to other objects, where these exo-relations irreversibly transform the local manifestation of the object. All asymmetrical qualities are of this sort. These events also harbor the power of transforming the endo-structure of objects, leading to the genesis of new singularities, powers, attractors, or vector fields in the virtual proper being of an object.

The great error to be avoided lies in conceiving the virtual or potential in teleological terms, or in believing that the entity could be captured or fully grasped by summing up all possible points of view on the object. The relation between virtual proper being and local manifestation is not a teleological relation or a relation between an agency and a goal. Throughout the last three chapters, I have attempted to argue that objects can be fully concrete without locally manifesting themselves or actualizing themselves in qualities. Another way of putting this is to say that local manifestation is not the *fulfillment* of objects. Local manifestation is something that objects *can* do, but an object that does not locally manifest itself is not *lacking* in some way, nor is it somehow incomplete. Nor is it the case that we would encounter the complete being of a substance if only we could see it from everywhere at once. Where the local manifestations of a substance are concerned, these manifestations are, in principle, *infinite*. There is no limit to the number of local manifestations that an object can actualize, precisely because there is no limit to the exo-relations an object can enter into and the exo-relations it can consequently produce. Yet even if God exists and is capable of perceiving an infinity of local manifestations, the being of objects is nonetheless radically withdrawn even from God for the subterranean dimension of substance, its virtual proper being, is in excess of any of its local manifestations. The virtual proper being of objects consists not of qualities, but of powers and these powers are never exhausted by local manifestations. In this regard, there is never a complete mapping of any phase space, but rather only ever a limited mapping of a phase space dependent on the exo-relations into which the object has been placed.

Here I see no reason to follow Bhaskar in privileging closed systems over open systems. Bhaskar's thesis seems to be that the events we witness when a substance is placed in the closed system of an experimental setting constitute the true being of an object. Here, I believe, Bhaskar betrays his fundamental insight: that substances can be out of phase with the qualities or events of which they are capable, and that there is therefore a fundamental difference between substance and qualities. All that takes place in the closed system of an experimental environment is the situating of an object within a particular set of exo-relations such that particular events take place. Nothing about this suggests that the substance thus situated is *exhausted* by this setting or that we have been brought before the *true* being of the object. That being is always withdrawn and in excess of any of its manifestations. As every cook knows, when placed in other exo-relations other local manifestations take place.

As I reflect on Harman's vigorous critique of potentiality, it seems to me that the real motivating desire behind this critique is the desire to preserve the *concreteness* of objects. As Harman writes,

> The recourse to potentiality is a dodge that leaves actuality undetermined and finally uninteresting; it reduces what is currently actual to the transient costume of an emergent process across time, and makes the real work happen outside actuality itself. The same holds true if we replace 'the potential' with 'the virtual', not withstanding their differences. In both cases, concrete actors themselves are deemed insufficient for the labour of the world and are indentured to hidden overlords: whether they be potential, virtual, veiled, topological, fluxional, or any adjective that tries to escape from what is actually here right now.[126]

However, if what Harman says here is true, I fail to see how it is possible for an object to change while remaining the same substance. Rather, this thesis seems to lead us to the punctualistic atomism of Whitehead's actual occasions, where each change constitutes an absolutely *new* entity. Here, perhaps, we should distinguish between the concrete, the actual, and the virtual. Harman appears to treat the concrete and the actual as synonyms of one another. Yet if we treat the concrete and the actual as synonyms of one another, then we're forced to go the route of Whitehead and treat every change in an actual entity as an absolutely new entity. With each stroke of the keyboard, with each movement of my finger, with each beat of my heart, I am, under this model, not the same entity now writing this essay, but rather am an absolutely new and distinct entity. This seems like a high ontological price to pay for preserving the concrete and seems to lead to the thesis that entities are created *ex nihilo* precisely because no entity contains potentials by which a new entity could be produced.

It is far better, in light of these concerns, to distinguish between the concrete, the actual, and the virtual. Within this framework, all entities are absolutely concrete, but have virtual and actual dimensions. The virtual is not the possible, nor is it an entity or substance that doesn't yet exist. Rather the virtual is a fully concrete, real, and existing dimension *of* objects.

Nor does it indenture objects to hidden overlords, rendering actuality irrelevant. This would only hold if the *true* being of objects were their virtual dimension, but as we have seen, the virtual is but a dimension of objects and actuality plays a key role in objects; not the least of which lies in unleashing potentials within objects when they enter into exo-relations. Here, in many respects, I sense that my position and Harman's are much closer than might initially be suggested. In *Guerilla Metaphysics*, Harman remarks that "[a]n object may drift into events and unleash its forces there, but no such event is capable of putting the object fully into play".[127] Without the dimension of potentiality or virtuality, it's difficult to see how it would be possible for objects to unleash their forces in this way. In his most recent work, Harman distinguishes between real objects and real qualities, and sensuous objects and sensuous qualities. Real objects and qualities refer to objects and qualities withdrawn from all relation to other objects, while sensuous objects and qualities refer to how one object encounters another object. Between Harman's real objects and sensuous objects, I sense more than a passing resemblance between my virtual proper being and local manifestations.

3.5. Žižek's Objecting Objects

Characterizing objects as split-objects onticology naturally invites comparison with Žižek's conception of objects as developed in his ontology. In concluding this chapter, I will discuss both where onticology is in agreement with Žižek and where it diverges from his thought. In *The Parallax View*, Žižek remarks that,

> Many times I am asked the obvious yet pertinent question about the title of my longest book (the present one excepted): "So who or what is tickling the ticklish subject?" The answer, of course, is: *the object*—however, *which* object? This, in a nutshell (or, rather, like a nut within the shell), is the topic of this book. The difference between subject and object can also be expressed as the difference between the two corresponding verbs, to subject (submit) oneself to object (protest, oppose, create an obstacle). The subject's elementary, founding,

gesture is *to subject itself*—voluntarily, of course: as both Wagner and Nietzsche, those two great opponents, were well aware, the highest act of freedom is the display of *amor fati*, the act of freely assuming what is necessary anyway. If, then, the subject's activity is, at its most fundamental, the activity of submitting oneself to the inevitable, the fundamental mode of the object's passivity, of its passive presence, is that which moves, annoys, disturbs, traumatizes us (subjects): at its most radical the object is *that which objects*, that which disturbs the smooth running of things. Thus the paradox is that the roles are reversed (in terms of the standard notion of the active subject working on the passive object: the subject is defined by a fundamental passivity, and it is the object from which movement comes—which does the tickling. But, again, *what* object is this? The answer is the parallax object.[128]

The parallax object of which Žižek here speaks is "the apparent displacement of an object (the shift of its position against a background), caused by a change in observational position that provides a new line of sight".[129]

The concept of the parallax summarizes a long line of development in Žižek's thought revolving around the non-identity of the One with itself. As Žižek remarks elsewhere, "[t]he Hegelian Twosome, rather designates a split which cleaves the One from within, not into two parts: the ultimate split is not between two halves, but between Something and Nothing, between the One and the void of its Place".[130] As a consequence, "the Real is the 'almost nothing' which sustains the gap that separates a thing from itself".[131] With respect to the ontology of objects, Žižek's concept of the parallax functions to surmount the Kantian opposition between the thing-in-itself and phenomena or between reality and appearance.

It will be recalled that one of Kant's central claims is that we only ever have access to phenomena (appearances) and never things-as-they-are-in-themselves (reality). As a consequence, in the best case scenario, we are unable to determine whether reality or things-in-themselves are anything like they appear to us, while in the worst case scenario it is possible that reality or things-in-themselves are entirely different from how they appear to us. The Hegelian gesture for overcoming this duality advocated by Žižek lies not in showing how we can overcome appearances, but rather in arguing that this split between phenomena or appearances and things-in-themselves arises from within *appearance* itself.[132] In other words, the split between reality and appearance is a sort of illusion of *perspective*. As Žižek remarks,

> [A]ppearance implies that there is something behind it which appears through it; it conceals a truth and by the same gesture gives a foreboding thereof; it simultaneously hides and reveals the essence behind the curtain. But what is hidden behind the phenomenal appearance? Precisely the fact that there is nothing to hide. What is concealed is that the very act of concealing conceals nothing.[133]

In short, the parallax that Žižek effects with respect to the relation between appearance and reality is not to show us how we can get beyond appearances to reach or touch reality, but lies rather in showing how this *apparent* gap between appearance and reality lies, in fact, on the side of *appearance* itself. Not only is appearance internally split, but this split is *itself* an *appearance*, a sort of optical illusion. If, then, this constitutes a parallactic shift, then this is because where, in the first figure of subjectivity, we experience ourselves as trapped within appearances, unable to touch reality, we now see this as an illusion *qua* illusion. Put differently, we come to see that appearances themselves are structured in such a way as to produce this very illusion. It is for this reason that we can say, in Žižek's sense, that objects are *split*. And as a consequence, reality is not something beyond or behind appearances, but is rather appearance itself.

But why do objects or phenomena produce this sort of illusion whereby phenomena *appear* to be manifestations of an inaccessible reality? Žižek's answer is that this *effect* arises from the split in the object embodied in the relation between the object and the void of its place. As Žižek remarks, the

> identity of an entity with itself equals the coincidence of this entity with the empty place of its "inscription". We come across identity when predicates fail. Identity is the surplus which cannot be captured by predicates—more precisely (and

this precision is crucial if we want to avoid a misconception of Hegel), identity-with-itself is *nothing but* this impossibility of predicates, *nothing but* this confrontation of an entity with the void at the point where we expect a predicate, a determination of its positive content ("law is…".). Identity-with-itself is thus another name for absolute (self-referential) negativity, for the negative relationship towards all predicates that define one's—what?—*identity*.[134]

Because entity, according to Žižek, is this non-identical identity divided between the object and the empty place of its inscription, it creates a "reality effect" in the object such that the object *simultaneously* appears to be an appearance through predicates *and* the expression of an unreachable reality in excess of this appearance. As Žižek argues elsewhere,

> [*objet*] *a*, qua semblance deceives in a Lacanian way: not because it is a deceitful substitute of the Real, but precisely because it invokes the impression of some substantial Real behind it; it deceives by posing as a shadow of the underlying Real. And the same goes for Kant: what Kant fails to notice is that *das Ding* is a mirage invoked by the transcendental object. *Limitation precedes transcendence*: all that "actually exists" is the field of phenomena and its limitation, whereas *das Ding* is nothing but a phantasm which, subsequently, fills out the void of the transcendental object.[135]

And, as Žižek will go on to remark a moment later,

> What we experience as "reality" discloses itself against the background of the lack, of the absence of it, of the Thing, of the mythical object whose encounter would bring about the full satisfaction of the drive. This lack of the Thing constitutive of "reality" is therefore, in its fundamental dimension, not epistemological, but rather pertains to the paradoxical logic of desire—the paradox being that this Thing is retroactively produced by the very process of symbolization, i.e, that it emerges from the very gesture of its loss. In other (Hegel's) words, there is nothing—no positive substantial

entity—behind the phenomenal curtain, only the gaze whose phantasmagorias assume different shapes of the Thing.[136]

The key point not to be missed is precisely that the "reality effect" is a result of *inscription* in the *symbolic*. Everywhere Žižek is careful to remark that the fundamental opposition is *not* between a signifier and an opposing signifier such as the opposition between wet and dry, but rather that the fundamental opposition, the founding opposition, is between a signifier and its *place* of inscription.[137] However, insofar as a signifier simultaneously embodies itself and the *emptiness* of its place of inscription, it is always non-identical to itself in its identity, thereby suggesting an excessive *being* beyond itself. Yet this excessive being or reality is something that can never be reached precisely because it is a radically void or empty place. In other words, this being, this transcendence, is an "optical illusion".

The fundamental point is that it is *not* a domain distinct from the symbolic, but rather is a peculiar twist in the symbolic. As Žižek explains,

> the bar which separates [the symbolic and the real] is *strictly internal to the Symbolic*, since it prevents the Symbolic from "becoming itself". The problem for the signifier is not its impossibility to touch the real but its impossibility to "attain itself"—what the signifier lacks is not the extra-linguistic object but the Signifier itself, a non-barred, non-hindered One.[138]

In short, the real is not something *other* than the symbolic, but rather is a sort of *effect* of the symbolic resulting from the difference that haunts every signifier by virtue of the split between the signifier and its place of inscription. Because the signifier always embodies this difference between itself and its place of inscription, the signifier always and everywhere necessarily fails to attain identity with itself. However, this very failure to attain identity with itself is precisely the very essence of its identity. As Hegel playfully remarks in the *Science of Logic*, if A were identical with itself, why would I need to repeat it? The repetition of an identity in a tautology like "A = A" actually marks the difference or non-identity of A with itself. Along these lines, Žižek will compare the shift from viewing the real as a *prediscursive* reality that is then "chopped" up by mind to viewing the real as an *effect* of the symbolic, to the shift from special to general relativity in Einstein's theory of gravity.

> And is not the shift from purification to subtraction also the shift from Kant to Hegel? From tension between phenomena and Thing to an inconsistency/gap between phenomena themselves? The standard notion of reality is that of a hard kernel that resists the conceptual grasp—what Hegel does is simply to take this notion of reality more literally: nonconceptual reality is something that emerges when notional self- development gets caught in an inconsistency and becomes nontransparent to itself. In short, the limit is transposed from exterior to interior: there is Reality because and insofar as the Notion is inconsistent, doesn't coincide with itself. The multiple perspectival inconsistencies between phenomena are not an effect of the impact of the transcendent Thing—on the contrary, this Thing is nothing but the ontologization of the inconsistency between phenomena. The logic of this reversal is ultimately the same as the passage from the special to the general theory of relativity in Einstein. While the special theory already introduces the notion of curved space, it conceives of this curvature as the effect of matter: it is the presence of matter that curves space—that is to say, only empty space would be noncurved. With the passage to the general theory, the causality is reversed: far from *causing* the curvature of space, matter is its *effect*. In the same way, the Lacanian Real—the Thing—is not so much the inert presence that "curves" the symbolic space (introducing gaps and inconsistencies in it), but, rather, the effect of these gaps and inconsistencies.[139]

And to complete Žižek's sentence, we can say that the gaps and inconsistencies *in the symbolic* produce these effects of the *real*. The shift from the "special theory of the Lacanian Real" to the "general theory of the Lacanian real" is thus a shift from viewing the real as a prediscursive reality that is subsequently formatted by the symbolic and that perpetually

perturbs the symbolic, to a theory of the real as an *effect* of the symbolic
or deadlocks of formalization within the symbolic such that any reference
to a prediscursive real is *mythological* or a sort of optical illusion. As a
consequence, any defense of pre-discursive reality becomes the height of
dogmatic thought.

Returning, then, to the quotation with which I began this section, why is
it that the real or the split object in Žižek's sense "tickles" the subject? If the
real tickles or perturbs the subject, then this is because it creates the illusion
of the Thing that the subject simultaneously lacks access to and that blocks
its access to this Thing. This Thing is the illusion of something that would
satiate and satisfy the subject's unsatisfied desire.

> The Real is thus the disavowed X on account of which
> our vision of reality is anamorphically distorted; it is
> simultaneously the Thing to which direct access is not
> possible and the obstacle which prevents this direct access,
> the Thing which eludes our grasp and the distorting screen
> which makes us miss the thing.[140]

However, this Thing from which we are blocked is precisely an *effect* of
the internally split nature of the object between the object and its place of
inscription. If the object appears suggestive of a Thing, of a complete object
beyond appearances that would satisfy our desire once and for all, then this
is precisely because, at the level of appearances, predicates fail to capture
the object. However, if predicates fail to capture the identity of the object,
then this is precisely because the object is internally fissured by the void of
its place of inscription in the signifier, suggesting a fullness through its very
absence that can never be filled.

As a consequence, this split within the object becomes the site of social
antagonism. "The 'Real'" is "the traumatic core of some social antagonism
which distorts" our view of actual social organization. And, as Žižek goes
on to remark, "the parallax Real is [...] that which accounts for the very
multiplicity of appearances of the same underlying Real—it is not the hard
core which persists as the Same, but the hard bone of contention which
pulverizes the sameness into the multitude of appearances".[141] Earlier
Žižek remarks that the Real, the parallax gap, is "that unfathomable X

which forever eludes the symbolic grasp, and thus causes the multiplicity of symbolic perspectives".[142] Insofar as the symbolic is haunted by an irreducible and ineradicable kernel of the Real, it becomes the site of social struggle as different groups strive to fill in the void that perturbs the symbolic.

In the preceding pages I have not done nearly enough justice to the complexity of Žižek's ontology and his account of the relationship between the subject and the object, but have only sought to outline the most relevant features of his account of being. In the next chapter we will see how a good deal of Lacanian psychoanalysis and Žižek's critique of ideology can be retained within the ontological framework proposed by onticology. However, it is clear that ontologically onticology and Žižek must diverge markedly from one another. The first point worth noting is that for Žižek the object is a *pole* in a relation between subject and object. In other words, there is one type of being, the subject, and another type of being, the object. The object is always an object for a subject and the subject is always a subject for an object. As such, Žižek's ontology is a variant of absolute correlationism or the position that there is no being apart from the subject.

Within the framework of onticology, by contrast, there is no special category referred to as "the subject" that is necessarily and irrevocably attached to an object. Rather, the central thesis of onticology is that being is composed entirely of objects or primary substances. To be sure, objects differ from one another and have different powers or capacities. Moreover, there are objects which we refer to as persons. However, the category of objects composed of persons possesses no special or privileged place within being, nor are all beings necessarily related to persons in some form or another. As Latour remarks, the zebras gallop across the steppes just fine without the benefit of our gaze. Humans are *among* beings and are beings among being, they aren't at the center of being, nor are they the necessary condition for being. Were Žižek's claims true, there could be no being apart from the human insofar as language, no matter how alien and alienating, only exists for humans and perhaps some other animals.

By way of a second point, while both onticology and Žižek argue that objects are split, the two do so for radically different reasons. For Žižek, objects are split between their appearance and the void of their place of inscription in the *symbolic*. As a consequence of this divide between place-holder and place, objects can never be identical to themselves. Insofar as objects are split between their appearance and the void of their place of inscription, objects are *effects* of the symbolic or the signifier. Here Žižek directly follows Lacan, for as Lacan remarks in *Encore*, "[t]he universe is a flower of rhetoric".[143] The claim that the universe is a flower of rhetoric is the claim that the universe is an effect or product of rhetoric. The universe, for Lacan, is that which blooms out of language and speech. And indeed, earlier we find Lacan remarking that, "[t]here isn't the slightest prediscursive reality, for the very fine reason that what constitutes a collectivity—what I called men, women, and children—means nothing qua prediscursive reality. Men, women, and children are but signifiers".[144] Presumably Lacan would claim the same thing of flowers, zebras, subatomic particles, burritos, stars and all other entities.

The thesis that objects are an effect of the signifier, the symbolic, or language is a variant of what I call the "hegemonic fallacy". Put crudely, in political theory a hegemonic relation is a social, ideological, cultural, or economic dominance exerted over all other members of the social field. For example, Christianity and, in particular, evangelical Christianity, has a hegemonic influence on United States politics in comparison to other religious beliefs or the absence of religious belief altogether. Onticology shifts the concept of hegemony from the domain of political theory to the domain of ontology and might be fruitfully compared to the concept of ontotheology. Within the framework of onticology, the hegemonic fallacy occurs whenever one type of entity is treated as the ground or *explanans* of all other entities.

In treating language or the signifier as the ground of being or the universe as an effect of the signifier, this is precisely what takes place in Žižek and Lacan. Beings are hegemonized under the signifier or language, just as they are hegemonized under mind in Kant. Lurking in the background of Žižek's argument is, I suspect, a variant of the epistemic fallacy and actualism as discussed in the first chapter. Just as Locke rejected the coherence of the concept of substance on the grounds that we are not *given* any access to substance in consciousness, the grounds for rejecting anything like prediscursive reality would lie in the fact that we can only *speak* about prediscursive reality through signifiers or language and that, no matter how hard we strive to escape language, we only produce more signifiers. Here language is the actuality that is given and we are invited to think of all being in terms of the epistemological or how beings are given to us through language.

However, as we saw in the first chapter, this argument only follows if it is possible to transform properly ontological questions into epistemological questions. The reasoning through which we arrive at the existence of objects is found not in our access to objects through language or consciousness, but rather through a reflection on what the world must be like for our practices to be intelligible. And indeed, it is difficult to see how language could ever have the power to divide or parcel in the way suggested by the linguistic idealists were it not for the fact that the world is itself structured and differentiated. Absent a world that is structured and differentiated, the surface of the world, as a sort of formless flux, would be too slippery, too smooth, for the signifier to structure at all.

The point here is not that we should ignore the signifier, language, and signs, but that the signifier cannot function as the *ground* of being. Here the "hegemon" of the hegemonic fallacy needs to be taken seriously. A hegemon is a monarch that stands above, overdetermining everything else in a collective of objects. A hegomonic relation is a vertical relation from top to bottom, where the entity serving as the hegemon functions as a monarch governing all that falls underneath the hegemon. In Žižek-Lacan's schema, this is precisely how language functions. The hegemon of the hegemonic fallacy thus functions like an active form giving structure or formatting a passive, structureless matter. Rather than thinking in terms of hegemonic conditioning, onticology recommends that we instead think in terms of *entanglements* of objects. Without sharing all the conclusions of her agental realism (especially her relationist ontology), while nonetheless being deeply sympathetic to her project, I borrow the term "entanglement" from the work of Karen Barad.[145] Barad encourages us to think in terms of entanglements of different agencies and the diffraction patterns these entanglements produce. As described by Barad,

> diffraction has to do with the way waves combine when they
> overlap and the apparent bending and spreading of waves that

occur when waves encounter an obstruction. Diffraction can
occur with any kind of wave: for example, water waves, sound
waves, and light waves all exhibit diffraction under the right
conditions.[146]

The concept of diffraction patterns proposed by Barad embodies a
much "flatter" conception of being than the sort of vertical conception of
being we encounter in hegemonic ontologies. Where a hegemonic ontology
treats one agency as making all the difference, an ontology premised on
entanglements is attentive to how a variety of different objects or agencies
interact in the production of phenomena. Just as new patterns emerge when
waves intersect one another or encounter an obstacle *with no one agency
entirely responsible for the pattern*, networks of objects interacting with one
another produce unique patterns that cannot be reduced to any one of
the agencies involved. Thus, Barad remarks, "diffractions are attuned to
differences—differences that our knowledge-making practices make and the
effects they have on the world".[147] And here the crucial point is that "these
entangled practices are productive, and who and what are excluded through
these entangled practices matter: different intra-actions produce different
phenomena".[148] Within an entanglement and a diffraction pattern there can
be no hegemon, which isn't to say that some objects might not contribute
more differences within a particular constellation than other objects. It is
precisely this tangled contribution of differences that an obsessive focus on
the signifier blinds us to. And once again, the point here isn't that signifiers
and signs don't contribute differences, but that we need to be attentive to
the role played by other, non-signifying differences within a collective.

With reference to Barad, we thus arrive at the profound difference
between Žižek's conception of split objects and the conception of split-
objects proposed by onticology. For Žižek, the object is internally split
between its appearance and the void of its place of inscription within the
symbolic order, whereas for onticology objects are split between their
manifestation and their virtual proper being. Here local manifestion is not
manifestation to a subject or humans, but rather actualization in the world.
Moreover, local manifestation would take place regardless of whether
or not any humans existed to receive it and whether or not the symbolic
existed. And, in this respect, the multiplicity of perspectives Žižek discusses

are not the product of the split between appearance and the void of the place of inscription in the symbolic, but rather are a product of different intra-actions among objects. As we saw in our discussion of virtual proper being, the virtual dimension of objects is such that it can actualize itself in different ways as a function of the various exo-relations into which an object enters with other objects. There is nothing special or privileged here about the human-object relation. What is true of the human-object relation is true of any object-object exo-relation, regardless of whether or not humans are involved or exist. And insofar as this is true of object-object relations regardless of whether or not humans exist, it follows that the signifier cannot play a constitutive role in the constitution of objects. The key point here is that local manifestations are, in part, a product of how objects *act* on one another when they enter into exo-relations. Salt brings about different local manifestations in water than, for example, wood.

However, while local manifestation is a phenomenon that takes place regardless of whether or not humans exist, the concept of exo-relation and local manifestation does encourage us to be particularly attentive to questions of how humans act on objects through their instruments and under specific conditions in the production of local manifestations. In short, so long as we remain within the framework of representation, asking how we *mirror* or *reflect* objects, we have posed the questions of epistemology poorly. The logic of representation, based as it is on visual metaphors of reflecting and mirroring, raises only the question of whether there is a *similitude* between the representation and the represented. As such, it necessarily misses the field of exo-relations and inter-actions among objects in the production of local manifestations. What onticology instead recommends is a particular attentiveness to fields of action among objects that enter into exo-relations with one another, examining how these inter-actions produce a variety of local manifestations in a diffraction pattern.

Chapter 4
The Interior of Objects

What those who use hermeneutics, exegesis, or semiotics
say of texts can be said of all [objects]. For a long time it
has been agreed that the relationship between one text and
another is always a matter of interpretation. Why not accept
that this is also true between so-called texts and so-called
objects, and even between so-called objects themselves?

— Bruno Latour[149]

...[E]very prehension consists of three factors: (a) the
'subject' which is prehending, namely, the actual entity in
which that prehension is a concrete element; (b) the 'datum'
which is prehended; (c) the 'subjective form' which is how
that subject prehends the datum.

— Alfred North Whitehead[150]

4.1. The Closure of Objects

In chapter 2, I argued that, far from being a paradox, the very essence
of objects consists in simultaneously withdrawing and self-othering. If
objects simultaneously withdraw and are self-othering, then this is because,
on the one hand, substances never directly manifest themselves in the

world while, on the other hand, they perpetually alienate themselves in qualities and states as a consequence of their own internal dynamics and the exo-relations they enter into with other objects. In the last chapter, I analyzed the self-othering of objects in terms of the relationship between the perpetually and necessarily withdrawn virtual proper being of objects and the local manifestations of objects that take place through the internal dynamics of substance and the exo-relations they enter into with other objects. The claim that substances withdraw from one another suggests that it is impossible for objects to directly encounter one another. If this is the case, then this raises the question of how objects relate to one another or how we are to think the interior of objects with respect to other objects.

In this chapter, I will discuss the manner in which one entity, to use Whithead's vocabulary, "prehends" another entity, producing what Graham Harman has called "sensuous objects" on the interior of a real entity. Here "prehension" refers to the manner in which one entity grasps or relates to another entity. Whitehead carefully distinguishes between the subject that prehends (what I call a substance or object), what is prehended (another substance or object), and *how* that other substance is prehended. In this chapter, I focus on the first and third dimension of prehension in terms of autopoietic systems theory. In underlining the "how" of how one substance prehends another entity, Whitehead implicitly captures the sense in which entities or substances withdraw from one another insofar as no entity encounters another entity in terms of how that entity itself *is*, but rather every entity reworks "data" issuing from other entities in terms of the prehending substance's own unique organization. However, the position I develop here diverges markedly from Whitehead's own ontology in rejecting the thesis that in "the analysis of an actual entity [...] into its most concrete elements" the entity is disclosed in its most concrete elements "to be a concrescence of prehensions".[151] While substances do indeed prehend other entities, substances must exist, it is argued, for these prehensions to take place. In other words, I seek to maintain a much stronger distinction between the subject/substance doing the prehending and the how of prehensions than the one Whitehead seems to suggest in his thesis that substances *are* a concrescence of prehensions. Part of this distinction was already developed in the last chapter with respect to the endo-structure of objects or their being as multiplicities. While prehensions can, as we will see, lead to the modification of the endo-structure of objects, the point throughout my analysis of inter-object relations is that objects must have a structure for the "how" of prehensions to take place at all and that this endo-structure constitutes the substantiality of objects.

It is to this issue that I now turn by drawing on the resources of autopoietic systems theory as developed by Maturana, Varela, and especially Niklas Luhmann. At the outset, it is important to note that my thesis is *not* that *all* objects are *autopoietic* machines. In their early founding essay, "Autopoiesis: The Organization of the Living", Maturana and Varela distinguish between autopoietic machines and allopoietic machines.[152] Later I will explain the distinction between these two types of objects in greater detail, but for the moment it is sufficient to note that when Maturana and Varela refer to autopoietic machines, they are referring to living objects, while when they refer to allopoietic machines they are referring to non-living objects. Luhmann expands the domain of the autopoietic beyond living organisms to include social systems within the purview of autopoiesis, but for the moment this rough and ready distinction is sufficient for our purposes. With a few qualifications, I accept Maturana and Varela's distinction between autopoietic and allopoietic machines. However, if the work of Luhmann is so vital to this project, then this is because he ontologizes autopoietic systems, treating them as real entities, whereas Maturana and Varela advocate a radical constructivism that treats autopoietic systems as constructed by an observer. As Luhmann writes at the beginning of the first chapter of the sublime *Social Systems*, "[t]he following considerations assume that there are systems. Thus they do not begin with epistemological doubt".[153] For Luhmann, systems are really existing objects in the world. I believe that I have shown in the first chapter why, following Roy Bhaskar, this supposition is warranted.

Additionally, it might come as a surprise to enlist a thinker like Niklas Luhmann in defense of object-oriented ontology. In essays like "Identity—What or How?" Luhmann levels a substantial critique against the very idea of ontology. There Luhmann remarks that "ontology is understood to be a certain form of observing and describing, to wit, that form that consists of the distinction between being and nonbeing".[154] A moment later, Luhmann goes on to remark that "[a]mong the consequences of an ontological dissection of the world, one that differentiates being and nonbeing is this one: that the identity of what is [*des Seienden*] must be presupposed".[155] I will discuss Luhmann's concept of distinction in more detail in the next section. Here what is to be noted is the manner in which Luhmann deconstructs ontology. Luhmann's point is that a particular distinction *precedes* the identity of an entity, such that the identity of an entity is an *effect* of the distinction that allows for observation, not a substantial reality that *precedes* observation. To understand Luhmann's point we must refer back to Spencer-Brown's calculus of forms. Spencer-Brown opens *Laws of Forms* with the thesis that indication is only possible on the basis of a *prior* distinction. As Spencer-Brown writes, "[w]e take as given the idea of distinction and the idea of indication, and that we cannot make an indication without drawing a distinction".[156] An indication might be, for example, a reference to anything in the world. Spencer-Brown's point is that any indication requires a distinction if the indication is to be made. A distinction cleaves a space in two, defining an outside and an inside. For example, we can imagine a piece of paper populated by a plurality of x's. We draw a circle on this paper (the distinction), and can now indicate x's within the circle and x's outside of the circle. Every distinction thus contains a marked and an unmarked space. The marked space is what falls within the distinction (in this instance, what is inside the circle), while the unmarked space is everything else. This unity of marked and unmarked space generated by a distinction is what Spencer-Brown calls a "form". There's a very real sense in which distinction is "transcendental" with respect to indication. Form is the *condition* under which indication is possible. As a consequence, the indic*ated* does not *precede* the distinction, but is the condition under which the indicated comes into being *for the system drawing the distinction*. The point, of course, is that while distinctions or forms obey rigorous laws once made, the founding distinction itself is contingent in that other distinctions could have always been made.

By analyzing ontology in terms of how its indications are possible through a prior distinction, Luhman, in effect, deconstructs the grounding premise upon which ontology, as he understands it, is based. By tracing ontology back to the being/non-being distinction upon which it becomes possible to observe beings as identical, Luhmann effectively shows how this distinction is *contingent* such that identity is no longer the ground of being but an effect of a distinction that enables observation. The point, then, is that insofar as distinctions are *contingent*, they can be drawn *otherwise*, producing other objects as effects. As a consequence, objects become not autonomous substances that exist in their own right, but rather what Heinz von Foester called "Eigenvalues".[157] As von Foester articulates the concept,

> Eigenvalues have been found to be ontologically discrete, stable, separable, and composable, while ontogenetically to arise as equilibria that determine themselves through circular processes. Ontogenetically, Eigenvalues and objects, and likewise ontogenetically, stable behaviour and the manifestation of the subject's "grasp" of an object cannot be distinguished. In both cases, the objects appear to reside exclusively in the subject's own experience of his sensori-motor coordinations.[158]

In other words, the object is not something that exists substantially in its own right, but is rather something that is constructed by the cognizing system through the production of stable equilibria in perception that can be returned to again and again. Elsewhere, Gotthard Bechmann and Nico Stehr sum up this line of thought when they remark that Luhman "describes the old European style of thought as concerned with the identification of the unity underlying diversity [...] Ontology refers to a world existing objectively in separation from subjects aware of it, capable of unambiguous linguistic representation".[159] It is precisely this model of being that Luhmann challenges.

What we have here is a variant of the epistemic fallacy and actualism as discussed in the first chapter. In treating objects as Eigenvalues, Luhmann conflates substances with what substances are for a particular observing system. However, he cannot coherently get by without the category of substance. Although Luhmann everywhere focuses on epistemological issues, he requires the *existence* of systems in order to launch these epistemological inquiries. These systems are characterized by unity, autonomy, and endurance, which are precisely the marks of substance.

As a consequence, it is necessary to distinguish between substances as such and what other substances are *for* a substance. Here onticology and object-oriented philosophy encounters an unexpected ally in the anti-realism of autopoietic theory and Luhmann's autopoietic systems theory in particular. Insofar as Luhmann's systems are characterized by autonomy, they avoid the holism of relationism and therefore present us with a picture of the universe that is parceled or composed of units. As I argued, following Graham Harman, in the last chapter, objects are characterized by withdrawal such that they never directly encounter one another. In their account of how systems always encounter other systems in terms of their *own* organization, Luhmann and autopoietic theory provide onticology and object-oriented philosophy with powerful conceptual tools for fleshing out the concept of withdrawal. The sort of ontological realism Bechmann and Stehr rightly denounce only pertains to those accounts of substance premised on presence. Yet where substances perpetually withdraw from other substances and from themselves such that they are characterized by closure, we encounter an ontology adequate to the critique of ontotheology and the metaphysics of presence.

What interests me in autopoietic systems theory is not so much its account of life or society, as its account of *operational closure*. As Maturana and Varela elsewhere define it, "their identity [the identity of autopoietic machines] is specified by a network of dynamic processes whose effects do not leave that network".[160] The concept of operational closure as it applies to autopoietic machines embodies two key claims: First, the claim is that the operations of an autopoietic system refer only to *themselves* and are products of the system itself. For example, if, as Luhmann has argued, social systems are composed entirely of communications, if communications are the elements that compose social systems, then communications refer only to other communications and never anything outside of themselves. Here communication is not something that takes place *between* systems but is strictly something that takes place *in* a system. Another way of putting this would be to say that a system cannot communicate with its environment and an environment cannot communicate with a system.

Second, the claim is that autopoietic systems are closed in on themselves, that they do not relate directly to an environment, that they do not receive *information* from an environment. As a consequence, it follows that information is not something that *pre-exists* an autopoietic machine, waiting out there in the world to be found. To be sure, objects outside an autopoietic machine can *perturb* or *irritate* an autopoietic machine, but this perturbation or irritation does not, in and of itself, constitute information for the system being perturbed. Rather, any information value the perturbation takes on is constituted strictly by the distinctions belonging to the organization of the autopoietic machine itself. As I argue in what follows, this closure of machines or objects in terms of perturbations is not unique to *autopoietic* machines, but to *both* autopoietic machines *and* allopoietic machines. Both autopoietic and allopoietic machines possess only selective relations to the world around them, such that both self-referentially constitute that to which they're open. Thus, while allopoietic machines do not reproduce themselves through their own operations as is the case with autopoietic machines, allopoietic machines nonetheless constitute the way in which they are open to other entities in the world.

In "Autopoiesis: The Organization of the Living", Maturana and Varela argue that "[a]n autopoietic machine

> is a machine organized (defined as a unity) as a network of processes of production (transformation and destruction) of components that produces the components which (i) through their interactions and transformations continuously regenerate and realize the network of processes (relations) that produced them; and (ii) constitute it (the machine) as a concrete unity in the space in which they (the components) exist by specifying the topological domain of its realization as a network.[161]

The unity of a system is what I call the system's "endo-consistency", its virtual proper being, or a multiplicity. As unities, systems, whether allopoietic or autopoietic, are substances. Autopoietic machines, systems, or substances are unique in that not only are they unities, not only are they operationally closed to the rest of the world, but they also *constitute* their own elements. As Luhmann puts it elsewhere, "[i]n contrast to what ordinary language and conceptual tradition suggest, the unity of an element [...] is not ontically pre-given. Instead, the element is constituted as a unity only by the system that enlists it as an element to use it in relations".[162]

Perhaps no one has gone further in formalizing, radicalizing, and developing the implications of autpoietic systems theory than Luhmann in his autopoietic sociological theory. Although I will here discuss elements of Luhmann's sociological theory, it should be borne in mind that my main aim is to outline the general features of autopoietic and allopoietic systems, rather than to focus on Luhmann's conception of society as an autopoietic system. Before proceeding, it is important to note that there are significant differences between how Maturana and Varela think autopoietic systems, and how Luhmann thinks them. For Maturana and Varela, autopoietic machines are homeostatic in character. "Autopoietic machines are homeostatic machines".[163] That is, they are systems that attempt to maintain a particular equilibrium across time. By contrast, Luhmann's autopoietic machines, at least in the case of meaning systems, are inherently characterized by unrest. "[W]e begin, without attempting reductive 'explanation,' from the fundamental situation of basal instability (with a resulting 'temporalized' complexity) and assert that all meaning systems, be they psychic or social, are characterized by such instability".[164] In a communication system, for example, the system aims not simply at maintaining equilibrium or homeostasis, but rather it is always necessary to find something new to say if the system is to continue to exist. Consider, for example, a conversation. Were the participants in the conversation to simply keep repeating themselves, the conversation would cease. It's necessary to find something new to say for the conversation, as a system, to continue its existence. Indeed, Luhmann will remark that both absence and remaining unchanged can therefore function as impetuses for change. As Luhmann remarks,

> On the one hand, given the capacity to process information,
> things that are not present can also have an effect; mistakes,
> null values, and disappointments acquire causality insofar
> as they can be grasped via the schema of difference. On the
> other, not just events but facts, structures, and continuities

stimulate causalities insofar as they can be experienced as differences. Remaining unchanged can thus become a cause of change.[165]

The key problem for any autopoietic system is how to get from one element to another in the order of time. Every autopoietic system is challenged by entropy and must find ways of staving off a collapse into entropy or disorganized complexity. The elements of autopoietic machines within the Luhmannian framework are events. As events, they disappear as soon as they occur. As a consequence, every autopoietic machine faces the problem of how it can reproduce itself or generate new elements from moment to moment. Confronted with an absence of change, that absence of change itself becomes the instigator of new events or elements in the ongoing autopoiesis of the system. Only through the production of subsequent elements or events is the autopoietic machine able to persist or continue existing. It is for this reason that meaning systems, at least, must necessarily be basally unstable. Here it should be noted that the substance of autopoietic systems resides not in the materiality of its parts—these parts can be and are replaced while the substance continues to exist—but rather by virtue of their structure or organization which I have referred to as multiplicities or the "endo-structure" of substances.

In arguing that the elements that compose autopoietic systems are not ontically pre-given, it is argued that these elements are not themselves *substances*, but rather only exist for the endo-consistency of the substance or multiplicity that *constitutes* them. The point is *not* that nothing exists apart from a system—everything must be built out of *other things* as Aristotle observed—but rather that what constitutes an element for a system does not pre-exist the system that constitutes or constructs it. Luhmann observes that we "must distinguish between the *environment* of a system and *systems in the environment* of this system".[166] If the distinction between the environment *of* a system and systems *in* the environment of a system is crucial, then this is because the former refers to how one substance encounters other substances in the world through its own closure and organization, while the latter refers to actually existing systems or substances that would exist regardless of whether or not the system encountering them existed. These actually existing systems, whether autopoietic or allopoietic themselves, can and do serve as material through which systems constitute their elements.

In his sociological systems theory, Luhmann develops the closure of systems to dramatic effect. For autopoietic systems theory

> the point of departure for all systems-theoretical analysis must be the *difference between system and environment*. Systems are oriented by their environment not just occasionally and adaptively, but structurally, and they cannot exist without an environment. They constitute and maintain themselves by creating and maintaining a difference from their environment, and they use their boundaries to regulate this difference. Without difference from an environment, there would not even be self-reference, because difference is the functional premise of self-referential operations.[167]

Insofar as onticology maintains that substances are fully autonomous, it parts ways with Luhmann in the thesis that substances or systems cannot exist independently of an environment. Nonetheless, onticology also recognizes that many systems would produce less than ideal local manifestations were they separated from an environment of exo-relations with other entities of a particular sort. A cat, for instance, is unable to exercise all sorts of powers of acting in the absence of oxygen. The important point here is that the distinction between system and environment is *self-referential*. Although this distinction refers to two domains (system and environment), the distinction itself originates from *one* of these domains: the system. The distinction between system and environment is a distinction drawn by each system. This is not only one of the origins of the operational closure of systems, but is also a condition for the *autonomy* of systems as individual and independent substances.

In the case of autopoietic machines, the distinction between system and environment emerges "because for each system the environment is more complex than the system itself".[168] As a consequence, "[t]here is [...] no point-for-point correspondence between system and environment".[169] Were there a point-for-point correspondence between system and environment, there would be no distinction between systems and their environments.

Moreover, this would require systems to respond or react to every event that takes place in their environment, thereby overburdening the system. Consequently, one way of thinking about autopoietic systems or substances is as strategies of selection or continuance within an environment that they are unable to completely anticipate and which they are certainly unable to dominate or master by virtue of the greater complexity that each environment possesses when compared to the complexity of systems.

A similar point holds with respect to the elements that systems produce or constitute. In the case of elements composing the endo-consistency of a multiplicity or system, these elements only exist in relation to one another. "Just as there are no systems without environments or environments without systems, there are no elements without relational connections or relations without elements".[170] Here we must carefully distinguish between substances and elements. Elements are always elements *for* a substance. They only exist as elements within the endo-structure or endo-composition of a system and do not, as we have seen, have any independent ontological existence of their own. Substances, by contrast, always enjoy an autonomous ontological existence in their own right, and therefore only exist in relations that are *external* to them. That is, substances are capable of breaking with their relations and entering into new relations, or of existing completely without relations at all. With an increase in the complexity of a system or the number of elements it must maintain to exist, special problems emerge. As Luhmann observes, "when the number of elements that must be held together *in a system* or *for a system as its environment* increases, one very quickly encounters a threshold where it is no longer possible to relate every element with every other element".[171]

Three interesting consequences follow from this endo-complexity of systems. First, insofar as it is not possible to feasibly connect every element of the system to every other element, it follows that systems must maintain selective relations among their elements, such that, they "[omit] other equally conceivable relations [among elements]".[172] These selective relations among elements are thus strategies for contending with an environment that is always more complex than the system itself. Luhmann emphasizes the *contingency* of these relations and the manner in which they involve *risk*. However, second, because not every element relates to every other element in a complex system, but rather relations are contingent strategies for contending with the environment, it follows that "very different kinds of systems can be formed out of a substratum of very similar units".[173] In other words, when speaking about the virtual proper being of an object or a multiplicity, it is not so much the substance's *elements* that constitute their substantiality, but rather how their elements are *organized* or *related*. It is for this reason that I speak of "endo-relations" in relation to the endo-consistency of the virtual proper being of an object. Finally, third, because systems constitute their own elements it follows that "systems of a higher (emergent) order can possess less complexity than systems of a lower order because they determine the unity and number of elements that compose them",[174] along with the relations among these elements.

One paradoxical feature of the system/environment distinction at the heart of any system, whether autopoietic or allopoietic, is that this distinction is not a distinction between two entities in their own right, but is rather a distinction that arises from *one side* of the distinction. In short, it is the *system* itself that "draws" the distinction between system and environment. As Luhmann remarks, "[t]he environment receives its unity through the system and only in relation to the system".[175] An environment is thus an environment *only* for the *interior* of an object or substance. Two consequences follow from this: First, the environment is not a *container* of substances or systems that precedes the existence of substances or systems. There is no environment "as such" existing out there in the world. Put otherwise, there is no *pre-established* or pre-given environment to which a system must "adapt". Rather, we have as many environments as there are substances in the universe, without it being possible to claim that *all* of these systems are *contained* in a *single* environment. As Timothy Morton puts it in a very different context, "[t]here is no environment as such. It's all 'distinct organic beings.'"[176] The environment is not a *container* lying there present at hand, awaiting the system to adapt to it. Rather, there are as many environments as there are systems, and the environment is nothing more than other systems that in turn "draw" their own system/environment distinctions. As we will see in chapter six, this leads to the conclusion that *the* world does not exist. Second, the distinction between system and environment is, as a consequence, paradoxical and *self-referential*. Insofar as the distinction between system and environment is a distinction "made" by the system, this distinction is also self-referential or a distinction belonging to the system itself. As we will see in a moment, this has significant consequences for how systems or substances relate to other entities.

To illustrate these points, take the example of the humble tardigrade. The tardigrade is a microscopic multicellular organism with eight legs, two eyes, and antennae and which looks somewhat like an alien pig. The tardigrade is particularly interesting because it is capable of surviving extreme variations of heat and cold without dying. Thus, for example, it can be subjected to extremely high temperatures such as those that occur when a meteor enters the Earth's atmosphere. When this occurs, all the water in the tardigrade's body steams away and it withdraws its legs into its trunk, becoming a hard pellet that appears to be dead. However, if water is introduced back into the tardigrade's environment, the tardigrade plumps back up and is walking around again within a few hours as if nothing happened. Returning to some themes of the first chapter, it is highly unlikely that substances like cats or humans belong to the environment of the tardigrade. As a microscopic organism, it perhaps crawls in and out of the different fissures in the skin and bodies of larger scale organisms, completely unaware that such organisms even exist. Nor, we can say, do these larger scale organisms function as that to which the tardigrade must adapt. The point is not that these larger scale organisms don't exist or that tardigrades get to decide what exists and what does not exist. To claim this, one would be confusing the environment of a system with systems or substances in a system's environment. Rather, the point is that substances maintain only selective relationships to their environment.

The self-referentiality of the system/environment distinction is one of the meanings of operational closure, and is common to both allopoietic substances and autopoietic substances alike. It is a common feature of all substances that they are one and all closed to the world, relating to systems in their environment only through their own distinctions or organization. As a consequence of this closure, systems or substances only relate to *themselves*. Put differently, while substances can enter into exo-relations with other substances, they only do so *on their own terms* and with respect to their own organization.

Luhmann draws startling conclusions from this thesis in his analysis of society. If societies are autopoietic systems or substances, and if autopoietic substances both constitute their own elements and are operationally closed, then it follows that *humans* are *not* a part of society. Luhmann's conception of society is thus radically at odds with that found in the humanist tradition. As Luhmann writes,

> The point of difference is that for the humanistic tradition human beings stand within the social order and not outside it. The human being counts as a permanent part of the social order, as an element of society itself. Human beings were called "individuals" because they were the ultimate, indivisible elements of society.[177]

Here it is important to note that, far from denying the existence of humans, Luhmann is *defending* their existence. Were we to claim that humans are products or effects of society as Althusser, for example, does in his essay on the ideological state apparatus and elsewhere, we would be conflating the existence of humans with that of elements in the system of society. However, just as societies are operationally closed systems, so too are humans. "If one views human beings as part of the environment of society (instead of as part of society itself), this changes the premises of all traditional questions, including those of classical humanism".[178]

Humans belong not to *society*, but rather the *environment* of society. Paradoxically, then, humans are *outside* of society. For Luhmann, society, by contrast, consists of communications and nothing but communications. And insofar as humans belong to the environment of society, they do not participate in society. As Luhmann puts it elsewhere, "one could say that the environment of the social system cannot communicate with society".[179] Likewise, systems or substances cannot communicate with their environments. If this is the case, then it is because systems only relate to themselves and "[i]nformation is [...] a purely system-internal quality. There is no transference of information from the environment into the system".[180] Put a bit differently, systems or substances communicate only with themselves. If, then, society is not composed of persons or humans, what is it composed of? As Luhman remarks, "[i]n the end, it is always people, individuals, subjects who act or communicate. I would like to assert in the face of this that only communication can communicate and that what we understand as "action" can be generated only in such a network of communication".[181] The elements that compose society consist of nothing but communications and the production of new communications in responses to communications. It is not persons that communicate, but rather communications that communicate.

To be clear, Luhmann is not advancing the absurd thesis that societies can exist *without* humans. Social systems are autonomous from humans, they are distinct substances in their own right, but they require the perturbations or irritations of humans in order to come into existence. As Luhmann puts it in *Social Systems*,

> Psychic and social systems have evolved together. At any time the one kind of system is the necessary environment of the other. The necessity is grounded in the evolution that makes these kinds of systems possible. Persons cannot emerge and continue to exist without social systems, nor can social systems without persons.[182]

How, then, are we to understand this jaw droppingly counter-intuitive thesis that humans do not belong to society and that they are incapable of communication insofar as only communications communicate? Elsewhere Hans-Georg Moeller explains this point well:

> The Old European philosophical tradition and Indo-European grammatical habits have contributed to the establishment of the "conventional assumption" that human beings can communicate—but it is an empirical fact that the "essential" elements of what is understood to constitute the human being cannot. Neither brains nor minds can communicate. We cannot say what our brainwaves are "oscillating", and we can't even say what we think. What is said in communication is never equal to what is thought and felt in the mind. It is impossible for me to adequately represent on this page what is going through my mind— intellectually, emotionally, "perceptionally"—while I am

writing this sentence. And the same is true for every sentence I say or write—there is no one-to-one correspondence between communication and mind. I suppose the same is true in regard to your reading of what I write. What you think and feel while reading this sentence will be, in each single case, entirely different from what is communicated in this sentence. Communication systems and mental systems are operationally separate.[183]

Minds are operationally closed with respect to brains. Minds relate to themselves through thought alone, whereas brains relate to one another through electro-chemical reactions alone. Neither of these systems *knows* anything of the other. Likewise, the communications of society are operationally closed with respect to minds such that communications can respond only to communications. In each of these cases we have systems and their environments.

To illustrate Luhmann's thesis, I turn to the simple example of a humble dialogue. For the last few years I have been fortunate to have the friendship of my colleague Carlton Clark, a rhetorician at the institution where I teach. Within a Luhmannian framework, this dialogue is not a communication *between* two systems (Clark *and* myself), but rather *is* a system in its own right. In this respect, Clark and I belong not to the *system* of this dialogue, but to the *environment* of this dialogue. We are outside the system constituted by this dialogue insofar as neither of us have access to the thoughts or neural system of the other. What communicates in this dialogue is thus neither Clark, nor myself, but rather *communications*. Moreover, this dialogue continually makes self-references (references to events that are within the dialogue and communications that have been made in the past of the dialogue) and other-references (references to the environment of the dialogue). In other words, the dialogue is organized around what is internal to the dialogue itself, to the system that has emerged over time, and to what is outside the dialogue or in the environment of the dialogue constituted by the dialogue itself. An event that has taken place at the college, for example, is treated as belonging to the environment of the dialogue, as outside the dialogue, while it can also become a topic within the dialogue that is related to according to the meaning-schema that the dialogue has developed over time. Over the course of this lengthy dialogue, the dialogue as a system has evolved its own distinctions, themes, topics, and ways of handling these themes and topics. Some of these topics and themes include rhetoric, teaching, philosophy, family, college politics, politics, and so on. The distinctions inhabiting the dialogue are the implicit ways in which these themes and topics are handled or the meaning schema that regulate the dialogue. Events in the environment of the dialogue can *perturb* or *irritate* the dialogue, providing stimuli for new communicative events. For example, a new book can be published that becomes a stimulus for the production of new communications within the system. However, the publication of this new book does not enter the dialogue *qua* book, but is integrated into the dialogue according to the distinctions and organization of the dialogue itself. In this respect, the dialogue is an entity itself that constitutes its own elements (the communication events that take place within it) and that is something Clark and I are bound up in without being *parts* or *elements* within the dialogue. Just as Meno is not *himself* an element in Plato's dialogue *Meno*, Clark and Bryant are not elements in this dialogue.

From our discussion of the operational closure of autopoietic objects, we have thus learned four important features of the nature of objects. First and foremost, objects relate only to themselves and never to their environment. Here it is as if the universe were populated by solipsists, Aristotle's First Cause, Unmoved Mover, Leibnizian monads, or, as Harman has put it, vacuums. Second, every substance or system is organized around a distinction between system and environment that the system itself draws. As a consequence, this distinction between substance and environment is self-referential. Third, autopoietic substances, in contrast to allopoietic substances, constitute their own elements or perpetually reproduce themselves through themselves or their own activities. In the case of autopoietic substances, the elements composing the autopoietic substance constitute one another and are constituted by one another. Finally, substances are such that we can have substances nested within substances, while these substances nested within substances nonetheless belong to the *environment* of the substance within which they are nested. This is the case, for example, with societies. Humans are nested within societies but do not belong to the social system but rather the environment of the social system.

In many respects, humans are the matter upon which social systems draw to construct themselves insofar as they constantly perturb social systems, without the humans being the ones doing the constructing. Instead, it is communication that constructs communications. To see this point, think of the way in which our intentions get entangled in communications. We make, for example, a claim that contradicts some claim we made in the past and the subsequent communication that follows points out this contradiction, regulating, as it were, our subsequent communications. We find an analogous case of substances nested within substances with respect to the relationship between cells and the body. Each cell is its own closed autopoietic system, yet the body employs cells in the construction of itself through its own autopoietic processes. Here we encounter, once again, the strange mereology of onticology and object-oriented philosophy where objects can be nested in other objects while nonetheless remaining independent or autonomous of those objects within which they are nested. This mereology destroys organic conceptions of both society and the universe, where all substances are thought of as parts of an organic whole.

One important consequence that follows from the operational closure of substances is that this closure renders unilateral control of one substance by another substance impossible. As Luhmann puts it,

> An important structural consequence that inevitably
> results from the construction of self-referential systems
> deserves particular mention. This is *abandoning the idea of*
> *unilateral control*. There may be hierarchies, asymmetries, or
> differences in influence, but no part of the system can control
> others without itself being subject to control. Under such
> circumstances it is possible [...] that any control must be
> exercised in anticipation of counter-control.[184]

In this context, Luhmann is speaking of subsystems of a system and how they relate to one another. Because each subsystem of a system is itself founded on an operationally closed, self-referential system/environment distinction, one subsystem of the social system cannot control another subsystem of the social system. For example, the political subsystem cannot control the economic subsystem because each subsystem relates to its own environment in its own unique way as a function of its peculiar organization. The economic subsystem of the social system, for example, encounters perturbations from the political subsystem of the social system *in terms of economics*. What holds for subsystems within a larger system holds equally and even more so for relations between different systems or substances. Each substance interacts with other substances in terms of its own peculiar organization. As a consequence, there can be no unilateral transfer of actions from one system to another system, such that the content or nature of the initiating system or substance's action is maintained as identical. As we will see in the next chapter, this requires us to rethink relations of constraint between substances in what Timothy Morton has called "meshes" or networks of substances.

4.2. Interactions Between Objects

If, then, objects or substances are operationally closed, if they only relate to themselves, how do objects interact? While substances are closed to one another, they can nonetheless perturb or irritate one another. And in perturbing or irritating one another, information is produced by the system that is perturbed or irritated. However, here we must proceed with caution, for information is not something that *exists* out there in the environment waiting to be received or detected. Moreover, information is not something that is *exchanged* between systems. Often we think of information as something that is transmitted from a sender to a receiver. The question here becomes that of how it is possible for the receiver to decode the information received as identical to the information transmitted. However, insofar as substances are closed in the sense discussed in the last section, it follows that there can be no question of information as exchange. Rather, information is purely system-specific, exists only within a particular system or substance, and exists only *for* that system or substance. In short, there is no pre-existent information. Instead, information is constructed by systems. As Luhmann remarks, "above all what is usually called 'information' are purely internal achievements. There is no information that moves from without to within a system".[185] Elsewhere, Luhmann remarks that "[i]nformation is an internal change of state, a self-produced aspect of communicative events and not something that exists in the environment of the system".[186] Consequently, information is a transformation of perturbations of an object into information *within* a system.

This point can be illustrated with respect to my relationship with my cats. When my cat rubs against me or jumps on my lap these events constitute perturbations for me. However, as a system I translate these *perturbations* into *information*, registering them as signs of affection. In response, I pet my cat to show my affection. By contrast, my cats might merely be seeking warmth or marking me with their scent so as to establish territory. The point here is that no *identity* of shared *information* need be present for this interaction to take place and maintain itself. My cat and I are perhaps occupied with each other for entirely different reasons, completely unaware that we have different reasons, yet an interaction and communication still takes place.

However, two points must be made here: first, substances are not capable of being perturbed in any old way. My eyes, for example, are not capable of being perturbed by infrared light. Dogs and cats, as I understand it, have a very limited range of color vision. Neutrinos pass straight through most things on the planet Earth. Rocks, as far as I know, are unable to see color at all. Electric eels sense the world through various electric signals, whereas cats very likely have no sense of what it would be like to experience the world in such terms. Consequently, all substances, whether allopoietic or autopoietic, are only selectively open to the world. Second, and in a closely related vein, not all perturbations are transformed into information. In the next section we will see that allopoietic machines and autopoietic machines relate to information events in very different ways. In the case of autopoietic machines, however, it is always possible for perturbations to which a system is open to nonetheless produce no event of information such that the perturbation is coded merely as background noise. As I am writing this, for example, my three-year-old daughter is dancing about the room, yet I scarcely notice her at the moment.

Information is thus not something that exists in the world independent of the systems that "experience" it, but is rather *constituted* by the systems that "experience" it. Nonetheless, this constitution does not issue entirely from the system constituting the information itself. Information is, as it were, a genuine event that befalls a substance or happens to a substance. The perturbations that function as the ground for the production of information can issue from either the environment or transformations in the system itself, but they are always events that must take place for information production to occur. Following Gregory Bateson, Luhmann treats information as a difference that makes a difference.[187] If information is a difference that makes a difference then this is because it selects system-states. As Luhmann writes, "[b]y information we mean an *event that selects system states*. This is possible only for structures that delimit and presort possibilities. Information presupposes structure, yet is not itself a structure, but rather an event that actualizes the use of structures".[188] Information is thus not so much a *property* of substances themselves, but is rather something that occurs within substances. In "Pathologies of Epistemology", Bateson articulates this point nicely. As Bateson writes,

1. The system shall operate with and upon *differences*.

2. The system shall consist of closed loops or networks of pathways along which differences and transforms of differences shall be transmitted (What is transmitted on a neuron is not an impulse, it is news of a difference.)

3. Many events within the system shall be energized by the respondent part rather than by impact from the triggering part.

4. The system shall show self-correctiveness in the direction of runaway. Self- correctiveness implies trial and error. [189]

Elsewhere, Bateson remarks that differences are "brought about by the sort of 'thing' that gets onto the map from the territory".[190] Here we can think of map and territory as system and environment, where the territory is always more complex than the map. Bateson's point seems to be that difference is not an identical unit that is transmitted from one thing to another—for example, from one neuron to another—but rather is a *perturbation* or *irritation* that is then transformed into information by the receiving entity. As such, information is constituted by the systems receiving the differences. Situated within the context of the thing-schema developed in chapter three, information, as that event that selects system states, actualizes virtual potentials belonging to the virtual proper being of an object, which are then deployed to produce local manifestations.

Later Luhmann will remark that "information is nothing more than an event that brings about a connection between differences".[191] Although Luhmann does not develop his thesis in this way, we can characterize the linkage of difference that events of information generate in terms of three dimensions. First, information differentially links an object to *itself* in a relation between the withdrawn virtual proper being of the object and its local manifestations. Here we encounter the process by which local manifestations take place within an object; or rather, the process of self-othering and withdrawal characteristic of every object whether that object be autopoietic or allopoietic. Through the selection of a system state, information affects a self-othering in the object whereby the virtual dimension of the object simultaneously withdraws and a quality is produced. These information events can take place both internally or as a result of external interactions of the object with other objects. Second, events of information link difference to difference through the linkage of perturbations to information. Perturbations are never identical to information precisely because information is object-specific, whereas the same perturbation can affect a variety of different objects while producing very different information for each object perturbed. Finally, third, events of information link difference to difference through a linkage of different withdrawn objects to one another. No object directly encounters another object precisely because all objects are operationally closed. As a consequence, no object is capable of representing another object or of functioning as a pure carrier of the perturbations issued from another object. This is because objects always transform or translate perturbations. Nonetheless, information links the different to the different in a substance-specific manner wherever substances relate to one another.

Because information is not a property of a substance, but rather an event that befalls or happens to a substance and which selects a system state, "[i]nformation [...] always involves some element of surprise".[192] For this reason, information plays a key role in the evolution and development of autopoietic systems, contributing to the formation of new forms of organization within existing autopoietic substances. Insofar as information selects object-states it always carries an element of surprise. As Luhmann puts it,

> a piece of information that is repeated is no longer information. It retains its meaning in repetition but loses its value as information. One reads in the paper that the deutsche mark has risen in value. If one reads this a second time in another paper, this activity no longer has value as information (it no longer changes the state of one's own system), although structurally it presents the same selection. The information is not lost, although it disappears as an event. It has changed the state of the system and has thereby left behind a structural effect; the system then reacts to and with these changed structures.[193]

Here whether or not a bit of information functions as information depends on the preceding object-state of the substance in question. If, after hearing that the value of the dollar has fallen, I shift to another news channel and hear the same thing once again, this bit of information has lost its status as information because it no longer selects a new cognitive state within my mental system. However, if I hear this bit of information a week or month later it can once again become information by virtue of how it contrasts with my preceding mental state. The value of the dollar has fallen *again*. And if this information selects a system state, this might be in the form—were I an investor—of not selling stocks at this particular time by virtue of the fact that I won't get a good return on my sale.

In order for information to take place as an event within a system it is thus necessary for distinctions to be operative within the system. As we will recall from the last section, indication can only occur based on a prior distinction that cleaves a space into a marked and unmarked space the unity of which Spencer-Brown refers to as a "form". Information is a sort of *indication* that an environment "forces", as it were, on a system. For example, when I awoke early this morning I saw that it was raining. Certainly I didn't conjure this weather state into existence through my own whim. However, for this weather state to function as information, there had to be a prior distinction at work in my cognitive system. Perhaps this distinction consists of something like the distinction between precipitation (marked state) and non-precipitation (non-marked state). It will be noted that this distinction doesn't tell me in advance *what* states exist in my environment. It doesn't tell me in advance whether the precipitation will be a torrential downpour, snow, sleet, a drizzle or whether the day is sunny or overcast. Nonetheless, for cognitive and communication substances, it is the distinction that allows for any of these states, and many others besides, to take on significance. Here the environment selects how this distinction will be actualized or filled with content, yet the prior distinction predelineates what environmental states can serve this function *for the system.*

There are a variety of ways in which such events select system-states. Not only do such events actualize the operative distinction in a particular way ("it's a heavy downpour!"), but they also play a role in subsequent operations of the system. For example, upon seeing that it is raining, I now conclude that I don't need to water my garden for the next couple of days, that I need to bring an umbrella if I go out, and that I need to dress in a particular way to keep warm and dry. In short, the information leads to subsequent events within the system.

Here it is important to note that the subsequent events that take place within the system are not of a determinate nature but could unfold in a variety of different ways. This is especially true of systems organized around meaning such as psychic systems and social communications systems. As Luhmann argues,

> the momentary Given that fills experience at any time
> always and irrevocably refers beyond itself to something
> else. Experience experiences itself as variable—and unlike
> transcendental phenomenology we assume organic bases
> for this. It does not find itself closed and self-contained, not
> restricted to itself, but is always referring to something that is
> at that moment not its actual content. This referring-beyond-
> itself, this immanent transcendence of experience, is not a
> matter of choice; rather, it is the condition on the basis of
> which all freedom to choose must first be constituted.[194]

Here, in his discussion of "experience", we encounter Luhmann's basic concept of meaning. Meaning is the *unity* of a difference between actuality and potentiality. Each actualized meaning *simultaneously* refers beyond itself to other meanings that *could have been* actualized. For example, while I conclude that since I am going out I must carry an umbrella, this actualization still refers beyond itself to the possibility of staying in. The phenomenon of meaning is such that while it actualizes a meaning, the negated or excluded alternatives remain, even though under the sign of negation. This is one reason every meaning has an air of contingency about it. Every meaning is haunted by the other potential meanings it has excluded. And this, incidentally, is why ultimate *foundations* are impossible within philosophy. Insofar as meaning is the unity of a difference between actuality and potentiality, every ground that purports to function as the final ground nonetheless refers beyond itself to other excluded potentials that could have functioned as grounds.

This account of meaning provides us with the means of distinguishing between information and meaning. As Luhmann writes,

> Meaning functions as the premise for experience processing in a way that makes possible a choice from among different possible states or contents of consciousness, and in this it does not totally eliminate what has not been chosen, but preserves it in the form of the world and so keeps it accessible. The function of meaning then does not lie in information, i.e., not in the elimination of a system-relative state of uncertainty about the world, and it cannot, therefore, be measured with the techniques of information theory. If it is repeated, a message or piece of news loses its information value, but not its meaning. Meaning is not a selective event, but a selective relationship between system and world.[195]

Information is an event that reduces uncertainty within a system by selecting a state based on a prior distinction ("what will the weather be like today?" "it's raining!"). Meaning, by contrast, maintains the unity of a difference between an actualized given and other potentialities or possibilities.

Because information is premised on a prior distinction that allows events in the environment to take on information value, it follows that systems, in their relation to other objects, always contain *blind spots*. What we get here is a sort of object-specific transcendental illusion produced as a result of its closure. As Luhmann remarks in *Ecological Communication*, "one could say that a system can see only what it can see. It cannot see what it cannot. Moreover, it cannot see that it cannot see this. For the system this is something concealed 'behind' the horizon that, for it, has no 'behind'".[196] If systems can only see what they can see, cannot see what they cannot see, and cannot see that they cannot see this, then this is because any relation to the world is premised on system-specific distinctions that arise from the system itself. As a consequence of this, Luhmann elsewhere remarks that, "[t]he conclusion to be drawn from this is that the connection with the reality of the external world is established by the blind spot of the cognitive operation. Reality is what one does not perceive when one perceives it".[197]

If reality is what one does not perceive when one perceives it, then this is because (1) objects do not relate directly to other objects, but rather relate to other objects only through their own distinctions, and (2) because objects do not themselves register the distinctions that allow them to relate to other objects in this way. Objects are thus withdrawn in a dual sense. On the one hand, objects are withdrawn from other objects in that they never directly encounter these other objects, but rather transform these perturbations into information according to their own organization. On the other hand, objects are withdrawn even from themselves as the distinction through which operations are possible, the endo-structure of objects, withdraw into the background, as it were, in the course of operations. When I note that it is raining, the distinction between precipitation and non-precipitation is not there before me for my cognitive system, but is rather *used* or employed by my cognitive system.

The transcendental illusion thus generated by the manner in which objects relate to one another is one in which the states "experienced" by a system are treated as other objects *themselves*, rather than system-specific entities generated by the organization of the object itself. In other words, the object treats the world it "experiences" as reality *simpliciter*, rather than as system-states produced by its own organization. Here it is important to note that the foregoing analysis does not require us to follow Luhmann or Spencer-Brown in the thesis that such system-states are produced by *binary distinctions*. All that is required is that these states be produced as a consequence of an object's endo-structure or virtual proper being. It could be that binary distinctions are only operative in "more advanced" objects such as cognitive systems and communication systems, with other systems simply having an endo-structure composed of networks of relations defining a particular organization that can only be perturbed in various ways along the lines described by Bateson in terms of a transmission (or better yet, production) of differences. It could be that "more advanced" systems are non-linear networks of this sort as well. What is important is not whether or not information is produced through binary distinctions, but rather that information is a product of the organization of the system in question, not a transfer of information as self-identical from one object to another.

Between Luhmann's account of how systems relate to the world and Graham Harman's object-oriented ontology, we find remarkable points of overlap. Like Harman's objects, Luhmann's systems are autonomous individuals that are closed and independent of other systems. In his most recent work, Harman has argued that all objects are quadruple in their structure.[198] Without going into all the details of his account of objects, Harman distinguishes between real objects and real qualities, and sensuous objects and sensuous qualities. Here we must proceed with caution, for Harman's sensuous objects 1) do not refer solely to objects that are merely fictional, and 2) are not restricted to humans and animals alone. Rather, *all* objects, whether animate or inanimate, relate to other objects not as *real* objects, but as sensuous objects. Evoking a sort of quasi-Lacanianism, we can say that "a sensuous object is an object for another object". Sensuous objects are not the real object itself, but are, rather, what objects are for other objects. In this respect, sensuous objects are very similar to Luhmann's information events and system-states.

Unlike real objects, Harman's sensuous objects exist only on the *interior* of a real object. These sensuous objects can arise both from the interior of the real object that encounters them or from other real objects. In *Prince of Networks*, Harman gives the examples of "Monster X" and a friend's cat that he is taking care of.[199] Monster X is a monster that Harman generates through his imagination and whose qualities he refuses to share with us (he assures us that this is the most fearsome and frightening monster ever imagined). Now, unlike a real object, Monster X only exists in the interior of Harman's imagination, is not withdrawn, and ceases to exist when he falls asleep at night or ceases thinking about it. Monster X is capable of acting on Harman through a sort of auto-affection of Harman by Harman, but it is not an object out there in the world that is capable of being perturbed by other objects. The case is similar with the cat Harman was taking care of when writing about Monster X. The cat is, of course, a real entity out there in the world that is an "autonomous force unleashed in Harman's apartment" regardless of whether he is aware of its activities. However, *for* Harman, the cat is *also* a sensuous object that exists on the interior of Harman. Like Monster X, the cat *qua sensuous* object ceases to exist when Harman ceases to think about it or when he goes to sleep. However, unlike Monster X, the cat *qua* real object continues to be an autonomous force unleashed in the world even when he ceases to think about it.

In this context, the important point to take away from Harman's quadruple objects is that objects only ever relate to other objects through *sensuous* objects. No object ever encounters another object as a real object. If we translate Harman's thesis into Luhmannian terms, we can say that systems or real objects only ever encounter other objects as information and system-states. Harman's fearsome Monster X would be an example of a system-state. Monster X is not an event produced within a system as a consequence of a perturbation from the environment, but rather is a meaning-event that Harman produced on his own. By contrast, Harman's friend's cat is a combination of information and meanings. When the cat perturbs him in a particular way, the cat functions as information, selecting a particular system-state within Harman. Various thoughts Harman might have about the cat would be meaning-events produced by Harman. Yet in both cases, what we have are purely internal system states that differ from whatever other objects might happen to be in the environment. As a consequence, we only ever encounter other objects as sensuous objects rather than real objects, such that we are both withdrawn from these real objects and they are withdrawn from us.

4.3. Autopoietic and Allopoietic Objects

Returning to the themes of the last chapter, we can now situate the
functioning of systems with respect to how they produce and respond to
information in terms of virtual proper being and local manifestation. As I
observed in 4.1, Maturana and Varela distinguish between autopoietic and
allopoietic machines. Autopoietic machines are machines or objects that
produce their own elements and "strive" to maintain their organization
across time. Our bodies, for example, heal when they are cut. The key
feature of autopoietic machines is that they produce *themselves*. Not only do
autopoietic machines constitute their own elements, but they paradoxically
constitute their own elements through interactions among their elements.
By contrast, allopoietic machines are machines produced by something else.
Generally the domain of allopoietic machines refers to inanimate objects.
Here it's worth noting that the distinction between autopoietic objects
and allopoietic objects is not a hard and fast or absolute distinction, but is
probably a distinction that involves a variety of gradations or intermediaries.

Despite the differences between allopoietic machines and autopoietic
machines, I want to argue that both undergo actualizations through
information and both involve system/environment distinctions that
constitute their relations to other objects. Here a major difference between
autopoietic machines and allopoietic machines would be that allopoietic
machines can *only* undergo actualization through information, whereas
autopoietic machines can both be actualized in a particular way through
information *and* can actualize themselves in particular ways through
ongoing operations internal to their being. Here it might appear strange
to speak of information in relation to allopoietic or inanimate objects.
However, we must recall that information is neither *meaning*, nor is
information a *message* exchanged *between* objects. Rather, as we have seen,
information is a difference that makes the difference or an event that selects
a system state. In this regard, there is no reason to restrict information
to autopoietic objects, for such events take place within allopoietic
objects as well.

Before proceeding to discuss the differences between how these
two types of objects relate to information, it is important to make some

points regarding the system/environment distinction as it is deployed in autopoietic theory. Maturana, Varela, and Luhmann tend to speak of the distinction between system and environment as a distinction that systems *draw* such that this distinction allows systems to *observe* their environment. In my view, these are conventions that should be abandoned, or rather, that should be evoked in highly system-specific contexts. Rather than claiming that systems *draw* distinctions between themselves and their environment— implying that there's a homunculus that does the drawing—we should instead say that systems *are* their distinction or form. Here it will be recalled that "form", as Spencer-Brown understands it, is the *unity* of the marked and unmarked space produced by a distinction. The distinction that generates the marked and unmarked space is, of course, self-referential in the sense that it belongs to one side of the distinction: the system. Insofar as objects are autonomous and independent, they are necessarily self-referential in that their separation from the environment is produced by the object itself. It is the distinction between system and environment that both constitutes the closure of objects and their particular form of openness to other objects. In the case of more "advanced" systems like cognitive systems, social systems, and perhaps some computers, we get the ability to actively draw distinctions and follow through their consequences or what subsequent operations they generate, but in many other instances it's unlikely that systems have any real freedom in how the distinction between system and environment is constituted.

Likewise, rather than claiming that systems *observe* their environment through their distinctions, we should instead claim that objects *interact* with other systems through their distinctions. The emphasis on observation, in my view, is one of the greatest drawbacks of various strains of autopoietic theory. Observation implies a distinction between self-reference or reference to internal states of the system and other-reference or references to the environment. The distinction between self-reference and other-reference, in its turn, requires a *doubling* of the distinction between system and environment *within* the system itself. That is, systems that distinguish between self-reference and other-reference are systems where the distinction between system and environment re-enters the system that draws this distinction so that the distinction between system and environment can itself be observed. In other words, self-reference and other-reference requires a self-referential operation whereby the system observes how it observes and thereby distinguishes between what arises from within the system itself and what comes from without. Rather than simply undergoing a perturbation, I now treat this perturbation as something that issues from the environment *and* register that this perturbation comes from the environment. This doubling of the system/environment distinction is a necessary condition for observation.

In their discussions of autopoietic theory, Maturana and Varela often evoke cells as a prime example of autopoietic systems. However, this example, above all, indicates just why we should not talk about the self-referential distinction upon which any system or object is founded in terms of *observation*. Although cells cannot exist without a boundary between system and environment that is constituted self-referentially by the cell itself, it is misleading to suggest that there's any meaningful sense in which cells observe their environment or make other-references to the world independent of them. To be sure, cells interact with their environment and are, like any other system, perturbed by their environment, but there's no meaningful sense in which they refer to their environment. To suggest otherwise is to imply that entities like cells operate according to *meaning*. Rather than speaking in terms of observation and other-reference, both of which are far too epistemological and cognitive in their connotations, we should instead speak in terms of how systems are selectively open to their environment and how they interact with their environment. Other-reference and observation, rather, seems to be something that only emerges with more complicated systems such as tardigrades, frogs, and perhaps certain computer systems.

The term "information" is fortunate in that it contains within itself a certain productive polysemy that allows it to resonate in a variety of ways. In addition to treating information as an event that selects system states, we can also read the term "information" *avant la lettre* to play on the more literal connotations of the term. When we break information into its units, we can say that information refers to what is *in formation*. Here information refers to the genesis of local manifestations as ongoing processes rather than as fixed identities. The identity of objects is not fixed, but is rather a dynamic and ongoing identity that is in formation. While there is indeed an identity to the object, in the sense that it has a virtual endo-structure that persists across time, this identity is always manifesting itself in a variety of ways. Similarly, we can also read information as "in-form-ation". Here information does not refer to the ongoing genesis and openness of objects—that which is "in formation"—but rather refers to the manner in which objects take on new form or come to embody new form with their actualizations in local manifestations. Returning to the distinction I drew between the topology of objects and the geometry of objects in the last chapter, information as in-form-ation here refers to the transition that takes place within an object from the domain of virtual proper being and the potentialities populating virtual proper being to the geometric actualization of a form or quality in an object. In other words, in-form-ation refers to the local manifestation of an object embodied in a specific quality.

In both allopoietic and autopoitic systems, information is an event that makes a difference by selecting a system-state. However, information functions in very different, yet related, ways in the case of allopoietic and autopoietic systems. In both cases, information is non-linear and system-specific, existing only for the system in question and as a function of the organization or endo-structure of the object. In saying that information is non-linear, my point is that it is an effect of the *endo-structure* of the *object* as it relates to its environment and how this endo-structure resonates within the field of differential relations that define that structure. Information is not *in* the environment, but is a product of the system perturbed by its environment. In the case of allopoietic systems, information functions to actualize a degree in the phase-space of the virtual proper being of the substance, leading to the actualization of a particular quality in a local manifestation.

Here the point I wish to make is so basic as to appear trivial. However, this point has important consequences for how we analyze allopoietic objects in the world. When an allopoietic object is perturbed in a particular way, it produces an actuality proper to the endo-structure of its being. One and the same perturbation can produce very different local manifestations in different allopoietic objects. Thus, for example, water behaves differently than rocks when hit by another object or heated up. When water is heated up, it locally manifests itself in the quality of boiling. When a rock is heated up, heat is distributed throughout the rock. When water is hit by another object, it produces waves. When a rock is hit by another object, it begins to roll and perhaps vibrates.

These are obvious and familiar points about the objects that populate our world. We all recognize, even if only implicitly, that different objects or different types of substances respond differently to *one and the same* perturbation. However, while this is an obvious point, it is nonetheless a point that needs to be accounted for. It is precisely this which the concepts of virtual proper being, local manifestation, and information attempt to account for. When an allopoietic object is perturbed in a particular way, information is produced as a consequence of how the object in question is organized. This information, in turn, selects a system-state which actualizes a potentiality in the virtual proper being of the object in the form of a particular quality or local manifestation.

Now, there are two important points worth making here. First, as in the case of autopoietic objects, allopoietic objects are only *selectively* open to their environments. Many events can occur in the environment of an object without all of these events being capable of perturbing the object and thereby being transformed into information. While rocks, for example, are certainly open to sound waves, they are not, as far as I know, open to *signifiers*. Uluru or Ayers Rock, for example, is in-different to its *title* as Uluru or any special legal status it is given. It does not get offended when a stranger that has never heard of it fails to refer to it by its proper name, it doesn't answer to its proper name, nor does it likely worry itself over any sacred or legal preferences it might gain through being Uluru. Here reference to Uluru's in-difference to its name should be taken quite literally as signifying that Uluru's name cannot select system-states *within Uluru*. Uluru is entirely closed with respect to its name.

Lest one conclude that this sort of closure to its name is merely a feature of the difference between culture and nature, I offer an example of (non)relations between completely natural beings as well. Neutrinos are extremely small elementary particles that travel close to the speed of light. Because neutrinos are electrically neutral, they pass through most matter completely undisturbed and without disturbing that matter. This causes, of course, massive problems in the detection of neutrinos as most detection devices we might use to detect them cannot be perturbed by them due to the electric neutrality of the neutrino. Here the neutrino is a perfect example of a strongly closed entity that cannot be perturbed by other entities and that cannot perturb many other entities. Between the indifference of Urulu to its proper name and the indifference of neutrinos to most other entities, there's a difference in *degree* rather than *kind*. While it is important to recognize that most inanimate objects cannot answer to their name (computers are quickly calling this generalization into question), there is no reason to treat culture as a special domain or distinct realm unlike material interactions. In both cases, the issue is one of how entities are selectively open to their environment.

The second consequence that follows from treating allopoietic objects in terms of self-referential system/environment distinctions that are only selectively open to their environment is that allopoietic objects cannot be treated as bundles of qualities. Qualities are *results* of how allopoietic objects are actualized by their perturbations. They are things that objects *can* do, but they do not define the proper being of objects which consists of powers. As I tried to show in my discussion of Bhaskar in the first chapter, objects can be "out of phase" with the events they're capable of producing. When situated in terms of qualities, this means that objects can exist, they can be there in the world, either in a dormant state where they produce no qualities of a particular sort, or in a state where, due to the intervention of other generative mechanisms or objects they produce exo-qualities that inhibit the production of particular qualities of which the object is capable.

The key point not to be missed is that the qualities of an object are *variable*. Every object, allopoietic or autopoietic, is capable of a variety of *different* local manifestations. And we can say that perhaps every object is capable of producing an infinite number of different properties. This is among the reasons that we cannot treat objects as bundles of qualities. Qualities are products of how allopoietic objects are perturbed, how those perturbations are transformed into information, and how that information selects system-states producing local manifestations.

The question that emerges here is that of why, if objects cannot be equated with their qualities, we have such a persistent tendency to reduce objects to their qualities. I think there are two basic reasons for this. The first has to do with the type of objects we are. Like all objects, we are operationally closed and relate to the world only through the distinctions that regulate our openness to the world. These distinctions, like all distinctions, have a marked and an unmarked space, such that the unmarked space becomes invisible or disappears. In the case of our perceptual world, one operative distinction seems to be the distinction between identity and change. Here identity functions as the marked state, while change functions as the unmarked state. If this schema plays such an important role in our experience of the world, then this is because, as Bergson observed long ago, our perception is geared towards *action* and our ability to act on other objects. Since action requires a more or less stable platform to take place, change and difference is thrown over into the unmarked side of the distinction governing our perception and cognition. When I go to grab my beloved coffee mug, I register it not as a series of variations or different local manifestations, but *as a blue coffee mug.* I register my mug in this way even when the lights are out and the mug is no longer blue. Here the blueness of the mug functions as a marker for *returning* to the mug. "Oh, there's my mug!"

However, while the manner in which we translate objects plays a role in our tendency to treat objects as bundles of qualities, there are object-centered reasons for this tendency as well. While objects are, in principle, independent of their relations, objects are only ever encountered in and among relations to other objects. Terrestrial existence is such that these relations are more or less stable and enduring. The consequence of this is that allopoietic objects tend to be perturbed by other objects in their environment in more or less constant ways. Insofar as objects are perturbed in more or less constant ways by other objects in their environment, they tend to have fairly stable and ongoing local manifestations. As a consequence, the volcanic powers objects have folded within them remain largely hidden from view.

I refer to networks of exo-relations like this as "regimes of attraction". Regimes of attraction are networks of fairly stable exo-relations among objects that tend to produce stable and repetitive local manifestations among the objects within the regime of attraction. Within a regime of attraction, causal relations can be bi-directional or symmetrical or uni-directional or asymmetrical. Bi-directional causation is a circular relation in which two or more entities reciprocally perturb one another in response to each other. Like fireflies signaling to one another, one lightning bug lights up and another lights up in response, leading the first to light up again. Similarly, one object perturbs another, producing an act in the second object that in turn perturbs the first object that started the sequence. As a consequence of these sorts of relations, we get constant local manifestations. The moon's gravity affects the earth and the earth's gravity affects the moon. Likewise, we can have uni-lateral or asymmetrical relations of perturbation that bring about a largely constant state in an object.

Fire is a particularly good example for illustrating the idea of regimes of attraction. In its terrestrial manifestation, fire behaves in relatively predictable ways. It leaps up towards the sky and is characterized by pointed tongues of flame that dance and oscillate. As a consequence, we are led to think of this sort of behavior (these qualities) as constituting the essence of fire. However, in outer space, fire behaves more like water, rolling over things in waves, expanding everywhere like liquid on the surface of a table. In its terrestrial manifestation, fire behaves this way because of the gravity of the earth. Here fire exists within a particular regime of attraction that leads to very specific local manifestations. When situated in different regimes of attraction, fire behaves in a very different way.

The concept of regimes of attraction is of central importance to onticology and has profound implications for how we think about epistemology or inquiry. The concept of regimes of attraction entails that it is not enough for inquiry to merely gaze at objects to "know" them, but rather that we must vary the environments of objects or their exo-relations to discover the powers hidden within objects. Knowledge of an object does not reside in a list of qualities possessed by objects, but rather in a diagram of the powers hidden within objects. However, in order to form a diagram of an object we have to vary the exo-relations of an object to determine that of which it is capable. And here, of course, the point is that knowledge is gained not by *representing*, but, as Aristotle suggested in a different context in the *Nicomachean Ethics*, by *doing*. In the case of Aristotle, this doing consists of repeated actions so as to produce habits or dispositions of action. In the case of other forms of knowledge, by contrast, this doing consists in *acting upon* objects to see what they do under these conditions.

As should be obvious, the concept of regimes of attraction is crucial to our understanding of both allopoietic and autopoietic objects. In "A Developmental Psychobiological Systems View", biologist Gilbert Gottlieb recounts his early doctoral research on the sensitive period for imprinting in ducklings.[200] Imprinting refers to any time-sensitive phase of learning that occurs very quickly and appears to be independent of behavior. As one might suspect, lurking in the background here is the issue of innateness or whether certain phases of imprinting are innate or learned. While Gottlieb did indeed discover a critical period of imprinting before and after which imprinting could not occur, he *also* discovered that the developmental age for imprinting could be moved around through a manipulation of the duckling's early *environment*. As Gottlieb puts it, "[t]he sensitive period for imprinting was not exclusively a function of maturation but depended also on the nature and extent of the bird's prenatal and postnatal experiences prior to entering into the imprinting situation".[201] Here maturation, of course, refers to factors of innateness. The crucial experiences that played a role in the timing of the onset of imprinting (or, presumably, lack thereof) had to do with whether or not the duckling was reared with visual and social experiences with other ducklings, or whether it was raised in complete darkness and in complete social isolation.

What we encounter here is the importance of regimes of attraction as they function in the development of allopoietic objects. The point here is that, if we don't attend to the regime of attraction in which the autopoietic system develops, we fall prey to a tendency to treat local manifestations as strictly resulting from innate factors in the system, rather than seeing them as results of an interaction between both system-specific properties of the system and perturbations from the environment that are translated into information which then selects system-states. Here the conclusion seems to be that development does not have any one particular attractor in the teleological sense. Rather, through entering into different exo-relations with other objects in the world, an allopoietic object can develop in a variety of different ways. This entails that a key component of inquiry consists in 1) mapping the exo-relations in which particular local manifestations take place, and 2) varying the exo-relations into which an object enters to determine the variations of which it is capable.

Nonetheless, there are significant differences between how autopoietic and allopoietic systems respond to information events. With allopoietic systems, the selection of a system-state is a *terminal* process. When the water is frozen in response to a change in temperature, it is frozen. There are no additional operations that take place within the system until it is once again perturbed in a new way. By contrast, in autopoietic systems, there are continuous operations that take place within the object even after the selection of a system-state through information. Taking an example from a social system, a news report that the value of the dollar has risen selects a system-state within the economic system. This information event, in its turn, kicks off a variety of subsequent operations within the social system. For example, people begin selling their stocks to maximize their profit. The point here is that, even in the absence of *new* information events, these subsequent operations continue apace. These system-states and operations are, of course, local manifestations of the autopoietic system in question.

Another, perhaps counter-intuitive, difference between autopoietic systems and allopoietic systems is that there's a way in which the local manifestations of allopoietic systems are more *elastic* than the local manifestations of autopoietic systems. As I noted in a previous chapter, it is necessary to distinguish between symmetrical and asymmetrical qualities. In the current context, the important nuance of this distinction is that symmetrical qualities are *reversible* qualities, while asymmetrical qualities are *irreversible* qualities. While there are certainly asymmetrical qualities that characterize a number of local manifestations for allopoietic objects (paper yellowed with age comes to mind), many qualities of allopoietic objects are symmetrical in character. I turn out the lights and my beloved coffee mug becomes black. I turn the lights on and the mug becomes a shade of blue once again.

In the case of autopoietic objects, by contrast, asymmetrical qualities seem to be the rule rather than the exception. Developmental processes, for example, appear to be largely irreversible, changing the structure of an autopoietic object's local manifestation irrevocably. In communication systems, a statement that is repeated is no longer the *same* statement, but has now taken on ever so slight new resonances. In the structural coupling of psychic systems and communications systems, I cannot read the same book twice because the very act of having read the book through once to the end already changes how the beginning of the book reads the second time when I begin it anew. As Bergson recognized at the beginning of the last century, the presence of memory as a dimension of all living, psychic, and social experience transforms each event, no matter how apparently repetitious in the brute sense, into a novelty.

However, where allopoietic systems often appear to have a greater degree of elasticity with respect to qualities, autopoietic systems seem to have a greater degree of elasticity with respect to distinctions or what we might refer to as "channels". It will be recalled that distinctions play a key role in how closed systems are open to their environment or other objects in their environment. One of the crucial features of autopoietic systems is that they have the ability to develop new distinctions, thereby enhancing their capacity to be irritated or perturbed by other objects. This occurs in a variety of ways that are subject to very different degrees of freedom. Thus, for example, it is likely that many plants can only transform the distinctions through which it is possible for them to be irritated by their environment through evolutionary processes of random variation and natural selection. Throughout the animal world, we seem to get increasing degrees of freedom in forming new distinctions through developmental processes that take place through learning rather than innate structure. The same holds true of social systems. And finally, it appears that computers are slowly developing the ability to revise their own distinctions, broadening their ability to be irritated by their environment.

What is important here in these reflections on the difference between autopoietic and allopoietic objects is that both types of objects are organized around a system/environment distinction, both objects are operationally closed, both types of objects are only selectively related to their environment, and both objects transform perturbations into information that selects system-states presiding over local manifestations. In the case of both allopoietic and autopoietic systems, local manifestations are a product of actualizations of virtual proper being rather than fixed properties in substances.

4.4. Translation

In light of the foregoing, we can now make sense of Latour's thesis, cited in the epigraph to this chapter, that objects "interpret" one another. Insofar as all objects are operationally closed, no object can transfer a force to another object without that force being transformed in some way or another. This generates a specific set of questions when analyzing relations among entities in the world. On the one hand, in any discussion of relations among entities, we must first determine whether the receiving entity even has channels capable of receiving perturbations from the acting entity. Because substances only maintain selective relations to their environment, they are not open to all perturbations that exist in their environment. As we saw in the last section, for example, rocks, as far as we know, are indifferent to our speech. This sort of selectivity is true not only of relations of objects between different sorts, but also of relations between objects of the same sort. Many, I'm sure, have experienced and been baffled by conversations with others from very different theoretical backgrounds and orientations. In such discussions, points and claims you take for granted as obvious seem not even to be registered or noticed by the interlocutor when made. Here we have different forms of selective openness among humans in discourse.

On the other hand, in those cases where an entity is open to perturbations of a particular sort, we must nonetheless be attentive to the manner in which the entity that receives that perturbation *transforms* it according to its own organization. In other words, we cannot begin with the premise that the effect is already contained in the cause, but must instead be attentive to how the cause is transformed into something new and unexpected. In *The Four Fundamental Concepts of Psychoanalysis,* Lacan contrasts laws and causality in a way that resonates nicely with this point.[202] As Lacan remarks,

> Cause is to be distinguished from that which is determinate
> in a chain, in other words the *law*. By way of example, think
> of what is pictured in the law of action and reaction. There

is here, one might say, a single principle. One does not go without the other.[203]

Lacan goes on to remark that,

> Whenever we speak of cause, on the other hand, there is always something anti- conceptual, something indefinite. The phases of the moon are the cause of the tides—we know this from experience, we know that the word cause is correctly used here. Or again, miasmas are the cause of fever—that doesn't mean anything either, there is a hole, and something that oscillates in the interval. In short, there is cause only in something that doesn't work.[204]

Lacan concludes "there remains essentially in the function of the cause a certain *gap*".[205] In characterizing causality in terms of a gap and something that "doesn't work", Lacan emphasizes the manner in which the effect of a cause always contains an element of surprise or something that can't simply be deduced from the cause. Here there's a way in which the effect is always in excess of the cause. And the claim that the effect contains something in excess of the cause is the claim that the entity being affected *translates* the cause producing something *new*.

Lacan's concept of causality is deeply related to his understanding of *objet a*, the object-cause of desire, and the unconscious. Without going into all the details of Lacan's understanding of the unconscious, *objet a*, and desire, we can here make a few brief remarks as to how this is to be understood. The first point to note is that *objet a* is not the object *desired*, but the object that *causes* desire. In other words, the object desired can be quite different from the object-cause of desire or the *objet a*. The *objet a* is rather that *gap* that generates desire. Desire is the *effect* of *objet a*, and *objet a* is the cause of desire. Put otherwise, we can say that it is that point where the symbolic *fails* and that it is the explanation of the effects of this failure. To illustrate this point, take the example of someone who desires an expensive luxury car. The car is the object of desire, but not the *object-cause* of desire. Rather, the object-cause of the desire for the car is perhaps the gaze of others who will envy the car or attribute status to the owner of the car.

This relation can be illustrated in terms of Lacan's discourse of the master, first introduced in Seminar XVII:

$$\uparrow \frac{S_1 \rightarrow S_2}{\text{\$} \;//\; a} \downarrow$$

Each of Lacan's four discourses has four positions and defines a structure.[206] In the upper left position we have an agent, addressing an other in the upper right position, producing a product in the lower right position, with an unconscious truth in the lower left position.

One way of reading Lacan's discourse of the master is in terms of how signifiers relate to one another. We have a master-signifier, S_1, relating to another signifier, S_2, producing a *remainder*, *a*. The point is that in all speech or utterances something *escapes*. When we utter something, we feel as if we never quite articulate what we wish to say. Indeed, we aren't even entirely sure what we wish to say in our own speech. On the other hand, when we hear another person's utterances, we're never quite sure *why* they say what they say. This is the gap that lies at the heart of all discourse. One way of thinking about Lacan's discourses is as diagrams of little machines in interpersonal relations. In the diagram above, it is paradoxically the *product*, the *failure*, *objet a*, that keeps the discourse going. Because I never quite feel that I've articulated what I wish to say and because I'm never quite sure if I've understood what the other has said, new utterances are produced that strive to capture this allusive remainder that perpetually recedes in the discourse.

Within a psychoanalytic context, the gap by which *objet a* functions as the object-cause of desire can be fruitfully thought in terms of the role played by the unmarked side of a distinction as it functions in psychic systems. Put a bit differently, while the unmarked side of a distinction is not indicated by a system employing a particular distinction, this unmarked side nonetheless has effects on how the psychic system functions. In his discussion of the cause, Lacan remarks that "what the unconscious does is show us the gap through which neurosis recreates a harmony with a real".[207] Here the unconscious is the network of unconscious signifiers, while the gap is the real. The psychoanalytic formation (the symptom) is the harmony recreated with the real.

To illustrate this point, I refer to an example from early in my own analysis years ago. During this time, I was just beginning to teach. This was back in the days when chalk was still used. Much to my dismay, I found that I was breaking multiple pieces of chalk during every class session. Indeed, this symptom was so pronounced and noticeable, that it became a running joke with my students. They even got together and left a chalk guard in my mailbox with a petition written in calligraphy imploring me to stop killing the citizens of "Chalkville" and a picture of a piece of chalk dressed in armor. Now, I found all of this quite upsetting as I felt it was undermining my authority in the classroom and revealing my incompetence. One day, in a session, I was rambling on about this little symptom. "I don't know what my problem is. I can't seem to modulate my pressure on the chalk. I try not to, but I always end up pressing too hard. Why can't I use less pressure?" And so on. As my ramble went on, my analyst, in a flat voice, intoned in a statement that was ambiguous as to whether it was a question or a statement, "pressure at the board?" "Yes", I responded, completely missing the polysemy of his remark, "pressure at the board! I just can't keep myself from using too much pressure!" After this session, I didn't think about the discussion of the chalk at all. Two weeks later, however, I noticed that I hadn't broken any chalk for two weeks. Somehow the desire embodied in my symptom had been articulated and therefore, from the standpoint of my unconscious, I no longer had to break chalk to articulate that desire.

Now where is the *objet a*, desire, and the unconscious in this example? Where is the gap through which the unconscious recreates a harmony with the real? Here the *objet a* is very likely the *gaze* of my students. That gaze poses a question: what am I for them? This gaze, however, was not the *object* of my desire, but the *cause* of my desire. It was that which set the desire in motion. In his various glosses on desire, Lacan said that "desire is the desire of the Other". This is a polysemous aphorism that has a number of different connotations. It can mean that desire desires the Other. Likewise, it can mean that our desire is not, as it were, truly our own, but rather is the Other's desire. That is, it can mean that we desire as the Other desires, as in the case of an adult who lives her life pursuing the career her parents wanted. Finally, it can mean that we desire to be desired by the Other. In this instance, my chalk breaking symptom did not seem to desire the Other (my student's here standing in the place of the Other), but rather seemed to be an articulation of *their* desire (or, rather, my *fantasy* of what they desired). Faced with the opacity or enigma of my students' desire, my unconscious sought to transform this traumatic and enigmatic desire into a specific *demand* or *judgment*: "You are not competent, you do not belong here!" In other words, through the breaking of the chalk I was perhaps unconsciously trying to satisfy my fantasy of what I took to be *their* demand. The breaking of the chalk at the board was both an articulation of how I was feeling ("pressured at the board") *and* a potential *solution* to the pressure I was experiencing: "if I'm incompetent then I won't have to teach!" The unconscious recreated a harmony with the real by giving content to the enigmatic gaze of my students through the symptom of breaking the chalk.

The gap functions in a very specific way in Lacan's conception of the mechanisms of the unconscious, but we can say that Lacan also makes a broader and more profound point about the gap and the relationship between cause and effect that holds for all inter-object relations. Here we can coin the aphorism, "there is no transportation without translation", or, alternatively, "there is no transportation without transformation". Here we must take care not to take Lacan's notion of the gaze too literally, but the point in this connection would be that the effects of the gaze as a perturbation cannot be anticipated in advance. Rather the effect that the gaze produces is an aleatory product of the organization or virtual proper being of the system that is perturbed by the gaze. Each substance *translates* perturbations in its own particular way.

Here, then, we can make sense of what Latour means when he claims that objects *interpret* one another. To interpret is to *translate*, and to translate is to produce something new. As Latour remarks, "[t]o interpret something is to say it in other words. In other words, it is to translate".[208] The translated is never identical to the original, but rather produces something different from the original. For example, if this book is some day translated into, say, German, it will very likely take on resonances that it doesn't have in English. My discussions of "existence" might be translated into *Dasein*. Yet the German term *Dasein* has connotations that English doesn't have, such as "there-being" or "here-being". In being translated into another language a text becomes something different. Likewise, when a perturbation is received by another entity, it becomes something different. As Latour says earlier in *Irreductions*, "[n]othing is, by itself, the same as or different from anything else. That is, there are no equivalents, only translations".[209] The point here is that no perturbation ever retains its identity or self-sameness when transported from one entity to another, but rather becomes something different as a consequence of being translated into information and then producing a particular local manifestation in the receiving object.

Along these lines, Latour elsewhere draws a distinction between mediators and intermediaries in *Reassembling the Social*. As Latour articulates this distinction,

> An *intermediary* [...] is what transports meaning or force without transformation: defining its inputs is enough to define its outputs [...]. *Mediators*, on the other hand, cannot be counted as just one; they might count for one, for nothing, for several, or for infinity. Their input is never a good predictor of their output; their specificity has to be taken into account every time. Mediators transform, translate, distort, and modify the meaning or the elements they are supposed to carry.[210]

All objects are mediators with respect to one another, transforming or translating what they receive and thereby producing something new as a result. By contrast, intermediaries merely carry a force or meaning without transforming it in any way. In this connection, we can say that the concept of intermediaries treats objects as mere vehicles of the differences contributed by another entity. In one of his most recent works, Latour drives this point home, remarking that,

> what should appear extraordinarily bizarre is [...] the invention of *inanimate* entities which should do nothing more than carry *one step further* the cause that makes them

act to generate the n+1 consequence which in turn are
nothing but the causes of the n+2 consequences. This conceit
has the strange result of composing the world with long
concatenations of causes and effects where (this is what is
so odd) *nothing is supposed to happen*, except probably at the
beginning—but since there is no God in those staunchly
secular versions there is not even a beginning [...]. The
disappearance of agency in the so called "materialist world
view" is a stunning invention especially since it is contradicted
every step of the way by the odd resistance of reality: every
consequence adds slightly to the cause. Thus, it has to
have some sort of agency. There is a supplement. A gap
between the two.[211]

Our treatment of objects in terms of autopoietic and allopoietic
machines has explained just why this is the case. Insofar as all entities
draw a system/environment distinction and transform perturbations into
information as a function of their own internal organization, they always
contribute something new to the perturbations they receive.

The concept of translation, coupled with the distinction between
mediators and intermediaries has profound implications for both theory
and practice. In the docile bodies chapter of *Discipline and Punish*, we
encounter a prime example of theories and practices organized around the
conceptualization of substances in terms of mere intermediaries.[212] There
Foucault analyzes a disciplinary structure of power that aims to form the
soldier down to the tiniest detail.

By the late eighteenth century, the soldier has become
something that can be made; out of a formless clay, an inapt
body, the machine required can be constructed; a posture
is gradually corrected; a calculated constraint runs slowly
through each part of the body, mastering it, making it pliable,
ready at all times, turning silently into the automatism of
habit; in short, one has 'got rid of the peasant' and given him
'the air of a soldier'.[213]

This conception of the formation of the soldier is premised on an implausible idea of causation where causes are transported from one object to another without remainder. Here the soldier is a pliable clay that can be formed however we like. Here information is conceived as something that is transported as self-identical, producing a univocal effect in the body of the soldier-to-be. What is entirely missed in such a model is the manner in which the entity receiving the perturbation transforms it according to its own organization.

In a very different context, biologist Richard Lewontin contrasts the difference between how applied biologists approach research into plants and animals and how developmental biologists in the laboratory approach plants and animals.[214] For the developmental biologist in the laboratory, a lot of research revolves around the manipulation of genes to see how they affect the phenotype. This encourages a conception of organisms in which genes are thought of as *already containing* the information whereby the phenotype is produced. In other words, genes are thought as a map or blueprint of the organism. By contrast, applied biologists investigating potentially new crops, test these crops for several years by growing variants of the crop in different environments or in different regions. As Lewontin notes, the crop that is eventually chosen for sale is not necessarily the crop that produces the largest yield but the one that produces the most consistent yield when grown in a variety of different regions.[215]

In Lewontin's example, we find a perfect instance of the difference between approaching the world in terms of intermediaries and approaching the world in terms of mediators. In treating information as already contained in the genes, the developmental biologist treats the organism as a mere intermediary. The blueprint is already contained within the genes and it is enough to merely manipulate the genes in a particular way to produce a particular phenotype. The point here is not that such manipulations don't produce particular phenotypes but that 1) these particular perturbations are a particular environment, and 2) in many instances environmental perturbations can produce similar transformations of phenotypes. As a consequence, we should see genes not as something that already contain information, but rather as one causal factor *among others*, where information is not *already there*, but rather where it is produced as a result of operations in the system/environment relation. In this connection, Susan Oyama calls for *parity* in investigating objects. As Oyama puts it, developmental systems theory (DST),

> makes extensive use of parity of reasoning. Descriptions and explanations of development are often asymmetric: the logic that is used (when there is a logic at all) to characterize certain factors as informing, coding, controlling, and so forth, could be, but typically is not, applied to other factors that play demonstrably comparable roles. In contrast, DST includes as full-fledged interactants many factors that are generally left in the background.[216]

In contrast to the developmental biologist described by Lewontin, the applied biologist's investigative practice implicitly indicates parity reasoning in its approach to new crops. In growing crops in different environments and regions, the applied biologist works on the premise that genes are not blueprints already containing information, but rather are one causal factor among others that can generate very different effects at the level of the phenotype when grown under different environmental conditions.

For the applied biologist, the entity (the seeds) are full-blown mediators. Between cause and effect there is here a *gap*, such that the effect is unknown. That is, we don't know what phenotypes will be produced under these circumstances. By contrast, the gap between cause and effect tends to disappear in the research practices of Lewontin's developmental biologist. Lewontin's developmental biologist, of course, begins with the premise that we don't know what phenotype will be produced if we manipulate this gene. The point, however, is that through the focus on genes alone, the developmental biologist tends to create the implicit conclusion that the information is *already* contained in the genes. In other words, the developmental biologist creates the impression that the effect is already there, requiring only a perturbation to take place. Lewontin's applied biologist, by contrast, works from the implicit premise that the phenotype is something that is constructed and that it is constructed in a way that can't be determined from the genes alone. One and the same genotype can produce very different results when cultivated in different environments.

As such, the seed is, for the applied biologist, a mediator. In short, there is no one-to-one mapping between genotype and phenotype. In this regard, we need to think the role that information plays in an object not as something that exists already in the entity, but as a cascade of events where information is simultaneously constructed and where information selects system-states. Needless to say, these selections have an impact on subsequent stages of development, playing a role in the determination of what subsequent information constructions are possible and excluding other possibilities.

Implicit assumptions about the transmissibility of information are rife in various forms of cultural studies as well. Whenever we speak of discourses, narratives, signifiers, social forces, and media as structuring reality and dominating people behind their backs, we speak as if persons were mere intermediaries or as if information can be exchanged without remainder. In other words, we ignore the manner in which systems are closed and how there is always a gap between cause and effect. Yet social systems, which are always themselves objects or substances, have a tough go of it as the objects of which these objects are composed never quite cooperate. All communication, as Lacan said, is miscommunication. And if this is the case, then it is because all systems produce their own information according to their own organization. As a consequence, every object or system is beset by its own system *internal* entropy as a consequence of the other objects or systems of which it is composed. Because objects are not intermediaries but rather mediators, the elements that a system constitutes never quite behave in the way the system anticipates.

The point here is that society cannot, as Latour said, be treated as an explanation but is precisely what has to be explained.[217] What is remarkable is that any stable social relations ever emerge at all. In *A Sociological Theory of Communication*, Loet Leydesdorff raises a similar question with respect to the self-organization of scientific discourse. How is it, we might ask, that something like a Kuhnian paradigm comes into existence? Leydesdorff proposes that first we have a field of heterogeneous communication acts, or a field that might be characterized by a high degree of entropy. Now, one of the remarkable and important features about human communication is that it is self-reflexive. That is, we can communicate about our communications or talk about our talk. At the second stage, reflexive discourse begins to set in. As Leydesdorff puts it,

> if reflexive analysts begin to communicate among themselves
> not only in terms of how they analyze data, but also at the
> reflexive level, e.g., about standards of analysis, the standards
> may become de-personalized; they begin to circulate in the
> communication system of this community, and thus begin
> to form a supra-individual dimension of quality control for
> the actors.[218]

With the reflexive moment of communication, distinctions and selections begin to emerge, determining a marked state or that which is selected and an unmarked state or that which is excluded. Over time, this talk about talk spreads through the community and becomes a sort of assumed background of those involved in communication, such that communications that deviate from these newly formed norms, themes, and distinctions are simply coded out as noise. In other words, a social system organizes itself and now develops its own capacity for selection at the second-order level through the manner in which talk about talk has become sedimented in those participating in the discourse.

In this way, the system thereby attains closure, both being produced by its own elements and producing its own elements. The system only comes into being from the action of those participating in the communication, but their communications begin to play a constraining role and produce new elements in the form of both new communications within the framework of the distinctions and selections produced by the system, and to produce new communicators capable of participating within that system. The production of these new elements, of course, takes place through the training of those participating in scientific discourse. The important point to keep in mind, however, is that even while such a self-organizing system comes to constitute its own elements, these elements aren't *just* elements. Rather, they are substances in their own right as well. As a consequence, such systems always struggle against a system-specific entropy. Communications are perpetually emerging that either diverge from the system that has emerged, or that challenge that system. In other words, the elements of the system are never simple intermediaries. Communications within the system perpetually generate surprising results as they pass through the mediators in the form of the persons participating in the discourse.

The concept of translation encourages us to engage in inquiry in a different way. Working from the premise that entities are mediators, it discourages any mode of theorizing that implicitly or explicitly treats objects as mere intermediaries such that effects are already contained within causes. As Latour suggests, all entities are treated as having greater or lesser degrees of agency by virtue of having a system-specific organization that prevents the relation between cause and effect from being treated as a simple exchange of information that inevitably produces a particular result. Likewise, in approaching entities as mediators, we are encouraged to attend to the manner in which entities produce surprising local manifestations when perturbed in particular ways and to vary the contexts in which entities are perturbed to discover what volcanic powers they have hidden within themselves. That is, we begin to investigate the manner in which substances creatively translate the world around them. In this respect, we move from the marked to the unmarked space of much contemporary thought. Rather than treating deviations from our predications as mere noise to be ignored, we instead treat these deviations as giving us insight into the way in which entities translate their world.

4.5. Autopoietic Asphyxiation: The Case of the Lacanian Clinic

To illustrate these points about the nature of translation and the closure of objects, I now turn briefly to some schematic remarks about the ontological foundations of the Lacanian clinic. My aim here is twofold. On the one hand, my aim is to schematically outline why Lacanian analysts conduct themselves as they do with respect to the treatment of their analysands. On the other hand, I wish to head off the criticism that object-oriented ontology ignores humans or the subject. As discussed in the introduction, the thesis of onticology and object-oriented philosophy is not that we should ignore subjects and focus instead on objects, but rather that being is composed entirely of objects or substances. In this respect, subjects are not *other* than objects, but rather are a particular type of object that relates to the world in a specific way. Far from excluding subjects, onticology is completely able to integrate various theories of the subject. What onticology and object-oriented philosophy object to is thus not the category of the subject, but rather the modernist conception of the subject in which the object is always coupled to the subject or culture in some form or another. Onticology, by contrast, seeks to think a subjectless object or an object that is not merely a correlate of a subject.

The account of autopoietic systems and operational closure developed in the foregoing turns out to be quite consonant with Lacanian psychoanalysis. In many respects, this comes as no surprise for, as a brief glance at the index to Seminar II indicates, Lacan was well aware of cybernetics which is, in turn, deeply related to autopoietic theory.[219] One of the features that marks Lacan's account of the subject is that it is thoroughly "intersubjective". The subject is both constituted in the field of the Other and is a perpetual relation with the Other. This is reflected both in Lacan's theory of the various subject-structures (neurosis, psychosis, and perversion) and how analysis is conducted.

Speaking strictly in the context of neurosis, it is ordinarily a symptom that brings a person to analysis. Setting aside the intricacies and transformations Lacan's theory of the symptom undergoes over the course of his teaching, it is important to note that Lacan's conception of the psychoanalytic symptom is not that of an underlying pathology arising from organic causes—for example, a chemical imbalance—but rather of the expression of a repressed desire and a relation to the Other. In this respect, the symptom is a form of speech, an address to the Other, that speaks without speaking. For example, my breaking of the chalk was *saying* something to my students. In this regard, Lacan remarks "that symptoms can be entirely resolved in an analysis of language, because a symptom is itself structured like a language: a symptom is language from which speech must be delivered".[220] The symptom, in short, is a way of speaking or addressing the Other while simultaneously not speaking.

Yet the symptom is also an expression of desire. However, here we must recall that for Lacan "desire is the desire of the Other". As we saw in the last section, this can entail that desire desires the Other, that desire desires to be desired by the Other, and that desire desires as the Other desires. In each instance, desire marks an intersubjective relation to the Other or a way of relating to the Other. In the case of neurosis, the desire that underlies the symptom is a repressed desire that the analysand, for whatever reason, cannot acknowledge or embrace. In this connection, it is crucial to note that the aim of analysis is not to treat the *symptom*, but to transform the analysand's relationship to both their own desire and the Other. While psychoanalytic treatment can, indeed, dissolve many symptoms—I ceased, for example, breaking chalk after that session—those symptoms that are dissolved come to be replaced by other symptoms. This is because, in the case of neurosis, the subject very much *is* its desire. What Lacan aims for rather is an avowal of desire and a separation from the Other.

In many respects, the symptom can be seen as a way of responding to the enigma of the Other's desire. In Seminar X, Lacan asks us to imagine standing before a female praying mantis without knowing whether or not we are wearing the mask of a male or female praying mantis.[221] As is well known, the female praying mantis devours the male praying mantis after mating with him. This perfectly embodies the dilemma of desire. Insofar as we don't know which mask we are wearing, we don't know what we are for the female praying mantis. The symptom can thus be thought as a way of surmounting or filling out this enigma by forming a hypothesis of what the Other desires. Desire, it could be said, embodies our non-knowledge with respect to the Other's desire. Embodied in all intersubjective relations is the sense that despite the fact that we are being addressed by the Other, we nonetheless do not know *why* the Other is addressing us. Put differently, we do not know the desire that animates the Other's relation to us. In this regard, the desire of the Other closely mirrors the phenomenon of operational closure with respect to systems. The Other perturbs us in a variety of ways, but we are unable to determine what intentions lie behind the Other's interaction with us.

It is this non-knowledge with respect to the desire of the Other that generates the fantasy and the symptom. Within the Lacanian framework, the fantasy is not so much a wish for something we lack, but is rather an *answer* to the enigma of the Other's desire. Fantasy, we could say, is a hypothesis as to what the Other desires. Through fantasy, the anxiety the subject encounters in the face of the enigma of the Other's desire is thereby minimized. Even where the fantasy is rather grim ("the Other wants to beat and exploit me!"), the answer to the enigma of the Other's desire is nonetheless preferable to the anxiety-provoking non-knowledge of that desire. With the answer provided by the unconscious fantasy, the analysand can now set about either thwarting or satisfying what they unconsciously believe to be the Other's demand, while also providing themselves with a schema for understanding what the Other wants from her.

Within a Luhmannian framework, we can already see that fantasy serves a function deeply analogous to the role of distinction in the continuing operations of a system. Here it will be recalled that distinction is a necessary condition for indication. If a system is to be capable of indicating anything within its environment, then it must first draw a distinction. However, distinction embodies two blind spots. On the one hand, every distinction contains a blind spot in the form of its unmarked state or what falls outside of the distinction. On the other hand, the distinction itself embodies a blind spot insofar as in the *use* of the distinction to make indications, the distinction itself becomes invisible, disguising the manner in which it renders indication possible. Just as Lewis Carroll said that you can eat your food or talk to your food but not eat your food *and* talk to your food, distinction is such that you can use your distinctions to make indications or observe your distinctions, but you can't observe your distinctions *and* use your distinctions. As a consequence, the use or operation of distinctions in making indications or observations produces a "reality effect" where what is observed or indicated appears to be a direct property of the indicated itself, rather than an effect of the distinction that renders the indication possible. So it is with fantasy as well. The fantasy is that which recedes in the background while structuring relations to the Other. As such, fantasy creates an effect whereby the manner in which fantasy transforms perturbations from the Other into information appears to directly result from the Other or to be a property of the Other itself. As Žižek puts it, "[t]he role of fantasy [is to] mediate between the formal symbolic structure and the positivity of objects we encounter in reality—that is to say, it provides a 'schema' according to which certain positive objects in reality can function as objects of desire, filling in the empty places opened up by the formal symbolic structure".[222] However, it is not simply the holes in the symbolic structure that are at stake here, but the opacity of the Other in our relations to the Other that fantasy fills. In this regard, it can be seen that fantasy is a direct response to the withdrawal of objects or others, to their constitutive opacity borne out of the operational closure of other persons and the social field as a whole.

The operational closure of subjects and the role played by the fantasy pose special challenges in the analytic setting. If fantasy structures the analysand's interpersonal relations in such a way as to pre-interpret perturbations from others in a particular way, how can the analyst intervene in the psychic economy of the analysand without merely *reinforcing* the analysand's fantasy and confirming their unconscious conception of the Other? Already we see that this question is a question of how it is possible to relate to operationally closed objects that cannot be dominated or controlled. Expressed a bit differently, the point here revolves around the status of information as it functions in psychic systems. One psychotherapeutic approach might have it that information is something that can be exchanged between therapist and patient such that it retains its identity or the meaning of the message. This seems to have been the premise of Freud's early treatments where he would didactically explain the dreams of his patients and their symptoms as, for example, in the case of Dora. However, as Freud quickly learned, not only did such didactic explanations have little impact on the symptom or in transforming the relationship of the subject to the Other, but in certain instances, such as in the case of Dora, it actually led patients to flee the analytic setting. Somehow a practice had to be devised that allowed the analysands to arrive at these discoveries for themselves, and the reason for this revolves around how information functions in closed systems.

In *The Four Fundamental Concepts of Psychoanalysis,* Lacan argues that the end of analysis consists in traversing the fantasy and separating from the desire of the Other. In light of the foregoing, we are now in a position to understand what Lacan is getting at with these proposals. Traversing the fantasy consists in a shift in perspective from relating to the Other in terms of first-order observation *through* the fantasy to second-order observation *of* the fantasy. The analysand shifts from making indications based on the distinctions drawn by the fantasy, to observing how he or she observes; that is, observing the fantasy itself. Accompanying this shift is a realization of the *contingency* of the manner in which the fantasy has drawn distinctions or how the analysand might be *mistaken* about the Other's desire. In other words, the analysand is confronted with the *enigma* of the Other's desire and thereby freed from the unconscious belief that the Other is making a specific demand of the subject. Accompanying this shift is a separation from the desire of the Other. Where first-order observation based on fantasy creates the impression that it is the Other itself that is making a specific demand, the shift towards second-order observation reveals the manner in which the *subject's* fantasy formatted perturbations from the Other in such a way as to transform them into a specific demand. Like Harry Angel in Alan Parker's *Angel Heart*, the analysand discovers that what he took to be the Other's demand was his desire all along.[223] At this point, the analysand is in a position to avow his desire, which, in turn, is often accompanied by a quite significant shift in how the subject relates to his or her symptom.

Yet how is this shift accomplished within the psychoanalytic setting? This shift is brought about by the manner in which the analyst conducts herself. As has often been remarked, the analyst is an enigmatic and impassive figure who seldom responds to the analysand. Lacan goes so far as to compare the position of the analyst with playing dead. As Lacan remarks, "the analyst concretely intervenes in the dialectic of analysis by playing dead—by 'cadaverizing' his position, as the Chinese say—either by his silence where he is the Other with a capital O, or by canceling out his own resistance where he is the other with a lowercase o".[224] This activity of playing dead serves the important function of confronting the analysand with the enigma of the Other's desire. Where the analysand expects the analyst to say something, thereby giving him a framework by which to transform this enigma of the Other's desire into a specific demand that the analysand can then satisfy or thwart, the analyst instead presents the analysand with a blank screen, thereby bringing the analysand before an inscrutable desire or a question: What does the Other want? In the early sessions of my own analysis, for example, I recall asking my analyst how he was doing at the beginning of my sessions or would inquire about some aspect of an article that he had recently published. My analyst would respond with utter silence that would then be punctuated with a drawn out "so?" inviting me to begin free associating. In this way, the analyst gave me no foothold to transform his desire into a demand. Whatever I began talking about issued from me and me alone rather than taking place as a response to a demand. This impassivity of the analyst's position thus gradually brings the analysand before the manner in which he or she projects certain demands on to the Other. Insofar as the analyst makes no specific demands beyond the demand to free associate, the analysand increasingly becomes aware of the manner in which the Other makes a specific demand of him issues from himself rather than the Other. In this way, he gradually traverses the fantasy, coming to see how he throws the net of fantasy over the Other as a way of transforming the enigma of desire into demand.

However, it would be a mistake to suppose that the analyst merely sits there quietly. The analyst does ask questions and make remarks. Yet the remarks that the analyst makes are generally of an enigmatic and polysemous nature, amenable to a variety of different interpretations. Lacanian interpretation does not *tell* an analysand what such and such *means*, but is rather an enigmatic and polysemous speech-act on the part of the analyst wherein the *analysand* or the patient creates the meaning. In this respect, one way of understanding Lacanian interpretation is as systematic *misinterpretation*. A properly psychoanalytic interpretation does not register that the analyst has understood—this would reinforce the belief that information is transmitted between closed systems—but rather works on the statements of the analysand in a surprising way that creates new meaning. Returning to the example from the last section, when my analyst intoned "pressure at the board", this statement systematically misinterpreted my discourse and upset my anticipations by taking the discourse I was articulating around physiology and physics (placing too much pressure on the chalk) and formulated a polysemous statement that simultaneously articulated these points about physics and physiology while also transforming the meaning in such a way as to indicate *my* pressure and anxiety at the board.

This particular form or practice of interpretation serves two important functions within the clinical setting. On the one hand, insofar as the interpretation is never quite what the analysand expects and insofar as it always slightly misinterprets what the analysand is saying, it becomes an event capable of producing information or resonance within the analysand. That is, it functions as an event capable of selecting new system-states. Where an interpretation that merely indicates the analyst has understood produces no new information (information repeated is no longer information), the minimal surprise embodied in a psychoanalytic interpretation carries the possibility of generating new meaning and redrawing distinctions that structure the analysand's experience of the world. As such, it becomes possible to shift the symptom into new basins of attraction that might be far less painful for the subject. On the other hand, insofar as the interpretation seems to misunderstand the analysand, it systematically undermines the analysand's deeply held belief that he has access to the Other, thereby assisting in the process of separation from the Other.

This brief gloss on Lacanian practice hardly does justice to the depth and complexity of Lacanian theory. I have, for example, said nothing about the *objet a*, *jouissance*, the various subject-structures, the imaginary, symbolic, and the real, and so on. However, my point is that if Lacan is right, then the quandaries the neurotic subject finds himself in follow directly from the ontological withdrawal of objects and their operational closure as systems. The quandaries of the neurotic subject are quandaries that emerge when psychic systems are coupled to other operationally closed systems such as the social system into which they are born and relations to other people. The subject wonders what their place is in the social system, what they are for the social system, and what they are for other people. Yet because systems are operationally closed, because psychic systems are both outside other psychic systems and exist only in the environment of the social system, there is no univocal answer to these questions. The symptom and the fantasy are ways in which this dilemma is navigated. This is true even where the symptom has an organic foundation in, for example, the neurology of the analysand, for the psychic system must still give these perturbations coming from within its own internal environment a meaning. Lacanian theory and practice gives us insight into just what is entailed by the withdrawal of objects, how this withdrawal is organized, and the reality effect produced as a function of the way in which objects construct their openness to their environment.

Chapter 5
Regimes of Attraction, Parts, and Structure

> The final step in the integration of developmental biology into evolution is to incorporate the organism as itself a cause *of its own development, as a mediating mechanism by which external and internal factors influence its future.*
>
> — R. Lewontin[225]

> Each portion of matter can be conceived as a garden full of plants, and as a pond full of fish. But each branch of a plant, each limb of an animal, each drop of its humors, is still another such garden or pond.
>
> — G.W. Leibniz[226]

5.1. Constraints

In *Critical Environments*, Cary Wolfe, a strong defender of Luhmann's systems theory, develops an important critique of autopoietic theory. As Wolfe writes,

> We might say [...] that *Luhmann's* "blind spot", *his* unobservable constitutive distinction, is his unspoken distinction between "differentiation" and what historicist,

materialist critique has theorized as "contradiction", a
blind spot that manifests itself in Luhmann's inability or
unwillingness to adequately theorize the discrepancy between
the formal equivalence of observers in his epistemology and
their real lack of equivalence on the material, social plane.
It seems that the category of contradiction—insofar as it
names precisely this difference—proves much more difficult
to dispose of than Luhmann's systems theory imagines. Or
rather—to put a somewhat finer point on it—it is disposed of
by systems theory, but only "abstractly", as Marxist theorists
like to say, only in thought, but not in historical, material
practice.[227]

In point of fact, this shortcoming of autopoietic theory arises not simply
with respect to social relations, but rather besets all discussions of exo-
relations with respect to objects. In its focus on the operational closure of
objects, the self-regulation and self-production of objects, and the manner
in which objects constitute *their own* information, autopoietic theory tends
towards a utopianism that ignores material constraints on the activity of
objects when objects enter into exo-relations with other objects. In its
emphasis on the closure of objects, autopoietic theory often tends towards a
picture of objects in which they are completely *self-determining* and therefore
entirely sovereign. Each object is treated as an observer that observes
the world through its own distinctions, and all observers are treated as
absolutely equal. For example, we encounter Luhmann saying that objects
cannot be dominated. What is missed here, however, are inequalities among
objects that emerge as a result of how they are related to other objects
in networks.

In *The Eighteenth Brumaire of Louis Bonaparte*, Marx observes that,
"[m]en make their own history, but they do not make it just as they please;
they do not make it under circumstances chosen by themselves, but under
circumstances directly found, given and transmitted from the past".[228] What
Marx says here is true not only of human actors, but also of all nonhuman
actors. In many of its formulations, autopoietic theory threatens to invert
this thesis. That is, autopoietic theory tends towards a characterization of
the world in which entities not only make their own history, but make their

own history in *conditions* of *their own making*. What we get here is a sort of radical idealism, where every entity, by virtue of its operational closure, fully constructs its own world. As Paul Bains articulates it in *The Primacy of Semiosis*,

> There are nothing but interpretations. Maturana contends that reality as a universe of independent entities is a fiction of the descriptive domain and that the notion of reality should be applied to this domain of descriptions in which we, the describing system, interact with our descriptions *as if* with independent entities.[229]

As a consequence, Bains continues, "we can begin to see that Maturana and Varela oscillate between realist claims about the nature of the individuality of autopoietic systems independent of an observer and idealist and phenomenological claims wherein thought is not able to have a real relation with something other than itself".[230] Do Maturana and Varela contend merely that we cannot have a direct relation with other objects, or are they making the more radical claim that each object constructs all other objects? The two claims are very different. The first claim is broadly consistent with the claims of object-oriented philosophy and onticology, insofar as both hold that all objects withdraw from one another, encountering each other only on conditions of closure. The second claim seems to lead to incoherence in that it is not clear how there can simultaneously be no independent reality *and* be entities that construct other entities. In other words, minimally autopoietic theory requires the independent reality and existence of entities doing the construction.

However, the more significant problem with autopoietic systems theory is that in its focus on the internal functioning of the entity, it tends towards a conception of entities that carry out their functions in a purely frictionless space, where each entity is a complete sovereign encountering no constraints from the world around it. It is one thing, following Aristotle, to defend the autonomy and independence of substance. It is quite another to argue that this autonomy and independence of substance entails that *when* substances enter into exo-relations with other objects they nonetheless remain completely unconstrained. The absurdity of the thesis that there are no independent objects can be discerned by simply reversing Maturana and Varela's claims about observation. Are Maturana and Varela prepared to claim that *they* are constructed by the observations of *another* autopoietic system such as the tardigrade? If not, why? And if they do grant independent existence to themselves, why do they not follow Bhaskar in granting a similar autonomous existence to other objects? What we need is an account of exo-relations capable of doing justice to both the closure and withdrawal of objects as well as the constraints that other objects exercise on withdrawn objects.

In this connection, we can ask ourselves how it is possible for objects to be constrained despite their autonomy, independence, and self-determination. In many respects, it is the distinction between virtual proper being and local manifestation, coupled with the concept of regimes of attraction that allows us to theorize these constraints. For while, in their virtual proper being, objects withdraw from any of their actualizations in local manifestations, while every object always contains a reserve excess over and above its local manifestations, nonetheless local manifestations are often highly constrained by the exo-relations an object enters into with other objects in a regime of attraction.

The key point not to be missed is that while objects are only selectively open to their environments, this doesn't entail that objects are free to do whatever they might like with their environments. In the case of autopoietic systems, for example, the distinctions which organize a system's relation to its environment are more or less *anticipations*, selecting events that are relevant to the ongoing autopoiesis of the system. However, as anticipations, these distinctions can be *disappointed* and those disappointments play a role in the subsequent development of the system. What we need is a model of exo-relations that allows us to thematize these complex exo-relations between system and environment. In *Difference and Repetition*, Deleuze remarks that,

> A living being is not only defined genetically, by the
> dynamisms which determine its internal milieu, but also
> ecologically, by the external movements which preside over
> its distribution within an extensity. A kinetics of population
> adjoins, without resembling, the kinetics of the egg; a

geographic process of isolation may be no less formative
of species than internal genetic variations, and sometimes
precede the latter. Everything is even more complicated
when we consider that the internal space is itself made up
of multiple spaces which must be locally integrated and
connected, and that this connection, which may be achieved
in many ways, pushes the object or living being to its own
limits, all in contact with the exterior; and that this relation
with the exterior, and with other things and living beings,
implies in turn connections and global integrations which
differ in kind from the preceding.[231]

Deleuze here presents us with a model of objects in which the
development of objects unfolds in a relation between three environments.
In the case of the organism, there is the internal environment defined by
the genes of the organism. In addition to the internal environment of the
organism, there is the external environment of the organism defined by
relations to other organisms and entities out there in the world. Finally,
there is what we might call the "horizontal" environment of the organism,
consisting of the internal parts of the organism and the pressures they place
on one another requiring integration. When we think this threefold relation
between environments, we must not forget the dimension of time and
interactivity among these different domains. Development, which continues
throughout the entire life of the organism, unfolds interactively and in the
dimension of time, such that events in one of these environments impact
events in other environments, actualizing them in aleatory ways.

Missing in Deleuze's mapping of developmental relations, however,
is a role for the agent itself in its own construction. Formulated in terms
of Kenneth Burke's pentad, Deleuze's map of development is all scene
with no agent. Rather, the agent (object) ends up becoming an effect
of the dynamics taking place in the scene (the interactions among the
environments). Deleuze's mapping of exo-relations thus points us in the
right direction for thinking constraints or relations of dependency in local
manifestations, but suffers from treating the agent or object as a mere
effect of these relations rather than granting the agent a causal role in
these developmental processes. In my view, developmental systems theory

(DST) provides the resources for navigating the radical constructivism of autopoietic theory where each object is a sovereign constructing all other objects, and the extreme "environmentalism" of Deleuze's mapping of ecological relations where the object is merely an effect of relations between internal, horizontal, and external environments.

Although the focus of DST has revolved around debates in developmental biology, it nonetheless provides us with a general model of how objects behave in regimes of attraction or within fields of exo-relations to other objects. DST research has focused primarily on nature/nurture debates within biology and the social sciences, strongly contesting models of genetics that treat genes as blueprints pre-delineating the eventual form that the phenotype (what I would call the "local manifestation") of an organism will take. In her early groundbreaking work, *The Ontogeny of Information*, for example, Susan Oyama shows that while mainstream biology gives lip service to the interactionist hypothesis that the development of the phenotype results from the interaction between genes and environment, nonetheless biologists tend to discuss genes as *already* containing information that presides over the development of the phenotype as a sort of map. In contrast to this, DST theorists argue that,

> information "in the genes" or "in the environment" is not biologically relevant until it participates in the phenotypic processes. *It becomes meaningful in the organism only as it is constituted as "information" by its developmental system.* The result is not *more* information but *significant information.*[232]

Along the lines I argued in the last chapter, information is not something that exists out there in the world, but is rather something that is constituted and constructed. There is no pre-existent information in the environment, nor can it be said, in the context of genes, that genes already contain information. Rather, events that take place in the development of the organism, cell development, and protein production themselves have an effect on how genes are actualized and the activation of particular genes also impacts how other genes are actualized or set in motion. As a consequence, while genes are indeed a causal *factor*, they cannot be said to constitute a *map* or *blueprint* of the organism.

In the introduction to *Cycles of Contingency*—a collection of articles by developmental systems biologists and theorists—Oyama, Griffiths, and Gray outline six basic themes of DST research:

1. Joint determination by multiple causes—every trait is produced by the interaction of many developmental resources.

2. The gene/environment dichotomy is only one of many ways to divide up interactants.

3. Context sensitivity and contingency—the significance of any one cause is contingent upon the state of the rest of the system.

4. Extended inheritance—an organism inherits a wide range of resources that interact to construct that organisms life cycle.

5. Development as construction—neither traits nor representations of traits are transmitted to offspring. Instead, traits are made—reconstructed—in development.

6. Distributed control—no one type of interactant controls development.

7. Evolution as construction—evolution is not a matter of organisms or populations being molded by their environments, but of organism-environment systems changing over time.[233]

Here it is important to note that developmental systems theorists use the term "system" in a different way than I have been using it up to this point. For the DST's, the organism-environment relation constitutes a developmental system. By contrast, within the framework of autopoietic theory, systems are one side of a distinction between system and environment.

Despite these differences, however, there are strong points of resonance between the autopoietic conception of systems and that advocated by dynamic systems theorists. Like autopoietic theorists, DST emphasizes the manner in which organisms construct their environment. The construction of the environment does not simply consist in the construction of things such as ant nests and bird nests, but also involves the way in which organisms are *selectively* open to their environments. As biologist Richard Lewontin observes,

> Organisms determine what is relevant. While stones are part of a thrush's environment, tree bark is a part of a woodpecker's, and the undersides of leaves part of a warbler's. It is the life activities of these birds that determine which parts of the world, physically accessible to all of them, are actually parts of their environments.[234]

In short, environments cannot be treated as something that is simply given or there such that the organism subsequently fills a niche that already existed in the environment. Rather, organisms take an active role in constructing their environment, both through determining relevancies in the environment and through actively changing their environment through activities like building nests. In terms of autopoietic theory, systems (organisms/objects) determine that to which they are open or what is relevant in the world about them. In other words, there is no such thing as an "environment as such". Rather, we can only discover what constitutes the environment of an organism through a second-order observation of how the organism relates to the world around them.

A central axiom of traditional evolutionary biology is that "the organism proposes and the environment disposes". Here the theory runs that random variations within the population of a species are proposed as various *solutions* to the problem of the environment. Individual organisms are proposed as various solutions to the problem posed by the environment. The premise of such a thesis is that the environment is something there, present-at-hand, that the organism must adapt to. This thesis, however, becomes significantly complicated when we recognize that organisms construct their own environments. Here the organism can no longer be treated as a passive object, such that genes and the environment are the subjects forming this object, but rather the organism itself becomes a "subject" that plays a role both in how its genes are actualized and how its environment is constructed. This does not entail that the organism is a sovereign acting without constraint in a purely smooth space it can define at will, but it does entail a far more active role on the part of the organism in these processes.

Lewontin goes so far in this line of thought as to argue that species actually co-construct one another. As Lewontin remarks,

> It might be objected that the notion of organisms constructing their environments leads to absurd results. After all, hares do not sit around constructing lynxes! But in the most important sense they do. First, the biological properties of lynxes are presumably in part a consequence of selection for catching prey of a certain size and speed, i.e., hares. Second, lynxes are not part of the environment of moose while they are of hares, because of biological differences between moose and hares.[235]

Part of the reason lynxes are as they are has to do with how the properties of hares and other similar creatures have constructed them. In other words, those lynxes that were more adept at catching the speedy hare were more likely to reproduce. Likewise, we can say that hares are constructed by lynxes and other similar organisms.

One of the central themes in DST is the concept of extended inheritance. Where traditional evolutionary biology tends to treat genes as the only thing inherited by organisms, thereby leading to the neo-Darwinist thesis that genes are the true units of natural selection, DST emphasizes, how, in addition to genes, all sorts of environmental factors are selected as well. Ant larvae, for example, inherit the nest and traces of pheromones built and left by other ants. These inheritances play a role in the development of the organism's phenotype, determining, for example, what type of ant the larvae will become (worker ant, soldier ant, and so on). Needless to say, these are non-genetic inheritances. Likewise, humans inherit culture, infrastructure, practices, and so on.

Observations such as these lead DST to defend *parity* in explanations and to remodel the concept of natural selection. Parity reasoning is a form of reasoning in which the theorist refuses to grant one sort of agency— for example, genes –control of development. Rather, parity reasoning emphasizes *distributed* causality, where a variety of different causal factors contribute to the development of the phenotype. The thesis here is *not* that all causal factors contribute equally to the local manifestation of the phenotype or organism, but that the interaction or interplay of a variety of different causal factors play a role in the local manifestation of the entity. This has real consequences for how research is conducted in both biology and the social sciences. In biology, for example, we might conduct experiments where we keep the environment constant to see what effects this has on the phenotype, but *also* conduct experiments where we vary the environment while keeping the genes constant to see what effects these shifts have on the phenotype.

Returning to some themes from the introduction, we saw how a good deal of contemporary theory focuses on the subject's and culture's relation to the world. Within this framework, the framework of representation, the subject falls in the marked space of the grounding distinction of thought. Beneath the subject or culture, we find a sub-distinction referring to content that leads us to focus on signs, signifiers, and representations. While clearly signs, signifiers, and representations play an important role in how human relations come to be organized, we can see how parity reasoning would lead us to expand the focus of our analyses in the social sciences and in social and political thought. Jared Diamond, for example, raises the question of why Western Culture has enjoyed such a dominant position throughout world history.[236] Why, for example, did the West conquer the Americas, rather than the Americas conquer the West? If we begin from the standpoint of the subject and culture, thereby indicating signs, signifiers, and representations as our sub-distinction, we are led to explain these cultural differences based on something unique to Western systems of representation or narratives that allowed the West to conquer other groups. For example, we follow Heidegger in asserting something unique and singular about the "Greek event", or perhaps we follow the theology of Radical Orthodoxy promoted by figures such as John Milbank, locating a fundamental historical break for humanity in the "Christian event".

Through careful analysis, however, Jared Diamond emphasizes the environmental differences between different cultures and the advantages and disadvantages these created for various people. Thus, for example,

Diamond contends that there were few animals fit for domestication in the Americas. This had a profound impact on how Eurasian and American populations developed. Because Eurasian populations had far more domesticated animals, there was also a much higher degree of cross-species germ development in Eurasian history. This meant that Eurasians not only developed greater immunity to disease, but also had far more diseases in the environment. *One* reason European conquest of the Americas was so unilateral was precisely because there were a variety of diseases moving from Europe to the Americas without the reverse movement from the Americas to Europe. As a consequence, tens of thousands of Native Americans died, rendering the European conquest far easier in the long run. Again, the point here is not that semiotic differences make no difference, nor that disease alone (Diamond explores a variety of geographical factors) completely explain such brutal events. The point is that when we draw distinctions in particular ways, certain phenomena and causal factors become completely invisible. Diamond practices an exemplary form of parity reasoning in exploring these geographical factors. Continental social and political thought and theory needs to do a much better job in exploring the role played by non-semiotic actants such as natural resources, the presence or absence of power lines, road distributions and connections, whether or not cable internet connections are available, and so on, in their exploration of why certain social formations take the form they do.

Insofar as it is not simply genes that are inherited, but environments as well, it follows that natural selection must operate not only at the level of the organism or genes, but at the level of environments too. Here we must recall that many organisms quite literally construct their environments, building nests and so on. Those constructed environments that confer an advantage in the reproduction of the organism will tend to be selected and passed on through generations. Here it's worth recalling that Darwin nowhere specifies what the mechanism of inheritance is, only that in order for natural selection to take place there must be inheritance. There is thus no reason to suppose that genes alone are the sole mechanism of inheritance. Constructed environments such as ant nests and culture are also forms of inheritance. In their article, "Darwinism and Developmental

Systems", Griffiths and Gray give a striking example of such environmental inheritance (and a number of other examples as well). As Griffiths and Gray observe,

> Certain aphid species reliably pass on their endosymbiotic
> *Buchnera* bacteria from the maternal symbiont mass to
> either eggs or developing embryo. The bacteria enable their
> aphid hosts to utilize what would otherwise be nutritionally
> unsuitable host plants. Aphids that have been treated with
> antibiotics to eliminate the bacteria are stunted in growth,
> reproductively sterile, and die prematurely.[237]

The point here is that the *Buchnera* bacteria is not a part of the aphid's genome, but nonetheless plays a significant role in the development of the phenotype. Far from the genes already containing information in the form of a blueprint of what the organism will turn out to be, genes are one developmental causal factor among a variety of others. The phenotype is plastic in the sense that it can take on a variety of different forms. Here it goes without saying that the plasticity of the phenotype isn't entirely without constraint. The organism-environment system indeed constrains the development of the phenotype in a variety of ways, defining a topological space of possible variations. What's important here is that the information presiding over the genesis of the phenotype is something *constructed* in the process of development from a variety of factors, and, moreover, the qualities that the organism comes to embody are not located *already* in the organism in a virtual or implicit form, but are rather new creations in the process of development.

In light of the foregoing, we are now in a position to theorize the emergence of constraints within an onticological and object-oriented philosophical framework. The whole problem arises from the manner in which objects are operationally closed and the manner in which they constitute their own environment through their distinctions, defining that to which they are open and that to which they are not open. This, in turn, leads to Luhmann's thesis that objects can neither be dominated nor controlled. However, while objects indeed constitute their own openness to their environment, it does not follow from this that objects control or create their own environment. Here we will recall that the environment is always more complex than the object or system that unifies the environment through a determination of what is and is not relevant to it. Moreover, while openness to the environment arises from the manner in which the object or system is organized, this openness does not determine which *events* take place in the environment. Were this the case, then each substance would be controlling or "dominating" the other substances or systems that exist in its environment. Just as other substances in a substance's environment can only *perturb* the substance without determining what information events will be produced on the basis of these perturbations, the most the substance can do is attempt to perturb other substances without being able to control what sort of information-events are produced in the other substances. And these attempted perturbations can always, of course, fail. My three-year-old daughter, for example, might yell at her toy box when she bumps into it, yet the toy box continues on its merry way quite literally unperturbed.

Everything turns on recognizing that, while objects construct their openness to their environment, they do not construct the events that take place in their environment. When Luhmann observes that objects cannot be controlled or dominated, his point is not that objects are completely free sovereigns capable of creating whatever reality they might like, but rather that any event that perturbs them will be "interpreted" in terms of the system's own organization. As a consequence, objects cannot be steered from the outside. However, the events that do or do not take place in the environment of an object and to which the object is open nonetheless play a tremendously significant role in the local manifestations of which the object is capable. We see a significant example of this in the case of Griffith and Gray's aphids, where the presence or absence of the *Buchnera* bacteria makes a significant difference in the formation of the aphid's phenotype. Those other objects and events in the environment of the object define a regime of attraction with respect to the object, creating regularities in the local manifestation of the object and producing constraints on what local manifestations are possible.

Regimes of attraction should thus be thought as interactive networks or, as Timothy Morton has put it, meshes that play an affording and constraining role with respect to the local manifestations of objects.

Depending on the sorts of objects or systems being discussed, regimes of attraction can include physical, biological, semiotic, social, and technological components. Within these networks, hierarchies or sub-networks can emerge that constrain the local manifestations available to other nodes or entities within the network. Thus, for example, government officials and high ranking business leaders such as CEO's have access to both contacts and business information that gives them an advantage in the capture of wealth and power. This appropriation of wealth and power leads, in its turn, to an absence of resources for those without this access. As a consequence, local manifestations at less "connected" levels of the social sphere are severely limited in terms of what is possible for them in much the same way that aphids without access to the *Buchnera* bacteria develop in a particular way. While the particular texture of a regime of attraction does not *determine* what an object will become or be because such actualizations depend on the organization of the object in question, they can play a significant role in limiting what local manifestations are possible for an object.

Similarly, in another context, Marx discusses the manner in which the repetitive activity of factory work has the effect of de-skilling the worker and dampening his or her cognitive abilities.[238] Without going into too much detail, the factory form arises, in part, as a consequence of the development of wage-labor and the necessity it engendered for diminishing the cost of production so as to maximize the production of surplus-value. The paradox of the factory form is that through de-skilling labor as a result of highly specialized and rote, repetitive activity, the laborer becomes increasingly dependent on the wage-labor system that divests him of control of his own life and circumstance, reinforcing the very system that limits his own freedom. The knowledge and skills are lost that would allow him to do other tasks. As a result, he becomes trapped in the factory system in part through his own actions. Technology here plays a central role in both this de-skilling and the diminution of cognitive ability as a result of endless repetitive activities that require little thought or skill. As such, wage-labor, the factory, and technologies function as a regime of attraction that deeply influence local manifestations at both the societal level (the texture that society takes on) and at the individual level of the worker. Different activities, regimes of attraction, and modes of production might lead to very different local manifestations at the cognitive and affective level.

Within this context, one of the central roles of social and political theory ought to be the cartography of regimes of attraction. This cartography consists in mapping those networks of objects that play a significant role in the production of local manifestations at the level of individuals, groups, and the texture of societies at large. Through such cartographies, it becomes possible to strategically locate those places where bifurcation points within the social system are available, allowing for the possibility of new local manifestations at the level of individuals and society. In this regard, Marx was an exemplary cartographer. In *Capital*, at least, Marx did not use "society" and "class" as explanatory variables, but instead mapped the regimes of attraction within particular historical settings precisely to explain why society takes the form it does and how class structures come to exist as they do. However, in his cartography of the social sphere, Marx sought to map not only existing social relations, but also *virtual* social tendencies as well. That is, Marx sought to locate those tensions and lines of flight within existing social structures to determine where change might be taking place and where new forms of social organization might be emerging. Through a knowledge of regimes of attraction, the attractors that organize them, and the bifurcation points to which they are susceptible, it becomes possible to strategize practices that might intensify and accelerate these processes. The presence of a bifurcation point is no guarantee that a system will shift into a new basin of attraction. Consequently, cartography, a cartography of the virtual, becomes an indispensable dimension of practice, providing us with resources for determining how to activate these bifurcation points.

Above all, we must avoid the conclusion that regimes of attraction *determine* the local manifestations of objects or entities. While regimes of attraction play a significant role in the form that local manifestations take, objects are not merely *effects* of regimes of attraction. When objects enter into exo-relations with other objects, these other objects certainly perturb the object in a variety of ways, influencing its local manifestations, but objects, and above all, autopoietic objects, are also causes and actors in the world. A cat that finds that the heat of the fire in the fireplace is a bit too hot does not merely sit there and roast, but rather gets up, paces back and forth a bit, and finds a place to sit more amenable to its desired temperature. In this way, the cat takes an active role in modulating the production of its local manifestations in relation to the milieu in which it finds itself. Likewise, beavers construct imposing dams, creating optimal environments for themselves to live in. While the regimes of attraction we find ourselves enmeshed in might constrain us in a number of ways, through our movement and action we have the ability to act on these regimes of attraction, construct our environments, and therefore modify the circumstances in which we find ourselves. We are not simply acted upon by regimes of attraction, but act on them as well. Given the unpredictable nature of other actors, however, the question revolves around which form of action might be most conducive to enhancing our existence.

5.2. Parts and Wholes:
The Strange Mereology of Object-Oriented Ontology

Within Continental philosophy and theory, a lot of mischief has been caused as a result of failing to carefully think through issues of mereology or the relationship between parts and wholes. This has especially been the case for bodies of social and political thought deeply influenced by the structuralist turn arising out of Lévi-Strauss and a variety of other French thinkers. In its focus on social structure as a totalizing relational system without an outside, structuralism created a crisis in French social and political thought, raising questions as to how any sort of agency or social change is possible. For if structure consists in differential or oppositional relations between elements and elements cannot be said to exist independent of their relations, then the question emerges of how any action whatsoever is possible that doesn't merely reproduce the social structure. Matters were further complicated in the tendency of structuralism to treat the subject as an effect of impersonal and collective structures that function according to their own pulse and rhythm. In this connection, who can forget Althusser's pronouncements concerning the subject in "Ideology and Ideological State Apparatuses"? There Althusser remarks that,

> the category of the subject is constitutive of all ideology, but
> at the same time and immediately I add that *the category of the*

subject is only constitutive of all ideology insofar as all ideology has the function (which defines it) of 'constituting' concrete individuals as subjects. In the interaction of this double constitution exists the functioning of all ideology, ideology being nothing but its functioning in the material forms of existence of that functioning.[239]

Althusser's pronouncements about the subject immediately generated a crisis in French social and political theory, generating, in subsequent years, a series of responses from both his students and those deeply influenced by his thought and conception of the social.

In many respects, the problem is quite simple. If the subject is both constitutive of ideology and constituted by ideology, and if ideology is the means by which the social system "reproduces the conditions of production",[240] then it would appear that social and political thought is unable to account for how it is possible for social change to take place. This problem emerges from the relational conception of the social developed within the various structuralist frameworks. Insofar as the relations constituting structure are themselves *internal* relations in which all elements are constituted by their relations, it follows that there can be no external point of purchase from which structure could be transformed. As an element of structure, this would hold for the subject as well. Like anything else within the social system, the subject would necessarily be differentially constituted by the relations making up social structure.

With these grim pronouncements, a desperate search began to find a *free* or void point within structure, a point not overdetermined by the differential relations constituting social structure, such that the transcendental condition under which change is possible could be articulated. Surprisingly, the theoretical resources for such an account were already suggested in the early work of Lévi-Strauss. In his early *Introduction to the Work of Marcel Mauss*, Lévi-Strauss's theorization of the concept of *mana* suggested the existence of a paradoxical feature of structure that is simultaneously internal to structure and undetermined by structure. As Lévi-Strauss observes,

always and everywhere, those types of notions [*mana*],
somewhat like algebraic symbols, occur to represent an
indeterminate value of signification, in itself devoid of
meaning and thus susceptible of receiving any meaning at all;
their sole function is to fill a gap between the signifier and
the signified, or, more exactly, to signal the fact that in such a
circumstance, on such an occasion, or in such a one of their
manifestations, a relationship of non-equivalence becomes
established between signifier and signified, to the detriment of
the prior complementary relationship.[241]

Further on, Lévi-Strauss goes on to remark that,

I believe that notions of the *mana* type, however diverse they
may be, and viewed in terms of their most general function
[...] represent nothing more or less than that *floating signifier*
which is the disability of all finite thought (but also the surety
of all art, all poetry, every mythic and aesthetic invention),
even though scientific knowledge is capable, if not of
staunching it, at least of controlling it partially.[242]

To this list we can add politics. What this floating signifier suggested
was the possibility of a void point within structure, a point of complete
indetermination, marking a space where both the social might be
transformed and where the subject might exist as something more than a
patient or object of social forces.

And indeed, if we look at the trajectory of subsequent French social and
political theory, we see a variant of precisely this option being embraced.
The later work of Althusser comes increasingly to focus on Lucretius and
a discourse of the swerve and the void.[243] Rancière comes to emphasize
the role of the "part of no part" as that void point within the social order
(which he calls "the police") from which the social order comes to be
transformed.[244] Badiou emphasizes the manner in which every structured
situation is haunted at its edge by a void where entirely novel and
undecidable events can occur that a subject can then decide, inaugurating
truth-procedures that gradually change the organization of the structured
situation.[245] And Žižek emphasized the unrepresentable real at the heart of

the symbolic from whence a subject becomes possible that marks the failure of the symbolic and such that an absolute act that completely abolishes the subject and re-creates it is open. All of these themes, developed in so many different ways, appear to be variations of the floating signifier that simultaneously marks the limit of the social and its infinite transformability.

Closely connected with this recognition of the void or floating signifier that haunts every social structure was a growing awareness of the *contingency* of structure. In a certain respect, the contingency of structure had been a persistent theme of structuralist thought. Where Kant had proposed one universal transcendental structure of the world issuing from the transcendental subject, structural anthropology and linguistics had revealed a variety of different structures organized in very different ways. However, increasingly structure came to be thought as veiling an infinite multiplicity bubbling beneath structure without order or unity. No one has developed this line of thought with more rigor and in greater detail than Alain Badiou in his magnificent *Being and Event*. There, developing an ontology based on Zermelo-Fraenkel set theory, Badiou advances something of a dialectical ontology partitioned between what he calls inconsistent multiplicities and consistent multiplicities. Inconsistent multiplicities can be thought as a sort of chaos insofar as they are pure multiples without any structure or individuated entities. These multiplicities constitute being as such or being itself. Consistent multiplicities, by contrast, are structured and unified situations. Consistent multiplicities are formed from inconsistent multiplicities through an operation Badiou refers to as the "count-as-one" and, by virtue of being founded in inconsistent multiplicities, are always haunted by a chaos that bubbles just beneath the surface. As such, any consistent multiplicity is only a contingent organization of a situation.

It is not difficult to detect, lurking behind Badiou's ontology, the desire to rigorously ground revolutionary social theory. One of the main ways in which ideology functions is through the *naturalization* of the social world. In other words, ideology presents the structure and organization of the social world as the inevitable and natural order of things, such that other arrangements are impossible. One major form of ideological critique has thus historically taken the form of demonstrating the manner in which social formations are contingent or capable of being otherwise through maneuvers of historicization and so on. Badiou's thought provides an ontological grounding for this capacity to be otherwise. In many respects, such a conclusion is already internal to set theory. Recall that, within the framework of set theory, sets are defined strictly through their *extension* or the elements that belong to the set. Here we can distinguish between a set and a type based on whether or not membership in the collection is defined extensionally (by the parts that belong to it) or intensionally (by some shared feature among the elements). The collection of all dogs, for example, is a collection that is defined intensionally insofar as membership in it is a function of all elements belonging to the collection sharing a common characteristic or set of characteristics. In contrast to types, sets are collections defined purely in terms of their members, such that there is no necessity of these elements sharing a common characteristic. Nor must the elements of the set be ordered in any particular way. Insofar as sets are defined extensionally, the set $\{x, y, z\}$ is equivalent to the set $\{y, z, x\}$. In short, the elements of sets are *non-relational* or are not defined by the relations among their elements. The point here is that if social structures are sets, there is no one way in which they can be organized and a variety of other forms of social organization are possible.

Initially these issues pertaining to set theory might seem remote from issues of ideology and the naturalization of the social field. However, if it is true that being is "set theoretical" and that, at its most fundamental level, being consists of inconsistent multiplicities rather than consistent multiplicities, then it also follows that any social structure is contingent in the precise sense that relations among elements can be otherwise. From the foregoing, this can be seen in two ways. On the one hand, because sets are defined extensionally and without any ordering relations among the elements, it follows that there is no *necessary* relation among the elements. Here relations are external to their terms. Likewise, a similar point can be made through the power set axiom in set theory. The power set axiom allows us to take all possible subsets of a set, forming a new set out of this collection. Thus, for example, given a set $\{x, y, z\}$, its power set would be $\{\{x\}, \{y\}, \{z\}, \{x, y\}, \{x, z\}, \{y, z\}, \{x, y, z\}\}$. The power set can then be applied recursively yet again to generate an even larger set and so on. The "cash value" of the power set axiom at the level of ideology critique is that it reveals the manner in which social groupings are contingent and capable of being otherwise by being grouped in different ways. In effect, Badiou provides an ontological "foundation" for demonstrating the contingency of social relations, thereby underlining the manner in which they are always capable of being structured otherwise.

Through this maneuver, Badiou strikes a strong blow against the internalism of structuralism. Structuralism had argued that all relations are strictly internal to their elements, such that elements cannot be said to have any existence independent of their relations. Through an ontology of inconsistent multiplicities coupled with an account of the externality of relations, Badiou is able to show that while elements do indeed enter into temporary relations with one another, these relations are always and everywhere necessarily contingent and capable of being otherwise. As such, Badiou significantly broadens the possibility of our ability to think change within the social sphere, while also allowing us to maintain the best insights of structuralism through his account of consistent multiplicities.

Badiou's meditations on the relationship between sets and subsets is thoroughly mereological in character. In making claims about the extensional composition of sets (parts), Badiou underlines the manner in which the parts of a set are simultaneously objects in their own right while also being parts of larger objects, to wit, the sets from which they are drawn. What is interesting here is that the parts are not defined by their relations to other elements in the set, but are objects of their own that can be detached from their membership in the set. Here object-oriented ontology and onticology find an unexpected ally with Badiou and a surprising point of resonance. As we have already seen, Graham Harman argues that all objects are such that there are objects wrapped in objects wrapped in objects, such that we can simultaneously treat objects as relations among objects and discrete units in their own right. Badiou argues—and, I might add, argues well –that all sets are infinite in the sense that they are infinitely decomposable. This is the dimension of inconsistent multiplicity haunting every consistent multiplicity.

What we encounter here is what I call the "strange mereology" of onticology and object-oriented philosophy. Mereology is that branch of mathematics, ontology, and logic that studies the relationship between parts and wholes. The study of mereology is highly complex and formalized, however onticology and object-oriented philosophy are concerned with a particular mereological relation; namely, that relation between objects where one object is simultaneously a part of another object *and* an independent object in its own right. To understand why this mereology is such a strange mereology, we must recall that all objects are independent or autonomous from one another. Objects can enter into exo-relations with one another, but they are not constituted by their relations. Put differently, their being does not consist of their relations. Consequently, the strangeness of this mereology lies in the fact that the subsets of a set, the smaller objects composing larger objects, are simultaneously necessary conditions for that larger object while being independent of that object. Likewise, the larger object composed of these smaller objects is itself independent of these smaller objects.

Despite profound points of overlap between Badiou's mereology and the mereology advocated by onticology and object-oriented philosophy, there are nonetheless important points of divergence between the two ontological frameworks. While both Badiou and onticology and object-oriented philosophy endorse an extensionalism of relations *between* objects, onticology and object-oriented philosophy endorse an *intensionalism* of relations within individual objects. In short, objects are not merely aggregates of other objects, but have an irreducible internal structure of their own. However, it's important to note that the intensionalism advocated by onticology and object-oriented philosophy is not an intensionalism revolving around a predicate shared by a plurality of objects, but is rather an intensionalism pertaining to the relations composing the *internal* relations of *an* object. To avoid confusion, I thus follow Graham Harman's convention of distinguishing between "domestic relations" and "foreign relations". Domestic relations are relations that structure the internal being of an object and correspond to what I have called "endo-relations" in chapter 3. Foreign relations, by contrast, are relations an object enters into with another object and which I have referred to as "exo-relations". Foreign relations are external to objects in the sense that objects are not constituted by exo-relations and can be detached from these relations. Of course, such detachment can also bring about less than happy local manifestations. If I am launched into outer space by a giant catapult without any sort of life-support suit, I will undergo a local manifestation that freezes me solid and kills me. Domestic relations, by contrast, are those relations that constitute the internal being of an object, its internal structure, and therefore the essence of an object.

Where Badiou sees sets or objects as possessing only foreign relations among the elements composing the set—e.g., {x, y, z} is equivalent to {y, x, z}—onticology and object-oriented philosophy insist that objects contain domestic relations such that their elements cannot be related in any old way. I will have more to say about this in the next section, but for the moment it is sufficient to note that Badiou's account of the relationship between inconsistent and consistent multiplicities generates special problems for his ontology. I have already discussed some of these problems in the first chapter when addressing those ontologies that argue that being is composed of chaos or a one-All that is then subsequently carved up into units. A similar problem emerges with respect to Badiou's ontology concerning the question of just how the transition from inconsistent multiplicities without unity or one to consistent multiplicities that are unified such that "one-ification" takes place. To explain this transition from inconsistent multiplicity to consistent multiplicity, Badiou refers to operations of the "count-as-one". These operations somehow effect both a selection and a unification of elements within the field of inconsistent multiplicity, producing consistent multiplicities. Two questions emerge here: first, what is the agency that carries out this operation, and second, exactly how does this agency accomplish this feat of both making selections from the field of inconsistent multiplicity and producing unified collections? Despite the advancements of *Logics of Worlds*, it is my view that the answers to these two questions are significantly underdetermined in Badiou's ontology.

By contrast, object-oriented ontology begins with the premise that the world is composed of distinct entities or units, each of which has its own internal structure or set of endo-relations. The twist is that larger scale objects can emerge from smaller scale objects and larger scale objects are composed of smaller objects. Similarly, larger scale objects can break apart into a plurality of other independent objects under certain circumstances. Thus, while onticology maintains that there are ordering relations, domestic relations, or endo-relations among elements within an object, it also argues that larger scale objects contain *autonomous* smaller scale objects. In this connection, what constitutes the substantiality of a substance is not the *parts* that compose it, but rather the organization, domestic relations, or endo-relations presiding over the organization of these parts.

A variety of examples can be marshaled in defense of this thesis. Organic bodies, for example, continuously lose cells and generate new cells. Although a body cannot exist without its cells, it is clear that bodies cannot be reduced to their cells either. What constitutes the substantiality of a body is not its cells, but its organization or its endo-relations. This point might be readily granted, yet someone might object that while bodies and cells are distinct, it is a mistake to suggest that cells are independent objects in their own right insofar as cells only exist within bodies. However, this is not true. On the one hand, we can think of the various forms of cancer as relations between a body and its cells in which cells have begun to act autonomously. Likewise, organ transplants are dependent on the possibility of cells being separated from bodies. Recently, scientists in Surrey, England have created a monstrous hybrid of organic life and machine, splicing a certain number of rat brain neurons into a computer chip that sends radio messages to a robot that can sense the world and that develops pattern and cognitive skills over time.[246]

Various forms of social relations have this structure as well. The citizens of the United States, for example, are born, die, and sometimes renounce their citizenship, yet the United States continues to exist. While it is certainly true that the United States would not exist at all without any citizens, it cannot be equated with its citizens. Additionally these citizens must be linked in some way. In *Imagined Communities*, for example, Benedict Anderson shows how print culture, among other things, contributed to the formation of national communities.[247] My only caveat here would be that these entities aren't *imagined*, but are, once built, real entities in their own right. Moreover, the United States cannot be equated with a particular geography either. The United States was the United States when it was just thirteen small colonies. Similarly, were some sort of national catastrophe to occur, the United States would remain the United States even if located solely on an island like Hawaii, or, more radically, even if citizens scattered all over the world maintained its existence through the internet. Moreover, the citizens of the United States are not just *elements* of the United States, but are autonomous entities in their own right. They can plot against the United States, seek to bring about the demise of the United States, renounce their citizenship, and engage in many activities not related to how they are counted as citizens of the United States.

From a certain perspective it can thus be said that all objects are a crowd. Every object is populated by other objects that it enlists in maintaining its own existence. As a consequence, we must avoid reducing objects to the manner in which they are enlisted by other objects precisely because the objects enlisted are always themselves autonomous objects. Another way of putting this would be to say that there is no harmony or identity of parts and wholes. Parts aren't parts for a whole and the whole isn't a whole for parts. Rather, what we have are relations of dependency where nonetheless parts and wholes are distinct and autonomous from one another. In this respect, we must reject the thesis of holism. Latour remarks that when one object enlists another "the two join together and become one for a third [object]".[248] While I do not go as far as Latour in claiming that *every* relation between objects generates a third object, the important point is that the object that emerges out of other objects does not *erase* the objects out of which it is composed, but rather generates a third autonomous object related to these other autonomous objects. For example, if we treat romantic relationships and friendships as objects we must ask how many objects are before us. For the sake of simplicity, we can say that the romantic relationship is composed not of *two* objects, but of *three* objects. Here you have the two people involved in the relationship, as well as the amorous relationship itself. The amorous relationship is an object independent of the two persons in the amorous relationship. While initially this sounds very strange, we should here recall how couples talk about their relationships. They talk about being *in* a relationship, about how the relationship is going well or is in a state of crisis. Likewise, friends of couples often treat couples as units, behaving as if one person cannot be invited to dinner without inviting the other. Similarly, from a legal standpoint, a person is married regardless of whether or not she has renounced the marriage or has decided to step out on her spouse. In all of these cases, the relationship is an autonomous object that has an existence over and above the persons that it enlists in its own continuing existence.

The relationship between multiples and sub-multiples or larger scale objects and smaller scale objects is one in which sub-multiples provide constant perturbations to multiples and where multiples perturb sub-multiples. Each object is an operationally closed object that relates to the sub-multiples of which it is composed or the multiples that it composes only in terms of its own internal organization. Sub-multiples and multiples are only "interested" in one another in terms of the perturbations they provide for one another with respect to their own respective autopoietic processes. The United States, for example, only relates to American citizens *qua* citizens, being exclusively concerned with things such as taxes, votes, positions on a variety of issues determining strategies for Congress and administrations, whether or not their action is legal or illegal, and so on. Most of the things that occupy the personal life of individual citizens are completely invisible to an object such as the United States and are treated as mere noise. The United States, for example, is completely oblivious to what I cooked for dinner last night or the fact that I am now sitting on the floor before my computer. Put in terms of Spencer-Brown's theory of distinctions, things like what I had for dinner last night belong to the unmarked state of the distinctions deployed by the United States in defining its channels of openness to its environment. These are events that cannot perturb or "irritate" the United States in its processes of producing information.

These relations between multiples or larger scale objects and sub-multiples are thus relations of what Maturana and Varela refer to as "structural coupling". As they describe this relation, "[w]e speak of structural coupling whenever there is a history of recurrent interactions leading to the structural congruence between two (or more) systems".[249] In short, structural coupling is a relation in which two or more objects constantly perturb or irritate one another, thereby making contributions to the local manifestations of each other and the evolutionary development of one another. The key point here is that while these systems or objects perturb or irritate one another, each system relates to these perturbations according to its own organization or closure such that we can't treat relations between objects as simple input/output relations.

Because objects are operationally closed and are composed of other objects, it follows that tensions or conflicts can emerge between multiples or larger scale objects and sub-multiples or smaller scale objects. As Latour writes, "[n]one of the actants mobilized to secure an alliance stops acting on its own behalf [...]. They each carry on fomenting their own plots, forming their own groups, and serving other masters, wills, and functions".[250] Here it could be said that each object contends with its own system-internal entropy arising from the surprising and dissident role that other objects play within it. In enlisting other objects to produce them, larger scale objects must contend with the tendencies of other objects to move in other directions and act on behalf of other aims. Each object therefore threatens to fall apart from within, to have the endo-relations presiding over its own organization destroyed, and therefore must develop negative feedback mechanisms to maintain its own structural order.

For example, if a class is an object, the professor, an element or sub-multiple of the class, might conduct him- or herself in a way different from his or her prescribed role as professor, teaching nothing at all, talking about unrelated things, relating to students in inappropriate ways, and so on. In these circumstances, some or all of these students or perhaps administrators might relate back to the professor in such a way as to steer him or her back to his role as a professor. Indeed, today one major administrative trend in academia is to formulate ways of gauging the performance of professors by selecting samples of student work as well as student evaluations. At a higher system-specific level, these are ways in which the administrative level increases its capacities to be "irritated" or "perturbed" by classes that are difficult to directly observe on a day to day basis. Based on these ways of constructing openness to an inaccessible environment, administrations devise techniques to steer faculty or introduce negative feedback into the classroom that strive to normalize or codify academic standards and techniques. Meanwhile, many faculty who are called upon to construct educational rubrics for these purposes try to structure them in such a way as to minimize the intervention of administration into their classroom and while appeasing the desire of administrations to have a spread sheet that shows their institution is successfully instructing students. In other words, we get relations of counter-feedback where faculty attempt to steer administrations in such a way as to keep them out of their business. In this instance, we can see the operational closure of two distinct systems, the classroom and administration, that do not so much communicate with one another but rather produce very different information based on perturbations with respect to one another.

Returning to the themes with which I began this section, we can see that the issues of social change are far more complex than is suggested by both structuralist thought and the heirs of structural thought. On the one hand, I believe that Althusser and his heirs tend to over-estimate the role that ideology plays in reproducing the conditions of production. While it is certainly true that "subjects" can internalize ideologies and therefore act to "reproduce the conditions of production", the role that negative feedback plays in larger scale objects such as social systems, coupled with problems arising from operational closure, play at least as great a role if not a greater role in explaining why certain social systems tend to reproduce themselves in such a way that they are resistant to change. Moreover, we cannot blithely reduce subjects to effects of social structure. While social structures, like any other system or object, indeed constitute their own elements, it is also important to recall that they do so from other systems or objects outside the system itself. That is, they draw on systems in their environment as the "matter" out of which they produce their elements. However, these systems are themselves operationally closed, governed by their own distinctions and organization, and thus can never be reduced to mere elements within a higher order system. The result, as social and political theory inflected by Lacanian psychoanalysis has constantly reminded us, is that subjectification is never complete or entirely successful. Nonetheless, within the framework of activist politics, groups, which are themselves objects within larger scale objects such as societies, find themselves beset by negative feedback issuing from these larger scale objects that tend to stand in the way of producing the sort of change for which these groups aim.

Returning to the theme of ideology as only one element among others explaining why social systems take the form they have, we must not forget that individuals or psychic systems exist in regimes of attraction that might severely limit or impede their capacity for action. For example, a subject might very well know that he is getting a raw deal, that the political and social system within which he is enmeshed functions in such a way as to disproportionately benefit the wealthy and powerful, diminishing his wages, quality of life, benefits, and so on. However, such a subject must also eat, especially if he has a family, and must therefore have a job. In order to have a job, such a subject must have a place to live so as to eat, rest and be presentable, must have transportation, very likely requires a phone, etc., etc., etc. As a consequence, such a subject finds himself trapped within a regime of attraction and a form of employment that, while unsavory, is required for his existence. Taking action against such a system might very well amount to cutting off the very branch the person is sitting on to sustain his own existence. In this connection, I suspect that people are far more aware of the manner in which the cards are stacked against them by the broader social system and far less "duped" by ideology than one might initially suspect.

Similar observations can be made with respect to how people are dragging their feet with respect to responding to the growing environmental crisis. Here we are trapped between an awful knowledge that the environment is changing in ways that might very well affect human existence in a radical way and a social structure that is organized in such a way that nearly everything required for mere existence carries a significant carbon footprint. We need some form of transportation to get to work and, absent affordable electric cars or some equivalent, are therefore trapped within a system dependent on fossil fuels. We do not produce our own food and, due to the de-skilling of labor that has arisen as a consequence of the functional differentiation of society, are largely unable to do so on a scale necessary to sustain a family. Thus, we are dependent on food transported by vehicles that run on fossil fuels and that is produced in a way that harms our environment. Likewise, electricity, largely produced by fossil fuels, is now a necessity of life. Meanwhile, the broader social system is structured in such a way that it is very difficult to persuade politicians to change regulatory standards for industries like trucking to invest in alternative energies and so on because such changes would be detrimental to large businesses that both create jobs (which translate into votes) and which line the pockets of politicians through the campaign contributions they require to get re-elected. Closely related to this, we might note that many politicians enter the private sector as lobbyists and consultants after their terms of office, getting paid handsomely for the access they have to other politicians and agencies. Faced with the option of low-paying activist work that improves the world and high-paying consultant and lobbying work that largely benefits big corporations, they tend towards the latter and most likely are thinking about such a future while they're in office.

Finally, questions of political change are constantly beset by issues revolving around resonance between systems. Resonance refers to the capacity of one system to be perturbed or irritated by another system. As we saw in the last chapter, because systems or objects are operationally closed such that they only maintain selective relations to their environment, they can only see what they can see and cannot see what they cannot see. Most importantly, they cannot see that they cannot see this. Niklas Luhmann has argued that modern society is functionally differentiated (legal system, media system, economic system, and so on), such that it contains a variety of different subsystems each organized around its own system/environment distinction within the social system. In addition to these function systems, society is also inhabited by various groups that become objects or systems in their own right, organized around their own system/environment distinctions.

As a consequence of this, one of the major issues facing any collective seeking to produce change within a social system is that of how to produce resonance within the various subsystems in the social system. This issue can be seen with particularly clarity in terms of how the 1999 World Trade Organization (WTO) protests were reported by the media system in the United States. While there was indeed a great deal of reporting on these protests, one curious feature of this reporting in televisual media was that there was very little discussion of just what was being protested and why it was being protested in cable and network news. Rather, viewers were presented with images of massive throngs of people and acts of vandalism protesting the WTO, while being told little in the way of just why these activists were protesting the WTO. The positions and complaints of the protestors were almost entirely absent from media coverage. As a consequence, the manner in which the message resonated within the media system ended up working, in many respects, counter to the aims of the protestors. Within the media system, the protestors were coded or portrayed as anarchistic hooligans with no respect for private property and as "dirty hippies" filled with the enthusiasm of youth and its accompanying immaturity. There was next to no analysis of the protestor's arguments against how the WTO places countries in massive debt, forcing them to privatize various industries and local resources, bringing about massive environmental exploitation and the oppression of indigenous peoples, thereby causing a severe decline in wages and quality of life. Nor was there any discussion of how similar dynamics are occurring in "first tier" countries, causing significant inequalities of wealth and diminishing the ability of average citizens to represent their interests within the political system. In many respects, we can thus say that the manner in which the WTO protests perturbed or irritated the media system and the way in which those perturbations were transformed into information ended up working contrary to and against the very aims of the protestors. Within the psychic systems inhabiting the broader social system and coupled to the media system, it is likely that the protestors resonated as an anarchic threat against which the social system needs to be defended.

Similar points about system resonance or the lack thereof can be made with respect to the notorious response of the United States government to Hurricane Katrina. Everything about the government's delayed response to the events that were unfolding in Louisiana and New Orleans suggests that there was a lack of resonance between the political system and what was unfolding on the ground. Given the detail and pervasiveness of the reporting of these events in television and print media, this is difficult to believe yet, without such a thesis, it is difficult to account for how the Bush administration could have acted in a way so contrary to its own political interests. Here we should recall that the environment of a system or an object is always more complex than the system itself. As a consequence, there is much in a system's environment that a system cannot observe or register. The events following Hurricane Katrina suggest a form of system-closure at the level of government and administration that was structured in such a way that these entities lacked the capacity for resonance with these features of the environment occurring in both New Orleans and Louisiana and the media system. This lack of resonance with the media system is particularly difficult to explain. However, if we recall that within conservative circles the media has been branded as biased by liberal ideology and that the Bush administration had taken many steps to manage the media and control their access to government, it becomes plausible to conclude that the then current administration and Congress had ceased observing the media and instead created an "echo chamber" that severely diminished their openness to the environment.

In the *Critique of Cynical Reason*, Peter Sloterdijk argues that cynicism has become the new form of dominant ideology.[251] Cynicism differs from traditional ideology in that where traditional ideology is a false belief about the world and social relations, cynicism has a true knowledge of social relations, power, exploitation and so on, yet continues to participate in these oppressive forms of social structure as before. As Žižek puts it, "[t]he cynical subject is quite aware of the distance between the ideological mask and the social reality, but he nonetheless still insists upon the mask. The formula, as proposed by Sloterdijk, would then be: 'they know very well what they are doing, but still, they are doing it".[252] From this, Žižek concludes that ideology resides not at the level of what subjects *know*, but of what subjects *do*. In other words, if we are to locate ideology, we ought not look at the level of their beliefs, but at the level of their actions.

In his treatment of society at the level of ideology, Žižek returns social analysis back to the domain of content, meaning, or signification. Recalling figure 4 from the introduction, we can see that Žižek's engagement of the social structure is organized around the culturalist or humanist schema:

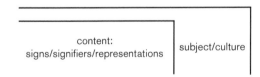

Within the field of this distinction, the subject or culture falls in the marked space of distinction and we get a sub-distinction where all other entities in the world are comprehended or related to as vehicles for signs, signifiers, meanings, discourses, narratives, or representations. To analyze a cultural practice or artifact according to this structure of distinction is thus to focus on its meaning-content in some form or another. Nonhuman objects and entities *qua* nonhuman objects and entities thereby fall into the unmarked space of the distinction.

Putting a finer note on this point, we can say that the culturalist or humanist approach to the world of objects treats any differences objects might contribute as *signifying* or representational differences. By way of analogy, we can say that the culturalist schema of distinction thinks about nonhuman objects in much the same way that we might think about the relation between a movie screen, a projector, and the images that appear on that screen. Objects are reduced to the status of screens and culture or subjects are treated as projectors. The only thing that becomes relevant to the analysis of social formations is thus the images that appear on the screen and how they are cultural or subjective projections. As a consequence, *non-signifying* differences contributed by nonhuman objects or actors are largely excluded from the domain of social analysis. Indeed, within the culturalist framework, objects aren't actors at all but are merely screens for the projection of human meanings and representations.

Within the framework of onticology and object-oriented philosophy, by contrast, we get an entirely different structure of distinction:

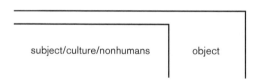

subject/culture/nonhumans   object

Here objects fall into the marked space, such that being is composed of only one sort of thing: objects or substances. While objects or substances, no doubt, differ from one another, being is nonetheless composed entirely of substances. As a consequence of this shift, we now encounter a subdistinction where subjects, culture, *and* nonhumans are placed on *equal* footing. In short, nonhuman actors are no longer treated as an opposing pole necessarily related to culture or human subjects, but rather are treated as autonomous actors in their own right. Thus, while we can and do indeed have relations between humans and nonhuman objects, these relations are no more privileged than relations between nonhuman objects and nonhuman objects. Moreover, insofar as nonhuman objects are themselves actors or agents, they can no longer be treated as passive screens for human and cultural projections.

In light of the foregoing, I hope it is now evident as to just why this redrawing of distinctions is of such crucial importance. Because the culturalist model of distinction places nonhuman actors or objects in the unmarked space of its distinction, regimes of attraction become largely invisible. Likewise, because the culturalist model focuses on content within the marked space of its sub-distinction, questions of resonance between systems or objects become largely invisible. The point is not that we ought not to analyze ideology or content, but that the manner in which we have organized our distinctions renders all sorts of other objects crucial to why society is organized as it is invisible or outside the space of discourse. As a consequence, we deny ourselves all sorts of strategic possibilities for engaging with the social world around us. In this regard, it is not enough merely to debunk the "ideological mystifications" from which we suffer. It is additionally necessary to raise questions and devise strategies for enhancing the resonance of other systems or objects within the social sphere so that change might be produced. Similarly, in his recent "Compositionist Manifesto", Latour proposes the practice of composition as an alternative to critique. Where critique aims at debunking, composition aims at *building*. Where critique focuses on content and modes of representation, composition focuses on regimes of attraction. If regimes of attraction tend to lock people into particular social systems or modes of life, the question of composition would be that of how we might build new collectives that expand the field of possibility and change within the social sphere. Here we cannot focus on discourse alone, but must also focus on the role that nonhuman actors such as resources and technologies play in human collectives. For example, activists might set about trying to create alternative forms of economy that make it possible for people to support families, live, get to work, and so on without being dependent on ecologically destructive forms of transportation, food production, and food distribution. Through the creation of collectives that evade some of the constraints that structure hegemonic regimes of attraction, people might find much more freedom to contest other aspects of the dominant order.

The point here is that the failure for change to occur despite compelling critiques of the dominant social order cannot simply be attributed to ideological mystifications. Social and political thought needs to expand its domain of inquiry, diminish its obsessive focus on content, and increase attention to regimes of attraction and problems of resonance between objects. The social space is far more free and informed than the structuralists and neo-structuralists, in their focus on content, acknowledge and it is more likely that the lack of change arises not from subjects being ideologically duped alone but from the manner in which we are entangled in life. It is not by mistake that often profound social change only occurs when the infrastructure of social systems encounter profound collapse, for in these circumstances psychic systems no longer have anything left to lose and live in the midst of a situation where the regime of attraction in which they once existed has ceased to be operative. Observations such as these teach critical theorists something important, yet the message of these events seems to be received with deaf ears. It is not an accident, for example, that the Russian Revolution took place in the middle of massive economic crisis and World War I. What examples such as these teach us are that content alone is not enough and that political theorists need to enhance their capacity of resonance with respect to nonhuman actors and regimes of attraction.

5.3. Temporalized Structure and Entropy

As we discovered in the last section, every object is threatened from within and without by entropy such that it faces the question of how to perpetuate its existence across time. Entropy refers to the degree of disorder within a system. Suppose you have a tightly closed glass box and somehow introduce a gas into it. During the initial phases following the introduction of the gas into the system, the gas will be characterized by a high degree of order or a low degree of entropy. This is so because the particles of gas will be localized in one or the other region of the box. However, as time passes, the degree of disorder and entropy within the system will increase as the gas becomes evenly distributed throughout the box. In this respect, entropy is a measure of *probability*. If the earlier phases of the gas distribution indicate a lower degree of entropy than the later stages, then this is because in the earlier phases there is a lower degree of probability that the gas will be localized in any one place in the box. As time passes, the probability of finding gas particles located evenly throughout the box increases and we subsequently conclude that the degree of entropy has increased.

In many respects, the real miracle is not that change takes place, but rather that change is not more frequent. This is especially mysterious in the case of higher-order or higher-scale systems or objects such as social systems. How is it that they maintain their endo-consistency or organization across time, such that they don't disintegrate into a high degree of entropy? Put differently, why do such objects not dissolve as objects? In what follows, I focus on Luhmann's analysis of the relationship between structure, complexity, entropy, and time as it pertains to biological, psychic, and social objects. I leave the analysis of structure and entropy as it functions in nonliving objects to others, noting that when suitably modified by an object-oriented framework, the work of DeLanda and Massumi is particularly promising in this connection.

There are a number of reasons that Luhmann's conception of structure is particularly promising. First, the tendency of structuralism was to fall into a sort of structural imperialism arising from a failure to note the manner in which systems distinguish themselves from their environment or are withdrawn. Structure became a sort of net thrown over the entire world without remainder or outside. To be sure, structuralists recognized that something other than structure exists, yet were unable to articulate what this might be because of the manner in which we are always-already situated within structure such that everything we might encounter is overdetermined by structure. This schema posed very difficult questions for structuralist thought with respect to the question of how change takes place. The structuralists recognized that structures are organized synchronically and evolve diachronically, yet were left without the means of accounting for just how this diachronic evolution takes place because their doctrine of internal relations, coupled with their formalism, prevented them from appealing to any outside as a mechanism of change. As a consequence, the development or evolution of structure became thoroughly mysterious.

I take it that I have already shown how, in the first chapter, we can speak of objects independent of us despite the fact that all objects are withdrawn. One major advancement introduced by Luhmann's concept of structure is to mark both the boundary of structure and the conditions under which structures can change or evolve. Closely connected to this is a pluralization of structure with respect to different systems, allowing us to conceptualize a variety of different structures embedded and entangled with one another, yet also operationally closed to one another, such that each one "comprehends" the entirety of the world in terms of its own organization. In this respect, Luhmann is able to account simultaneously for the particularity or finitude of objects and their curious universality. As Luhmann writes in *The Reality of the Mass Media*,

> [a]mong the most important consequences of [...] differentiation is the complementary relationship between *universalism* and *specification*. On the basis of its own differentiation, the system can assume itself, its own function, its own practice as a point of reference for the specification of its own operations. It does and can only do whatever has connective capability internally, according to the structure and historical situation of the system. It is precisely this, however, which also creates the conditions for being able to deal with everything which can be made into a theme for its own communication.[253]

In other words, each object or system is universal in the sense that it is able to comprehend the rest of the world in terms of its own distinctions. Nonetheless, each system is particular precisely because it relates to its environment or the rest of the world in terms of its own specific distinctions.

The rise of structuralist thought marked a growing awareness of this paradoxical simultaneity of universality and specificity. Replacing the universal Kantian transcendental subject, the structuralists recognized the *contingency* and plurality of different structures and how they relate to the environment through their own distinctions. Implicitly they thus recognized the manner in which objects are withdrawn from other objects. At the methodological level, they implicitly practiced second-order observation, observing how observers observe, by observing the manner in which other social systems or objects relate to the world. Yet this line of inquiry, as promising as it was, was itself under-theorized. On the one hand, having made the monumental discovery that there are other objects at a larger scale than human beings or subjects such as social systems, they made the move of treating lower scale objects such as humans as mere effects of structure so as to protect their important discovery and prevent all subjectivist or humanist attempts to ground these larger scale objects in the cognitive and affective capacities of psychic systems. Rather than adopting an ontological mereology of objects at a variety of scales and durations that are all operationally closed and that relate to each other only selectively, they instead attempted to banish these other lower-scale objects altogether. Yet, in making such a move, they swept the ground out from beneath themselves as they could no longer account for how their own discussion of structure was anything other than yet another formation being produced by structure itself.

On the other hand, having recognized system-specific universality in the plurality of structures they had uncovered in the domain of culture and language, they nonetheless tended to fail in properly theorizing the conditions under which they could make these claims. In other words, in their structuralist imperialism of treating structure as a net thrown over the entire world, they undermined the possibility of accounting for how second-order observation of *other* structures might be possible. In part, this problem emerged as a result of failing to properly mark or identify the limits of structure. A similar problem has more recently emerged in the radical constructivism of Maturana's autopoietic theory.

Among his major contributions to our understanding of structure lies Luhmann's treatment of structure in terms of the distinction between system and environment and the temporal problem of how structures reproduce themselves across time. It will be recalled that the environment is always more complex than any structure or environment. There is never a point-for-point correspondence between system and environment.

Were there such a correspondence, system would cease to exist. As a consequence, objects only maintain selective relations to their environment, and this entails that the relations a system maintains to its environment always involve contingency and risk with respect to the ongoing autopoiesis or existence of the object. As Graham Harman puts it, every object caricatures other objects when relating to them. Moreover, objects have an internal complexity such that every element is not related to every other element, but rather elements are only related in specific ways. Not only do the ongoing operations or events that take place within an object risk falling into entropy, but each object is threatened by disintegration from events in its internal and external environment. Structure names the mechanism or organization through which a system or object both makes use of entropy to continue its existence and resists falling into entropy. As Luhmann writes,

> [d]rawing on general systems theory and structuralism, we obtain an initial characteristic of the concept of structure by referring to problems of complexity. Structure transforms unstructured complexity into structured complexity—but how? Unstructured complexity is entropic complexity, which can at time disintegrate into incoherence. The formation of structure *uses this disintegration* and constructs order *out of it*. Out of the disintegration of elements (i.e, the necessary cessation of every action), it draws the energy and information to reproduce elements that therefore always appear within existing structural categories yet still always appear as new. In other words, the concept of structure defines more precisely how elements relate across temporal distance.[254]

The advantage of treating structure in terms of the system/environment distinction is that it allows us to think the manner in which structure is open to the world, thereby providing structure with events from the outside that play a role in how structure evolves or develops. Likewise, by treating structure in terms of entropy and complexity, we can see how structure is related to questions of how an object reproduces itself across time.

It is sometimes contended that structure consists of relations between elements. Luhmann rejects this thesis on the grounds that it is too broad and indeterminate. While it is indeed the case that within any structure elements are related to one another, these relations are of a specific kind. On the one hand, while it is the case that one and the same structure can be embodied in a variety of elements, it doesn't follow from this that a structure can be embodied in *any* element. This feature of multiple realizability is crucial to understanding structure and objects, for it is almost always the case that the elements that realize a structure are destroyed or pass away, while the structure remains and persists. For example, citizens are born and die in the United States, and offices are occupied by a variety of different politicians. It is thus not the parts that make an entity an entity precisely because these parts can change. However, it would be a mistake to conclude from this that structures can exist without their elements. Objects can be destroyed through their parts insofar as a point is reached where the endo-structure of an object can no longer embody or sustain itself. It is precisely because the elements that realize structure pass away that systems or objects face the question of how to perpetuate themselves across time. In the case of autopoietic objects, the object faces the question of how to produce new events or elements to maintain itself across time.

In short, each system or object must *reproduce* itself across time. In the absence of a reproduction of elements and therefore of relations, the object dissolves or falls apart. In this respect, we can see just how dynamic objects are. Objects are not brute clods that simply sit there unchanging until provoked, but perpetually reproduce themselves in the order of time. This structure of reproduction can be represented in terms of Bergson's diagram of attention and memory as presented in *Matter and Memory*.[255]

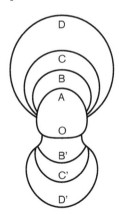

Bergson uses this diagram to outline the role of memory in the process of perception, yet it works equally well for thinking the reproduction of objects across time. In Bergson's schema, each moment of perception is overlaid by a memory image trailing off into the remote past. Bergson describes this as a "circuit" of perception and memory, where the two come to be ever more deeply intertwined. In the case of perception, the result is that each perception becomes increasingly overlaid by memory. Bergson's circuit of perception and memory is particularly illustrative of the dynamics of autopoietic objects in the order of time. ABCD refers to the subsequent reproduction of the object in the course of unfolding in time or in moving towards the future. By contrast, A'B'C'D' refers to the memory produced by the autopoietic object that can, in its turn, be reactualized in the present in a variety of ways. The object uses each prior phase, as well as stimulations from its environment, to reproduce itself across time. Similarly, in autopoietic objects, memory can be used to actualize new states in the present. As a consequence, objects are temporally elongated, tracing a path throughout time through their acts.

Why, then, if objects must reproduce themselves from moment to moment, do I not follow Whitehead in arguing that being, at its most basic level, is composed of "actual occasions" and that objects are but "societies of actual occasions"? Whitehead's actual occasions are instantaneous events that cease to exist the very moment that they come into existence. They are the true atoms of being, with the important caveat that these atoms are not enduring entities, like Lucretius's atoms, but events that flicker in and out of existence like the flickering of fireflies. As a consequence, from a Whiteheadian perspective, objects are a sort of illusion in the sense that they are not the true units of beings, but are rather multiple-compositions or societies of actual occasions that are continually coming into existence and passing out of existence. In this respect, Bergson's circuit of the object, coupled with Luhmann's thesis that objects must perpetually reproduce themselves in the order of time, would seem to be a mirror image of Whitehead's metaphysical thesis.

However, to treat actual occasions or instantaneous time-slices as the atoms or true units of being is to confuse the being of objects with their parts. An object is not its parts, elements, or the events that take place within it—though all of these are indeed indispensable—but is rather an *organization* or structure that persists across time. This brings us to Luhmann's second reason as to why structure cannot be identified with relations among elements *simpliciter*. As Luhmann remarks,

> relations acquire structural value only because the relations realized at any given time present a *selection from a plurality of combinatory possibilities* and thus introduce both the advantages and the risks of a selective reduction. And only *this selection* can be held constant across change in elements, that is, can be reproduced with new elements.[256]

From this Luhmann concludes that "structure, whatever else it may be, consists in *how permissible relations are constrained within the system*".[257] What Whitehead's account of objects as societies of actual occasions misses is that this organization, this constraint on permissible relations among elements, is not itself of the order of an actual occasion but is rather that which persists or endures across the existence of actual occasions. To be sure, these structures exist only in and through actual occasions, but this does not change the fact that these structures are irreducible to actual occasions for, without structure, there could be no regulation of how events are constrained and produced in the ongoing existence of the object.

A system in which all elements related to one another would be a system characterized by absolute entropy and would thus be no system at all because it would be unable to distinguish itself from its environment. There are thus three problems that beset each system and to which structure responds. First, there is the question of how events are to be constrained and selected within a system. For example, were all possible memories, thoughts, and imaginings to suddenly flood the mind, the mind would immediately collapse into absolute entropy, falling into an autistic jumble preventing any action or attention. Within a psychic system, there must be selectivity as to what events take place within the psychic system and how these events are linked to one another.

Second, and similarly, there must be selectivity or constraint with respect to the events that a system is open to from the world or its environment. Take the example of an object like a conversation at a cafe.

If such a conversation is to be possible, its relationship to its environment must be highly constrained, remaining open only to certain events within the coffee shop. Of course, this openness to the environment can shift with changing events within the system such that the system becomes open to events that it was previously closed to, but the point is that at any point in time the system only maintains selective relations to its environment. Within the cafe, all sorts of conversations are taking place, people are bustling about, waiters and waitresses are serving various customers, cappuccino machines are hissing their songs, music is playing, people are walking back and forth on the sidewalk, and cars are honking and screeching outside. Were the conversation as a system or object to share a one-to-one correspondence to all these events in the environment, the conversation would be impossible and would again fall into a maximum state of entropy. As a consequence, the conversation can only be selectively open to events in its environment, constituting itself as an object or system through a system/environment distinction that both constitutes the conversation as an object distinct from its environment and that institutes selective relations to the environment, allowing certain events occurring within the environment to perturb the system constituted by the conversation. Two young women heatedly discussing Sartre's *Being and Nothingness* and whether he stole his ideas from Simone de Beauvoir pause suddenly when an impending blizzard is announced over the radio. This event functions like a switch. Suddenly the conversation changes direction and the women begin discussing whether they should leave to beat the weather, only to turn back to Sartre's discussions of facticity and how they constrain choice. This event perturbs the conversation in a particular way, leading it to drift in another direction, yet what is more remarkable is all the other events in the environment that fall into the unmarked space of the distinctions regulating the conversation's relationship to its environment, becoming all but invisible. Only certain events from the environment are capable of influencing the local manifestations the conversation takes.

Finally, each system faces the question of how to produce subsequent events so as to continue its existence across time. Luhmann remarks that "one must radically relate the concept of event [...] to what is momentary and immediately passes away".[258] Because events are momentary and fleeting, and because structure can only exist so long as it is embodied in elements, each system or object faces the question of how to pass from one event to another so as to perpetuate its existence. As Luhmann observes, "we will constrain the concept of structure in another way: not as a special type of stability but by its function of enabling the autopoietic reproduction of the system from one event to the next".[259] In the space of a conversation, it is necessary to find something else to say if the conversation is to continue. The production of events can take place either through the internal domain of the system itself, as in those instances where one utterance in a conversation leads to another utterance or one secretion of a cell initiates processes in another cell in a body, or through perturbations coming from the environment.

Because objects face the question of how to get from one moment to the next, they are condemned to change and their identity is a dynamic identity that perpetually reproduces itself across time. As Luhmann argues,

> the event, if one may say so, suffers the consequences of the fact that no object can change its relationship to the course of time. To endure, objects must change in time. Events prefer to pass away. On the other hand, every event brings about a total change in past, present, and future—simply because it gives up the quality of being present to the next event and becomes past for it (i.e., for its future). This minimal displacement can change the perspective of relevance that structures and bounds the horizon of past and future. In this sense, every event brings about a total modification of time.[260]

In the case of autopoietic objects such as organisms, tornadoes, social systems, psychic systems, and conversations, events taking place in the present modify the substance's relationship to the past as well as the future. This is especially the case with respect to the role played by events that issue from the environment. Upon reading a book once, rereading the book produces a different impression of the book as a result of both how the first reading reconfigured my prior thoughts about the world and other texts and as a result of how the opening pages of the book now resonate differently as a result of my anticipation of what is coming. As a consequence, objects develop and evolve.

Information plays a particularly important role in the development and evolution of structures. Because structures operate within the framework of system/environment distinctions, they are selectively open to their environment and can therefore evolve and develop as a result of that openness to their environment. Objects constrain the sort of events to which they're open from their environment through their distinctions or organization. In the case of autopoietic objects, this entails that structures are anticipatory of what the future will bring. When events issue from the environment, information-events are produced selecting system-states within the system. This leads to the production of further events within the system, unfolding within a particular order and structured in a particular way. This can have the effect of reinforcing and intensifying certain developmental vectors within the object.

However, because structures are anticipatory, they can also undergo *disappointment* when events anticipated from the environment fail to materialize. However, it would be a mistake to conclude that the disappointment of an anticipation entails the absence of information. As we have seen, in more "advanced" objects, the absence of an event can itself function as information. In Sartre's famous example in *Being and Nothingness*, he walks into a cafe and discovers that his friend Pierre is not there.[261] Far from being an absence of information, the non-event of Pierre's appearance creates an event, information, that selects subsequent system-states. Depending on the magnitude of the disappointment, such information events can have the effect of propelling systems capable of self-reflexivity to revise their distinctions, modifying their system structure and developing new forms of openness to the world while foreclosing other forms of openness. Similarly, in the case of autopoietic objects or systems not capable of self-reflexivity, such disappointments can play a key role in natural selection, leading to the death of certain substances reliant on particular forms of perturbation to continue their existence and paving the way for other organisms to more effectively reproduce themselves. This can occur when massive environmental changes take place. Indeed, certain organisms unwittingly produce their own demise as in the case of pre-historic microorganisms that required carbon dioxide to continue their autopoiesis or self-reproduction and that produced oxygen as a bi-product of this process. One result of this process was that they eventually saturated their environment with oxygen, contributing to the construction of new niches in which other organisms could emerge and undermining the niche upon which they relied for their continued existence.

From the foregoing, we can thus see why selection, constraint, distinction, and organization involve risk at the level of structure. Structure is contingent in the sense that both the manner in which elements are related and the openness to events within the environment could always be otherwise. Insofar as structure is a strategy for staving off entropy so as to reproduce system-organization across time, the contingency of selection and constraint carries with it the risk of dissolution in those instances where the selections opening the object to the environment anticipate perturbations or irritations that fail to reliably appear. In these instances, we encounter less than fortunate local manifestations or death. Here death can take one of two forms. On the one hand, death can take the form of a substance continuing to exist but becoming incapable of producing certain local manifestations such as movement, affect, and cognition. On the other hand, death can take the form of absolute death, where entropy completely sets in and the substance is utterly destroyed such that it is no longer able to enlist other objects in maintaining its own organization and the other objects of which the entity was once composed now go their separate ways autonomously, enjoying their existence elsewhere. The first death generally leads to the second eventually.

The risk of selectivity and constraint can be seen with particular clarity with respect to the issue of climate change. At present, the world's various social systems and subsystems lack sufficient capacities for resonance to register the importance of changes taking place in the climate. To be sure, much of the world's various social systems are aware that climate change is taking place and that this will potentially have a massive impact on whether or not these social systems are able to sustain themselves. However, despite this knowledge, we don't see social systems making the sorts of changes necessary to avoid this destruction. Why is this? A good deal of the problem has to do with the nature of resonance between various subsystems within the social system and between the various social systems and psychic systems. We can only learn of climate change through the scientific system and the media system because the changes produced by climate change are so diffuse and spread out that they can only be observed through very specific techniques. At the level of the other social systems and psychic systems, this generates doubt in the science system as the environments of these other social systems and psychic systems do not register any significant differences. Like two shades of red that are extremely close to one another, we see the climate as largely unchanged. The media system, in its turn, creates constant noise around the issue, endlessly parading experts before the viewing audience that claim that there is a lot of dispute surrounding whether or not anthropogenic climate change is taking place and who suggest it is based on junk science. Insofar as the media system is selectively open to its environment in terms of *controversy* so as to maximize its possibility of new reporting on a daily basis, it generates the impression in psychic systems that there is broad disagreement regarding these issues when, in fact, it is a minority of scientists, often funded by energy companies, who hold such views.

The more significant problem emerges with respect to resonance between the science system, the political system, and the economic system. The code according to which the economic system functions is the profit/ no-profit code. In other words, the economic system encounters its environment in terms of whether or not it is capable of producing profit. As a consequence, the economic system is largely blind to the science system unless the findings of the science system create the opportunity for producing profit. Initially, it seems as if progress is being made in this regard as many businesses are adopting a "green orientation" that advertises an ecologically friendly orientation. However, the lion's share of our ecological problems issues not from whether we're using energy efficient light bulbs, but from farming practices (it's a dirty secret that livestock methane contributes more to climate change than the use of fossil fuels), industry, shipping, and the sort of energy we use. The sorts of changes required in these areas immediately fall into the "no-profit" side of the codes deployed by the economic system.

The political system, in its turn, finds itself entangled with the regimes of attraction governing the lives of psychic systems as well as the economic system. The code according to which the political system functions is that of power/no-power. In concrete terms, this code revolves around questions and issues of re-election. Many of the changes required to mitigate the effects of climate change would prove to be a significant hardship on lives of citizens, as it would require major changes in the regimes of attraction upon which they rely for their existence. This is especially the case in countries with developing economies where many are just trying to find a way to feed their families from day to day. While many might be abstractly supportive of taking action to mitigate the coming climate crisis, when concrete proposals are made, many of the suggested changes are deeply unpopular because these things would significantly impact how people live their lives (imagine how Americans would respond to being told to cut down on their meat consumption!) and might lead to the loss of jobs. This, in turn, translates into whether or not politicians get votes and get re-elected. As a consequence, it is likely that a Faustian bargain is made where the politician who is ecologically aware tells himself that at least he is making incremental change.

Nonetheless, it seems that a lot could be done by more heavily regulating the shipping industry, encouraging the trucking industry, for example, to switch over to alternative fuels, giving large tax breaks to families and individuals that drive hybrid cars, use solar panels, increase their energy efficiency, making the use of school buses and trains a patriotic action for high school students, and providing government subsidies to developing countries that provide and develop environmentally friendly industries for their citizens, and so on. However, here the political system encounters another entanglement with industry and business that makes such actions less than appealing from a political perspective. These changes all imply major economic hardship for a variety of businesses and industries that make massive amounts of money from their practices. In the United States at least, the 2010 Supreme Court decision in *Citizens United v. Federal Election Commission* opened the gates for corporations to use unlimited funds for political purposes. This entails that every U.S. politician must now think twice before proposing policy changes as they now face massive advertising campaigns—always conducted behind "front groups" implying that they're the work of average Americans and grass root activists—targeting the possibility of the politician's re-election.

The point of this rather pessimistic analysis of resonance within social systems with respect to issues of climate change is to underline the manner in which the constraints and selections governing openness to the environment always involve risk. Within our current social system, the distinctions governing resonance between the various social subsystems, psychic systems, and the broader environment have generated a quagmire that renders responsiveness to climate change very difficult. The forms of resonance that do exist, in their turn, create the very real possibility that these social systems will themselves collapse as a result of changes in their environments that abolish sources of perturbation upon which they depend. As climate change and population growth intensifies, it is very likely that there will be famines as a result of changes in the climate that destroy farming and water resources. This will generate a variety of social crises that will reverberate throughout all the different social subsystems.

The question of how certain forms of system resonance can be diminished and how other forms of resonance can be enhanced thereby becomes a key question for activists concerned with issues of climate change. In his book, *Collapse*, Jared Diamond notes that one reason Dutch citizens, politicians, and businesses seem to be more eco-friendly is not because they are more enlightened, but because much of their landmass is below sea-level, rendering climate change in the form of rising sea levels a potential threat to the majority of the population.[262] Likewise, Diamond notes how foreign logging companies depleted the rain forests of the Malay Penninsula, Borneo, the Solomon Islands, Sumatra, and the Philippines by logging these lands as quickly as possible once they were leased to them by the local countries and then declaring bankruptcy rather than replanting as it was more beneficial financially to do so. The citizens of these areas were then left to endure the ecological consequences of these practices, losing their own sources of food and industry.[263] One lesson of these contrasting examples seems to be that resonance is enhanced when a system or object has a direct stake in the long-term preservation of elements of the local environment or climate. Yet how such a suture to local climate is to be produced in various industries is a very difficult question.

Returning to some themes from the last section pertaining to mereology, we can also discern that a number of objects have some very peculiar properties with respect to space and time. It is fairly common to argue that objects are individuated by occupying a particular position in space and at a particular time. This, for example, was Locke's position. However, if it is true that it is the organization or structure, not the parts, that determine whether or not something is an object, it follows that objects can be discontinuous across time and can be vastly spread out across space. A conversation, for example, can cease and be resumed at a later point. Here the conversation falls out of existence for a time, it ceases to manifest itself locally, and comes back into existence at a later point in time. A variety of objects have this strange sort of temporal structure. An Alcoholics Anonymous group, for example, might only meet once or twice a week, thereby flickering in and out of existence. A number of groups and institutions only meet intermittently.

Not only do we encounter this strange temporality where objects can flit in and out of existence while remaining the same object, but there are also a variety of different temporal scales characteristic of different objects that are oddly simultaneous with one another yet working at very different temporal levels. It takes the sun, for example, 225 million years to make one rotation around the Milky Way. The Milky Way is one object, characterized by its own temporal duration, whereas the solar system is yet another object. Here we encounter one temporal duration embedded in another temporal duration, with very different cycles unfolding in each object. Similarly, societies, climates, and ecosystems each have their own heterogeneous durations, moving at different rates and characterized by their own unique organizations. In this regard, there's a very real sense in which duration is always system-specific such that each object is characterized by its own duration and relates to other durations in terms of its own. Different social groups, for example, exist in their own "plane of history", as can be observed with the old university professor who hasn't kept up with his reading and continues to fight philosophical wars that are decades past, or the Amish who live in a very different temporal frame both with respect to the structuration of their daily life and their relation to the broader social system in which they're embedded. The temporal rhythms of an organism are different from those of a population of organisms, and these, in their turn, are different from the temporal rhythms of an entire ecosystem. Between all these different temporalities are different forms of resonance, as well as different possibilities of conflict.

Similar features characterize the mereology of objects in space. Blog discussions involve participants located all over the world, integrating internet servers, various blogs, and participants so as to produce an evolving and developing object of its own. Increasingly a number of people work from home, yet various businesses still exist as entities in their own right. More recently, there's been a trend towards university courses being offered online, allowing students to enroll in courses at a specific university or college from all over the country and world. Indeed, a friend of mine makes his living teaching online courses "in" the United States from Israel. Currently, there are massive radio telescope arrays that span entire continents, drawing on many smaller radio telescopes to plumb the depths of outer space and using thousands of home computers volunteered by average citizens to increase their ability to compute the huge amounts of data they receive. And, were this not astonishing enough, the observations of these entities are not observations of entities existing in the present, but in the remote past!

At the level of object-oriented and onticological mereology, we cannot work from the premise that location in time and space is sufficient to individuate an object, nor that objects exist only at a particular scale such as the mid-range objects that tend to populate the world of our daily existence. Rather, entities exist at a range of different scales, from the unimaginably small to the unimaginably large, each characterized by their own duration and spatiality. Here a tremendous amount of work remains to be done in thinking these spatial and temporal structures. In my view, onticology and object-oriented philosophy have opened a vast and rich domain for thinking these strange structures of space and time. What is important, however, is the recognition that the substantiality of objects lies not in their parts, but in their structure or organization, and that objects are not brute clods that merely sit there, contemplating their self-perfection like Aristotle's

Unmoved Mover, but that they are dynamic and evolving as a consequence of their own internal dynamics and interfaces with their environment.

Chapter 6
The Four Theses of Flat Ontology

The rock was one of those tremendously solid brown,
or rather black, rocks which emerge from the sand like
something primitive. Rough with crinkled limpet shells and
sparsely strewn with locks of dry seaweed, a small boy has
to stretch his legs far apart, and indeed to feel rather heroic,
before he gets to the top. But there, on the very top, is a
hollow full of water, with a sandy bottom; with a blob of jelly
stuck to the side, and some mussels. A fish darts across. The
fringe of yellow-brown seaweed flutters, and out pushes an
opal-shelled crab— "Oh, a huge crab", Jacob murmured—

— Virginia Woolf[264]

6.1. Two Ontological Discourses:
Lacan's Graphs of Sexuation and Two Ways
of Thinking Being

Onticology proposes what might be called, drawing on DeLanda's term
yet broadening it, a flat ontology. Flat ontology is a complex philosophical
concept that bundles together a variety of ontological theses under a
single term. First, due to the split characteristic of all objects, flat ontology
rejects any ontology of transcendence or presence that privileges one
sort of entity as the origin of all others and as fully present to itself. In

this regard, onticology proposes an ontology resonant with Derrida's critique of metaphysics insofar as, in its treatment of beings as withdrawn, it undermines any pretensions to presence within being. If this thesis is persuasive, then metaphysics can no longer function as a synonym for "metaphysics of presence", nor substance as a synonym for "presence", but rather an ontology has been formulated that overcomes the primacy of presence. In this section, I articulate this logic in terms of Lacan's graphs of sexuation. Here I believe that those graphs have little to tell us about masculine or feminine sexuality—for reasons I will outline in what follows—but a great deal to tell us about ontologies of immanence or flat ontologies and ontologies of transcendence. Second, flat ontology signifies that *the* world or *the* universe does not exist. I will develop the argument for this strange claim in what follows, but for the moment it is important to recognize the definite article in this claim. The claim that the world doesn't exist is the claim that there is no super-object that gathers all other objects together in a single, harmonious unity. Third, following Harman, flat ontology refuses to privilege the subject-object, human-world relation as either a) a form of metaphysical relation different in *kind* from other relations between objects, and that b) refuses to treat the subject-object relation as implicitly included in every form of object-object relation. To be sure, flat ontology readily recognizes that humans have unique powers and capacities and that how humans relate to the world is a topic more than worthy of investigation, yet nothing about this establishes that humans must be included in every inter-object relation or that how humans relate to objects differs in kind from how other entities relate to objects. Finally, fourth, flat ontology argues that all entities are on equal ontological footing and that no entity, whether artificial or natural, symbolic or physical, possesses greater ontological dignity than other objects. While indeed some objects might influence the collectives to which they belong to a greater extent than others, it doesn't follow from this that these objects are more *real* than others. Existence, being, is a binary such that something either is or is not.

Apart from the fact that I believe these propositions to be ontologically true, the broader strategic import of the concept of flat ontology is to diminish the obsessive focus on the human, subjective and the cultural within social, political, cultural theory and philosophy. In particular, my ambition is to diminish an almost exclusive focus on propositions, representations, norms, signs, narratives, discourses, and so on, so as to cultivate a greater appreciation for nonhuman actors such as animate and inanimate natural entities, technologies, and such. To be clear, in seeking to diminish a focus on these sorts of actors, my aim is not to *exclude* these sorts of actors. Rather, I seek both to synthesize divergent trends within contemporary Continental social, political, cultural, and philosophical thought and broaden the field of inquiry available to these discourses and debates. Within the framework of contemporary Continental thought, it would not be too far off the mark to say that there are *two* highly different cultures. Within the one culture, we have a focus on lived experience, text, discourse, signifiers, signs, representation, and meaning. This is a form of inquiry dominated by figures such as the various phenomenologists, Derrida, Lacan, Žižek, and Foucault, for example. Here there is very little in the way of a discussion of the role played by nonhuman actors in collectives involving human beings. Rather, nonhuman entities are treated as screens upon which humans project their intentions, meanings, signs, and discourses, rather than as genuine actors in their own right. They are instead passive matter awaiting formatting by humans. This is not entirely fair to the theorists of this culture, as Foucault devotes a great deal of attention to institutions, architecture, and practices, while Derrida recognizes the importance of simple agencies like writing in the most literal sense and digital encoding, yet nonetheless, these are dominant tendencies within this culture or orientation of theory.

By contrast, the other culture ranges widely over nonhuman actors or objects and pays careful attention to the differences contributed by nonhuman agencies such as technologies, animals, environments, and so on. Here we might think of monumental intellects such as Donna Haraway and Katherine Hayles, the work of McLuhan, Kittler, Ong, and Stiegler, the later work of Deleuze and Guattari, the thought of Latour and Stengers, engagements with technology such as that found in Ian Bogost's work, pathbreaking work such as that found in Protevi, DeLanda, and Massumi, ecologists like Timothy Morton, Marx's meditations on how the money-form, technologies, and factories change our very identities, critical animal theorists such as Cary Wolfe, and a host of other thinkers. Within this culture, we find two important trends. On the one hand, there is a tendency to decentralize the human by describing the impact of the nonhuman in the form of technology and other inhuman agencies on collectives involving humans and how these agencies cannot be reduced to human intentions, signs, meanings, norms, signifiers, discourses, and so on.

On the other hand, there is, in this culture, a speculative tendency, deserving of the title of "Spinozism", that ranges freely over the "experience" of nonhuman entities, plumbing the worlds of other entities without being obliged to relate everything back to the human. Graham Harman's universe is a universe populated by circuses and clowns, vampires, unnamed monsters, fire and cotton, and a host of other frightening and delightful carnivalesque entities that erupt across his pages like so many apparitions that simultaneously withdraw and capture us with their inherent fascination and allure. Jane Bennett's universe is inhabited by the vital forces of abandoned bottle caps, dead rats, trash heaps undergoing various forms of bio-chemical decomposition, and a host of other objects. Ian Bogost is currently writing his *Alien Phenomenology*, which promises to bring us into the subterranean experience of all sorts of other entities such as computer software we scarcely notice in our day to day existence. Donna Haraway's universe is pervaded with wolves, microbes, lab reports and articles, various types of primates, plants, and all sorts of laboratory equipment. Karen Barad's universe is populated by all sorts of particles, instruments and waves.

What I aim for with the concept of flat ontology is a synthesis of these two cultures. I desire an ontology capable of doing justice to these strange nonhuman actors, capable of respecting these strange strangers on their own terms, and an ontology capable of doing justice to the phenomenological and the semiotic. Moreover, I believe that such a project is absolutely vital to the future of contemporary thought. The first of these two cultures is regnant in the contemporary world of theory. The aim of diminishing the primacy of the human is not nihilistic nor designed to exclude the human, but is premised on the thesis that, so long as the first culture maintains center stage, we are thoroughly unable to properly comprehend *human* collectives nor theorize strategic ways of transforming them. In this connection, flat ontology makes two key claims. First, humans are not at the center of being, but are *among* beings. Second, objects are not a pole opposing a subject, but exist in their own right, regardless of whether any other object or human relates to them. Humans, far from constituting a category called "subject" that is opposed to "object", are themselves one *type* of object among many.

The difference between philosophies of transcendence and philosophies of immanence such as those advocated by the flat ontology of onticology can be thematized in terms of Lacan's graphs of sexuation. Here my aim is to argue that onticology and its conception of objects aligns itself with the feminine side of Lacan's graph of sexuation. Before proceeding to outline this congruence and the difference between ontological discourses organized around withdrawal and ontological discourses organized around presence (the masculine side of Lacan's graphs of sexuation), it is first necessary to make some qualifications. Within the history of philosophy, there has been a long history of associating women with nature, being, and passivity coupled with an objectification of women that denies them agency as subjects in their own right. Onticology certainly does not wish to align itself with these unfortunate tendencies, yet doesn't it risk doing precisely this in arguing that the true discourse of being falls on the side of the feminine side of Lacan's graphs of sexuation? Moreover, doesn't it fall into an even worse plight in treating being as composed of objects?

There are a few points worth making in response to this entirely justified concern. First, and above all, it is necessary to recognize that it is difficult to see what, if anything, Lacan's graphs of sexuation have to do with sex or gender. As Bruce Fink articulates this point,

> [i]t should be recalled that sexuation is not biological sex:
> What Lacan calls masculine structure and feminine structure
> have to do not with one's biological organs but rather with
> the kind of *jouissance* one is able to obtain. There is not,
> to the best of my knowledge, any easy overlap between
> sexuation and "sexual identity", or between sexuation and
> what is sometimes referred to as "sexual orientation". [...].
> When I refer to men in the ensuing discussion, I mean those
> people who, regardless of biological sex, fall under certain

> formulas—what Lacan calls "the formulas of sexuation" –
> [...] and when I refer to women I mean those people who,
> regardless of their biological sex, fall under the [feminine
> side] of the formulas.[265]

Having spent more time than I care to admit with the Lacanian secondary literature and the seminars in which he develops his account of sexuation, I believe that Bruce Fink is essentially correct in this judgment. While Lacan does indeed articulate two different structures of the deadlocks that beset desire and *jouissance*, it is not at all clear why these two structures should be called "masculine" and "feminine". In my view, Lacan fails to establish any direct link between these structures and sex and gender. For example, any subject, whether biologically male or female—assuming, questionably, that we can even speak univocally of subjects being biologically male or female—can occupy either side of Lacan's graphs of sexuation. Put differently, biologically "male" subjects can enjoy or fail to enjoy as feminine subjects and biologically "female" subjects can enjoy or fail to enjoy as masculine subjects.

The strongest argument in favor of associating the graphs of sexuation with the masculine and the feminine arises from the fact that the masculine side of the graph of sexuation can be read as a highly abstract and formalized version of the structure of Freud's patriarchal Oedipus Complex and myth of the Primal Father in *Totem and Taboo*. If the Oedipus Complex and the myth of the Primal Father are understood to be intrinsically patriarchal and phallocentric structures, then there is some reason to associate the masculine side of the graph of sexuation with forms of *jouissance* and desire related to masculinity. However, here again we encounter the question of why the feminine side of the graph of sexuation should be associated with women. We could just as easily refer to the two sides of the graphs of sexuation as outlining logics of immanence (the feminine) and logics of transcendence (the masculine), or logics of the "not-all" (the feminine) and logics of exception (the masculine).

A second point to be made is that in arguing that the objects of onticology and object-oriented philosophy fall on the feminine side of the graphs of sexuation, it is imperative to recall that, within the framework of onticology, objects are neither passive nor a pole opposed to the subject.

Within the framework of object-oriented ontology, there are not two domains of being, one belonging to the domain of the subject, the other belonging to the domain of the object, but rather just one type of being: objects. On the one hand, we can thus say that subjects are not a pole opposed to objects, but are themselves a type of object. They are objects among other objects. To be sure, what we refer to as subjects have special powers and capacities, but they are nonetheless a sort of object in the world. On the other hand, far from being passive clods awaiting formatting from humans and getting worked over by humans, objects, as theorized by onticology, are themselves, following Latour, actors or actants that are themselves agents. In this regard, treating objects as falling on the feminine side of the graphs of sexuation in no way suggests that women are passive objects. To the contrary, the feminine side of the graph of sexuation turns out to be the side of agency.

With these caveats in mind, I now turn to Lacan's graphs of sexuation. I will first discuss the graphs of sexuation within the framework of Lacanian theory and then reformulate them in ontological terms. Lacan's graphs of sexuation attempt to symbolize or display certain deadlocks that occur whenever we attempt to totalize the symbolic order or the world. Lacan argues that whenever we attempt to totalize the world, certain deadlocks emerge preventing such totalities from being successfully accomplished. Because of the absence and metonymy introduced into the world of the subject by language, Lacan contends that each potential object of *jouissance* contains a remainder of absence or lack that prevents it from conferring complete enjoyment. Complete enjoyment would require the totalization or completion of the symbolic, yet such totalizations always fail. Moreover, there is not merely one way in which we attempt to totalize the world and for this totalization to fail, but rather two ways. These two ways of failing are what Lacan refers to as the "masculine" and the "feminine". These two forms of failure, in their turn, generate two very different structures of desire and *jouissance*. Put differently, depending on how the subject is structured as either a "masculine" or a "feminine" subject, different forms of *jouissance* will be available to the subject. The term "*jouissance*" is highly polysemous within Lacanian theory, however within the framework of the graphs of sexuation we can treat *jouissance* as the sort of enjoyment open to a subject. Put more precisely, the two graphs explain why our *jouissance* comes up *short* or lacking as a result of our being enmeshed within the symbolic order. As Bruce Fink remarks, "[w]e find the pleasures available to us in life inadequate, and it is owing to that inadequacy that we expound systems of knowledge—perhaps, first and foremost, to explain why our pleasure is inadequate and then to propose how to change things so that it will not be".[266]

Within the Lacanian framework, this deficit of *jouissance* is not accidental but rather *structural*. In other words, our deficit of *jouissance* arises not from an accidental lack such that if we could only find the appropriate object we would experience complete enjoyment, but rather is a structural feature of how we are enmeshed in language or the symbolic order. These structural impossibilities of complete *jouissance*, in their turn, generate fantasies to account for both why *jouissance* is lacking and how this lack might be surmounted. For example, racists are often particularly attentive to the *imagined jouissance* of other groups, believing these groups to both possess a greater *jouissance* than themselves, and believing that the other group has perhaps stolen their *jouissance* from them. The racist might endlessly talk about how the other group is lazy, how they get free rides from the government, how they are promiscuous, how they lack moral values, and so on. Based on such fantasies, the racist might imagine all sorts of ways to take action against these other groups so as to get back their stolen *jouissance*. It's not difficult to discern such mechanisms at work in misogyny and homophobia as well. The tragedy of this sort of *jouissance* is two-fold. On the one hand, these dark fantasies lead to the persecution of other people and groups based on an imagined *jouissance* that one believes these other groups have stolen. The pursuit of *jouissance* purported to be lost and stolen thus riddles the social field with conflict. On the other hand, the belief that total *jouissance* exists, that it is possible to attain complete *jouissance*, makes it all the more difficult to enjoy the *jouissance* that is available because it always falls short of imagined *jouissance*. As a consequence, the subject suffers from fantasies of total *jouissance* that transform life into cold ashes. Filled with envy at the *jouissance* one believes to be enjoyed by other groups, and crushed by bitterness at the absence of *jouissance* in one's own life, the subject becomes unable to enjoy anything.

To illustrate the structural deadlocks that arise when we attempt to totalize the symbolic order, Lacan resorts to the resources of symbolic logic:[267]

The upper portions of the graph filled with equations refers to the structural deadlocks that inhabit the symbolic. The left side is the masculine side, whereas the right side is the feminine side. These refer to logics of exception and the "not-all" respectively. The symbols that appear in the lower portion of the graph refer to the sorts of *jouissance* available to subjects depending on whether they fall under the left or right-hand side of the graph. Within symbolic logic, "∃" is what is known as an "existential quantifier". Existential quantifiers refer to partial collections such as "some", "many", "one" and so on. Thus, for example, the proposition "some cats are black" would be written in symbolic logic as follows: $\exists x Cx$ & Bx. Translated back into ordinary language, this would read, "there exists at least one entity such that this entity is a cat and this entity is black". The upper case letters are thus predicates qualifying a subject or entity, while the lower case letters are variables or arguments. Similarly, in symbolic logic, the symbol "∀" is what is known as a "universal quantifier". Universal quantifiers refer to expressions such as "all" and "every". Thus, the proposition "all humans are mortal" would be translated into symbolic logic as follows: $\forall x Hx \rightarrow Mx$. Translated into ordinary language, this would read, "for all entities, if x is human then x is mortal". The arrow thus reads as a conditional or an "if/then" statement. Finally it will be noted that over some of the expressions in the upper portions of Lacan's graph a bar appears. This bar denotes negation. Within what follows, I will use the following symbol to denote negation: "~".

In all four of the propositions populating the upper portion of Lacan's graph of sexuation we notice the symbol "Φ" appearing as a predicate qualifying "x". Within the framework of the upper portion of the graphs, this symbol refers to the phallic function. Like many of Lacan's mathemes, Φ is highly polysemous depending on the context in which it appears. Within the present context, Φ does not refer to the phallus—at least in the upper portion of the graph—much less to the male organ of the penis. Rather, Φ refers to castration, our submission to language, or our submission to the Law. In other words, Φ refers to the manner in which we must pursue *jouissance* through language and therefore encounter a priori restrictions or limitations to *jouissance*.

We are now in a position to read the propositions in the upper portion of Lacan's graphs of sexuation. The top and bottom propositions are to be read together or in relation to one another as embodying a sort of deadlock or contradiction. Thus, on the left or masculine side, the top proposition reads $\exists x{\sim}\Phi x$, while the bottom proposition reads $\forall x\Phi x$. Translated into ordinary language, the first proposition reads, "there exists an entity such that this entity is not subject to the phallic function", while the second proposition reads, "for all entities, x is submitted to the phallic function". When read together, the deadlock or contradiction embodied in these two propositions is that of a fantasy held by the subject in which complete enjoyment is possible, coupled with an existence where all *jouissance* comes up short by virtue of being subordinated to the phallic function.

One of the great advantages of Lacan's abstraction in these formulations is that it allows us to discern a common structure in a number of diverse domains. Not only does Lacan's handful of symbols allow us to discern the basic structure of the Oedipus Complex and the myth of the Primal Father in *Totem and Taboo*, but we can also see it as articulating the basic relationship between a monarch and his subjects, God and his creatures, the Cartesian subject and other objects, a celebrity and his fans, and so on. In each of these cases, we have the *fantasy* of a subject that either has complete knowledge, complete power, or complete enjoyment coupled with a plurality of subjects or entities that are lacking in knowledge, power, or enjoyment. In the case of the Primal Father, for example, we have an entity that has no limitations on his *jouissance*. Not only does he possess all the women of the tribe, he is also able to enjoy incest with his mother and daughters. Similarly, in the case of the Oedipus, the subject encounters a limit to his enjoyment in the incest prohibition. Likewise, in *The Concept of the Political*, Schmitt's monarch enjoys a strange status of exception, simultaneously being above and outside the law and therefore enjoying absolute power, while also being the origin of the law (castration/limitation).[268] What we thus get here is a logic of universality defined by exception. In order for the universal to establish itself in the form of the law, there must be a shadowy and phantasmatic exception that allows the boundary of the law to establish or ground itself. The sovereign need not truly have absolute power, nor must the Primal Father really have existed. All that is necessary is the unconscious belief in such exceptions to the failure of *jouissance*. If it proves impossible to totalize the symbolic order under this model, then this is because such totalization always requires an impossible exception outside that order, whereas the signifier is always differentially constituted without positive terms.

On the feminine side of the graph of sexuation, we get not a logic of exception, but a logic of the "not-all". The top proposition of the feminine side of the graph of sexuation reads, $\sim\exists x\sim\Phi x$, while the lower proposition reads, $\sim\forall x\Phi x$. Translated into ordinary language, the first proposition reads, "there does not exist an entity that is not submitted to the phallic function". By contrast, the second proposition reads, "not all of x is submitted to the phallic function". In other words, on the feminine side, something escapes from the law of language, castration, or the phallic function. It will be noted that whereas the masculine side constitutes a universal (the universality of the law) through an exception, we find no exception on the feminine side, nor do we find any universality. Instead of universality, what we find is the "not-all" or the "not-whole". Two consequences follow from this: first, insofar as there is no constitutive exception within the structure of feminine sexuality, this structure can be described in terms of *immanence*. Where the structure of masculine sexuality presupposes a transcendent term outside the world or law in some way or another, within the field of feminine structure we find only a flat plane with no transcendent outside or exception.

Second, the absence of a constitutive exception leads to Lacan's much maligned and misunderstood claim that *the* woman does not exist.[269] Here we must attend to the role of the definite article in Lacan's formulation.

Lacan's thesis is that, in order for a class to constitute itself as existing or universal, there must be an exception that defines the rule. If, according to Lacan, we can say what a male is, then this is because all men share the common characteristic of being castrated or subordinated by the Law defined by the phallic function. This law is guaranteed by the constitutive exception that allows the law to be determined. There is no analogous instance on the feminine side of the graph of sexuation, therefore it is impossible to constitute a universal class of women. The upshot of this is not that *women* do not exist, but rather that *woman*, the woman, does not constitute a closed and defined class. Put in more positive terms, women belong to the set of the *singular*, the individual, the different. They form an open set without any shared or overarching predicate defining a universal identity, thereby undermining any pretension to essence or identity.

In response to the failures of totalization found on both sides of the graph of sexuation, forms of *jouissance* appear as attempts to supplement and surmount this failure. On the masculine side we witness $, the symbol for the barred subject, pointing at *a*, the matheme for *objet a*. It will be noted that the form of *jouissance* that appears on the masculine side of the graph of sexuation also has the structure of Lacan's formula for fantasy, ($ <> a), read "barred subject punch *objet a*". In chapter four, we already saw that *objet a* is the remainder produced as a result of the subject's entrance into language. As a consequence, *objet a* is not an empirical or existing object, but a sort of remainder, excess, or irreducible fractional quantity marking that which cannot be integrated into the symbolic. Lacan refers to the *objet a* not as the object of desire, but as the object-cause of desire. *Objet a* forever propels the masculine subject forward, seeking a lost object he never had to begin with. Nonetheless, within the framework of fantasy, while *objet a* is not the object of desire but the cause of desire, various objects come to function as surrogates or stand-ins for *objet a*. Within the domain of unconscious fantasy, these surrogates are thought as that which, if destroyed or gained, would complete the subject, allowing the subject to surmount the lack that characterizes his being. In this respect, all fantasies are dual, organized like a Möbius strip, containing both a hypothesis as to what must be gained in order to surmount lack *and* a hypothesis as to what caused the loss of that object which would complete him. For example, the anti-Semite might believe that Jews are responsible for his economic woes and that money would provide the satisfaction that he seeks. This belief in the possibility of total *jouissance* arises from the upper proposition of the masculine side of the graph of sexuation, $\exists x{\sim}\Phi x$, and the unconscious belief that either an uncastrated subject exists or is possible.

Lacan often refers to phallic *jouissance* or the sort of *jouissance* found in *objet a* as deferred *jouissance*. As Bruce Fink puts it, "Lacan associates phallic *jouissance* with organ pleasure, the pleasure of the genitalia [...]; the idea here is that one must endlessly defer or altogether give up organ pleasure to obtain another kind of pleasure".[270] Part of the reason for this deferral is that, were the subject to actually reunite with the semblance of *objet a*, he would discover that the semblance of *objet a* is not "it". Thus, for example, Lacan argues that obsessionals, which are associated with masculine sexuation, have a desire for an impossible desire.[271] Through a fantasy structure organized around an impossible desire, the masculine subject can thereby sustain his desire and protect against the disappointment of *jouissance* coming up short.

In many respects, masculine *jouissance* can be described as solipsistic and masturbatory. In *Encore*, Lacan notoriously claims that there is no sexual relationship.[272] In the case of the masculine sexuated subject, whether biologically male or female and whether one's partner is male or female, we can see how this is the case. The masculine sexuated subject relates not to his partner *qua* subject, but rather to *objet a*. Returning to our discussion of the Lacanian clinic in chapter 4, the masculine sexuated subject attempts to reduce or abolish the subject as Other, as autopoietically closed, relating only to the Other's demand and *objet a*. I refer to this way of relating to the Other and the world as "Malkovichism". In Spike Jonze's *Being John Malkovich*, we are told the strange tale of a passage in an office building that allows you to enter John Malkovich's mind and experience what it is like to be John Malkovich for fifteen minutes. At a certain point in the film, John Malkovich becomes wise to what is going on and himself goes through the passage. When Malkovich goes through the tunnel and experiences his own experience, he has the harrowing experience of seeing everyone else, male and female, with his own head, speaking not ordinary language, but endlessly repeating his name: "Malkovich! Malkovich!

Malkovich!" In short, Malkovich is forcibly confronted with his own narcissism and phallic economy of *jouissance*. What we encounter here is correlationism in its purest form. Within the correlationist frame of thought, the world is reduced to a passive screen that merely reflects our intentions, meanings, signs, narratives, and discourses. Within the masculine economy of *jouissance*, one relates not to the partner but to Žižek's ticklish object which functions like a strange attractor bringing the subject into existence. In this connection, Lacan makes the joke that masculine *jouissance* is "*hommosexual*". Here Lacan is punning on the French "*homme*" or "male", and "homosexuality". His point is not that all men are homosexuals, but rather that masculinely sexuated subjects desire the same or identity and therefore strive to banish the alterity encountered in desire. Lacan's point is not that men only desire other men, but rather that masculine desire desires the *same* in the form of *objet a* or the fetish object.

On the feminine side of the graph of sexuation we encounter a very different form of *jouissance*. On the one hand, we see not one arrow, as in the case of masculine sexuation, but rather two arrows. On the other hand, we see not the barred subject, S, but rather the barred "*La*". *La* refers to non-existent woman that cannot be totalized under a single category or identity. In the lower portion of the feminine side of the graph of sexuation, we see an arrow pointing at Φ. Here we encounter the polysemy of Lacan's mathemes. In this context, Φ does not seem to represent the phallic function or castration, but rather power, potency, or a master. Lacan's somewhat sexist thesis here seems to be that the feminine sexuated subject, whether biological male or female, can find *jouissance* by identifying with a partner that embodies Φ. Such a subject might be someone that possesses political power, knowledge, celebrity, prestige, physical strength, skill, and so on. The idea would thus be that the feminine sexuated subject, who can find no signifier within the symbolic to define or fix her identity, identifies with Φ so as to confer an identity upon herself. Whereas *La* marks the inability for language to complete or totalize itself and therefore an inability to produce a fixed or stable identity within the symbolic, Φ creates the *illusion* of a fixed or stable identity. In this regard we can see the impossibility of the sexual relation in terms of feminine sexuation, insofar as the femine sexuated subject relates to his partner not as a subject but as a semblance of Φ.

This reading of $L\ddot{a}$ as it relates to Φ seems to recommend itself as a consequence of Lacan's discourse of the hysteric, which Lacan associates with the feminine. In the discourse of the hysteric, we have the barred subject addressing itself to the master or master-signifier, demanding to be told what it is:

$$\uparrow \frac{\text{\$}}{a} \xrightarrow{} \underset{//}{} \frac{S_1}{S_2} \downarrow$$

In the discourse of the hysteric, the subject addresses the Other or master from the standpoint of his split. This split results from the inability of the symbolic or language to provide the subject with a signifier that would fix or name his identity within the symbolic. In short, the hysterical subject calls on the other to tell him what he is. This inability of language to provide a signifier that would found the subject arises from the essence of language itself. As Lacan remarks in *The Logic of Fantasy*, "it is of the nature of each and every signifier that it cannot signify itself".[273] Insofar as the signifier cannot signify *itself*, it always requires *another* signifier to produce effects of signification. In this respect, signifiers have the structure of sets that do not include themselves, and Lacan does not hesitate to draw a parallel with Russell's paradox pertaining to the impossibility of a set of all sets that do not include themselves. The net result of this is that there cannot be a "universe of discourse" or totality of language because it will always be beset by paradox from within.[274] The consequence of this is that there can be no stable signifier that could ground the subject's identity, for each signifier will necessarily refer to another signifier without any possibility of completeness. It is this structure of language that accounts for the divided structure of the subject. Moreover, in the position of truth in the discourse of the hysteric, we encounter *objet a* as that remainder that is always lost within language. It is this remainder that literally drives the subject forward, forever looking for that signifier that would ground identity, and further alienating himself through his speech. The product of this discourse, we note, is knowledge, S_2, produced as a result of the hysteric's demand. Indeed, Lacan claims that the discourse of the hysteric is the only discourse that produces knowledge.[275] In this connection, we can treat Φ and the master or S_1 to which the hysteric addresses himself as equivalent.

At this point, there are a couple of points worth noting. Attentive readers will have noted that I have been referring to the hysterical subject in masculine terms. First, while Lacan associates hysteria with the feminine, any neurotic subject that undergoes analysis must enter into the discourse of the hysteric or begin asking the question "what am I for the Other?" Second, and more fundamentally, however, both Lacan and Freud argue that the subject is, at root, a hysterical subject. As Žižek puts it, "the status of the subject as such is hysterical. The subject is constituted through his own division, splitting, as to the object in him; this object, this traumatic kernel, is the dimension that we have already named as that of 'death drive', of a traumatic imbalance, a rooting out".[276] If the subject is hysterical at its core, then this is because both masculine and feminine neurotic subjects undergo the same alienation in language and therefore encounter the same paradoxical structure of language with respect to its inability to totalize or complete itself. In this vein, Žižek goes on to remark that,

> hysteria and obsessional neurosis are not two species of
> neurosis as a neutral-universal genus; their relation is
> a dialectical one—it was Freud himself who noted that
> obsessional neurosis is a kind of "dialectic of hysteria":
> hysteria as a fundamental determination of a neurotic
> position contains two species, obsessional neurosis *and itself as*
> *its own species.*[277]

At root, at the most fundamental level, the subject is hysterical in its structure such that obsessional neurosis is a subspecies of hysteria.

The importance of this observation is not to be underestimated. If it is true that subjectivity is at root hysterical, if it is true that obsession is a subspecies of hysteria, and if it is true that hysteria is associated with feminine sexuation and obsessional neurosis is associated with masculine sexuation, we find that we are able to invert a fundamental characterization of woman throughout Western history. Generally we hear that woman is characterized by masquerade, deception, semblance, inconsistency, and so on. However, in light of the foregoing, it would appear that in point of fact it is masculinity that is a charade, a semblance, a masquerade. And indeed, this is clearly visible in Lacan's discourse of the master.

$$\uparrow \frac{S_1}{\$} \overset{\rightarrow}{\underset{//}{}} \frac{S_2}{a} \downarrow$$

Lacan associates the discourse of the master with obsessional neurosis and therefore with masculine sexuation. In the position of truth in the lower left-hand corner of this discourse, we witness the barred subject, $\$$, which is nothing other than the hysterical subject. As a consequence, the master-signifier that appears in the position of the agent in the upper left-hand corner must be a charade, a semblance, or a masquerade. What the foregoing entitles us to claim is thus that the feminine side of the graph of sexuation is the structure of truth, whereas the masculine side of the graph of sexuation is the side of semblance. Moreover, we can now say that the totalization that masculine sexuation attempts to effect through the logic of exception is a semblance that strives to erase and cover over the constitutive split of being.

The second arrow on the feminine side of the graph of sexuation points not to Φ, but rather to $S(\overline{A})$. $S(\overline{A})$ refers to what Lacan calls "Other *jouissance*", which is a form of *jouissance* outside the symbolic that Lacan associates with the experience of mystics.[278] Because not-all of woman is subject to the phallic function, the feminine sexuated subject, whether male or female, is capable of a *jouissance* outside the symbolic. Echoing Lacan's thesis that masculine sexuated subjects are "hommosexual", we could say that in light of Other *jouissance*, $S(\overline{A})$, feminine sexuated subjects are the true "hetero-sexuals". Here the "hetero" of hetero-sexual should not be read as claiming that women only desire men, but rather that feminine sexuality is structured in such a way that it is capable of desiring *alterity* or the Other *qua* Other, regardless of whether the other subject is biologically male or female.

Having made this detour through Lacan's graphs of sexuation in terms of desire and *jouissance*, I now turn to the question of how these structures relate to flat ontology. We have already seen that Lacan's graphs of sexuation have no clear or unambiguous link to biological sex or gender. Biologically male subjects can occupy the feminine side, just as biologically feminine subjects can occupy the masculine side. Moreover, we have seen that, as structures, these graphs are able to represent a wide variety of diverse formations. Likewise we have seen that the graphs represent failures of totalization. Finally, we have seen that the masculine side of the graph of sexuation refers to semblance, whereas the feminine side of the graph of sexuation refers to truth.

Without excluding the reading of Lacan's graphs in terms of sexuation, desire, and *jouissance*, I propose to read these graphs in terms of ontological discourse and, in particular, in terms of withdrawal. This reading is not designed to have any argumentative or demonstrative force, but rather is designed to outline how the discourse of onticology and object-oriented ontology differ from other ontological discourses. Moreover, this treatment of onticology in terms of the graphs of sexuation will, I hope, allow us to see more clearly what is entailed by a flat ontology. Under this reading, the phallic function or Φ is no longer treated as the phallic function or castration, but rather as the ontological function of *withdrawal*. In the foregoing, we have already seen how objects are constitutively withdrawn from other objects. This withdrawal takes two forms: on the one hand, objects are withdrawn in the sense that they are always in excess of any of their local manifestations. Objects always have a virtual domain that is never exhausted by any of their local manifestations. On the other hand, objects are withdrawn in the sense that they are never directly perturbed or "irritated" by other objects, but rather always translate perturbations into information according to their own endo-structure, organization, or distinctions. Φ refers to this constitutive withdrawal of objects.

In this respect, the two sides of Lacan's graphs of sexuation refer to the manner in which different ontological discourses handle or treat this dimension of withdrawal within objects. Rather than referring to these structures as "masculine" and "feminine", I now refer to the two sides of Lacan's graphs as ontologies of presence and ontologies of withdrawal respectively. Likewise, ontologies of presence can be referred to as ontologies of transcendence, whereas ontologies of withdrawal can be referred to as ontologies of immanence. Ontologies of transcendence refer to ontologies where some being or term stands apart from the world, thereby immunized from withdrawal. Such ontologies are organized around the logic of exception outlined in the foregoing. By contrast, ontologies of immanence refuse any such term, treating all of being as composed of a single flat plane in which *all* beings are subject to withdrawal. Both forms that ontology takes relate to withdrawal but do so in very different ways.

On the side of ontologies of transcendence, we encounter the following propositions: $\exists x{\sim}\Phi x$ and $\forall x \Phi x$. The first proposition now reads, "there exists an entity such that that entity is not withdrawn". The second proposition now reads, "for all entities, these entities are withdrawn". As abstract as this formulation is, it allows us, I believe, to capture the core hypothesis of philosophies of presence or ontotheology. On the one hand, whether we're speaking of the God of ontotheology or the traditional subject of philosophy embodied in Descartes' thought, we encounter a term that is not itself withdrawn, but which is fully present to *itself*. This is true even of Hume's mind or Kant's structure of experience, where their critiques of metaphysics are premised on some form of consciousness or experience that is present to *itself*, but where there is no direct access to *other* objects. Hume, for example, is able to advance his critique of causality and the notion that objects are inhabited by "hidden powers" while arguing that cause and effect relations are associations drawn by *mind* on the grounds that mind is *present* to itself, whereas causal relations and powers are *withdrawn* from mind. Likewise, Kant is able to argue that substance, for example, is a category imposed by *mind* on the manifold of intuition producing phenomena, while also arguing that things-in-themselves are unknowable on the grounds that mind is present to itself, while objects are withdrawn. A good deal of philosophy influenced by the linguistic turn has this structure as well. Language here is treated as what is present, whereas objects are withdrawn. Finally, in theology, within this framework God is treated as a fully self-present term, while all of God's creatures are treated as finite, imperfect, and incomplete.

What we find in all variants of the ontologies of presence and transcendence is thus a term that is treated as present or immune to the function of withdrawal. As a consequence of this structure, withdrawal comes to appear as *accidental* rather than as an essential feature of all objects. Withdrawal is treated as something to be *overcome*, rather than as a structural feature of being. Here we encounter the function of *objet a* in ontologies of presence. *Objet a* is that remainder or leftover within representation that eludes complete presence. However, the premise here is that this remainder is not a constitutive feature of the being itself, but rather is an accidental feature of the relativity of our representations. Put a bit differently, objects are seen as withdrawn *for-us* and fully present *in-themselves*. In this regard, withdrawal is a sort of "optical effect" produced as a result of how *our representations* hook on to the world, rather than as a structural feature of *objects* themselves. This is true even of skeptical variants of ontologies of presence such as Hume's where the thesis is not that entities are in-themselves withdrawn, but rather where the thesis is that we have no direct access to entities by virtue of how we represent entities.

This discussion of ontologies of transcendence provides me with the opportunity to distinguish between epistemological realism and ontological realism, the latter of which is advocated by onticology and object-oriented philosophy. Any confusion of the ontological realism advocated by onticology and object-oriented philosophy and epistemological realism is doomed to be disastrous, as these two forms of realism belong to entirely different registers. Epistemological realism is a variant of the ontologies of presence that strives to bring objects or the world to presence in an adequate representation. The concern of epistemological realism is to represent the world and objects as they *are* and to sort between true representations, illusions, and superstitions. As such, epistemological realism treats the withdrawal of objects as an accident that can, in principle, be overcome by the proper form of inquiry. It is for this reason that epistemological realisms remain within the domain of ontologies of presence or ontotheology.

The ontological realism advocated by onticology and object-oriented philosophy, by contrast, is what Graham Harman has called a *weird* realism.[279] The realism advocated by object-oriented ontology and onticology is not an *epistemological* thesis, but an *ontological* thesis. This realism is not a thesis about how we know things, but rather about how things *are*. On the one hand, onticology refuses to reduce entities to *constructions* by other entities. To be sure, every entity translates the other entities to which it relates, yet these translations must be rigorously distinguished from the entities that are translated. In this regard, every entity is an irreducible entity in its own right. On the other hand, onticology and object-oriented philosophy are the thesis that entities are constitutively withdrawn from one another. In other words, withdrawal is not an accidental feature of how mind represents entities, but is rather a structural feature of what beings or entities are as such. In this regard, onticology and object-oriented philosophy are able to retain many of the insights of *anti-realism*, while situating them in *ontological* terms. Here, following Žižek, onticology and object-oriented philosophy can proclaim that we are healed by the spear that smote us.[280] Withdrawal, far from being an accident of how mind, representation, or language hooks on to being, is instead a constitutive feature of all beings.

Turning to the ontologies of immanence, we now encounter two very different propositions: $\sim\exists x\sim\Phi x$ and $\sim\forall x\Phi x$. If these propositions characterize an ontology of immanence, then this is because there is no longer a transcendental term that is exempted from withdrawal. Rather, as the first proposition reads, there does not exist an entity that is not subject to withdrawal. If, for example, God exists, God is necessarily withdrawn with respect to itself *and* God's creatures are withdrawn from *God*. In short, even God has no privileged or omniscient access to its creatures, nor even to himself. Likewise, subjects are both withdrawn from themselves and other beings are withdrawn from subjects. Withdrawal is thus not an accidental feature of beings, but is rather a constitutive feature of beings. Moreover, withdrawal is not simply a relation between one entity and another, but is the core of each entity itself. In this regard, *every* entity, up to and including God if God exists, is like a Lacanian divided or barred subject, $barred{S}$, such that, regardless of whether or not it is related to another entity, each entity is withdrawn with respect to itself. Put differently, no entity is fully self-present to itself, but rather every entity necessarily contains blind spots or is opaque to itself. Withdrawal here is the very structure of entities, not an accidental relation of how one entity relates to another entity. In short, such ontologies are ontologies of immanence in that no entity escapes withdrawal either for-itself or in-itself.

However, while there is no entity that is not subject to withdrawal, the side of the graph pertaining to ontologies of immanence also indicates that *not all* of entities are withdrawn. This thesis is expressed by the lower proposition on the feminine side of the graph of sexuation. Here something of the entity manifests or presents itself in the world through actualization or local manifestation. In short, withdrawal is never so thorough, never so complete, that local manifestation in one form or another is impossible. Returning to the themes of chapter two, we thus encounter the basic structure of objects in the relation between the top and bottom propositions on the feminine side of Lacan's graph of sexuation. There we saw that the basic structure of objects is to simultaneously be withdrawn and self-othering. No object directly relates to another object and every object is in excess of any of its actualizations, yet objects undergo self-othering through their local manifestations. Something of the object presents itself to the world. However, here we must be careful to note that this presentation or local manifestation is not a presentation to the gaze of a subject, but rather is an event that takes place in the world regardless of whether any entity is present to register this local manifestation.

The difference between ontologies of transcendence and ontologies of immanence is thus evident. In the case of ontologies of transcendence, withdrawal is an accidental feature of objects. Here, while objects might indeed be withdrawn *from us*, objects are entirely present *to themselves*. Moreover, subject, mind, and language are invariably treated as present or immune to withdrawal within these ontologies. In the case of ontologies of immanence, by contrast, withdrawal is not an accident, but a constitutive feature of all objects. Withdrawal constitutes the very structure or being of their being. Here objects are not only withdrawn *from themselves* such that every object is akin to a Lacanian divided subject, $barred{S}$, but objects are always withdrawn from one another. In this regard, local manifestation is not a presentation of an object that presents "part" of the withdrawn object such that, were there enough local manifestations, the object would be completely presented and withdrawal would be overcome. Rather, local manifestation is always the production or creation of a new quality that actualizes powers of the virtual proper being of the object without rendering virtual proper being itself present. Virtual proper being is necessarily abyssal such that it never comes to presence. In this respect, the agency of virtual proper being can only ever be inferred through the variety of qualities an object produces in its local manifestation. It can never itself be directly encountered for, as we saw in chapter 3, virtual proper being is structured without being qualitative.

Within discourses organized around ontologies of immanence, the mathemes populating the lower portion of the feminine side of Lacan's graphs of sexuation now take on a new valence. S(A) continues to signify Other *jouissance*, yet Other *jouissance* is no longer an ineffable *jouissance* outside the symbolic, but rather is an attentiveness to what Timothy Morton has called "the strange stranger". Describing the strange stranger, Morton writes,

> [t]he strange stranger [...] is something or someone whose existence we cannot anticipate. Even when strange strangers showed up, even if they lived with us for a thousand years, we might never know them fully—and we would never know whether we had exhausted our getting-to-know process.[281]

Indeed, the strange strangers can never be exhausted precisely because withdrawal is a constitutive feature of being. However, it would be a mistake to suppose that the strange strangers are objects *other* than *us*. To think the strange strangers in these terms would be to think them in terms of a binary based on identity. On the one hand, there would be the familiar, the *heimlich*, while on the other hand there would be the strange stranger, the unfamiliar, the *unheimlich*. The strange stranger would constitute itself as the strange stranger by virtue of its lack of proximity to the *heimlich* or the familiar. It would be that which is different *from*. And in being different from, it would be a difference based on identity or the same.

The concept of the strange stranger, however, is a concept without a binary. Rather the multiple-composition of being consists of strange strangers all the way down. And in this regard, we ourselves are strange strangers not only to other entities, but above all to ourselves insofar as withdrawal is not merely a relation of one entity to another, but also a relation of entities to themselves. Ontological discourses premised on immanence thus relate both to themselves and other objects *qua* strange strangers. Such discourses welcome the other as a strange stranger and acknowledge the strange stranger within themselves or their constitutive being as self-othering. In this regard, discourses of immanence are not unlike the ethics Lacan ascribes to the analyst. As Lacan remarks,

> [t]he analyst's desire is not a pure desire. It is a desire to obtain absolute difference, a desire which intervenes when, confronted with the primary signifier, the subject is, for the first time, in a position to subject himself to it. There only may the signification of a limitless love emerge, because it is outside the limits of the law, where alone it may live.[282]

Ontologies of immanence strive to relate to themselves and others as strange strangers, in and through their differences. They welcome that difference, remaining open to the possibility of surprise, refusing to reduce strange strangers to fixed identities. In this regard, they practice the difference between local manifestation and virtual proper being. In other words, philosophies of immanence recognize the locality of local manifestation and the openness and excess of virtual proper being, refusing any reduction of the being of beings to their local manifestations. It is this excess that accounts for the strangeness of the strange stranger. Strange strangers always harbor an excess within them that refuses any reduction to local manifestation.

The difference between how ontologies of transcendence and how ontologies of immanence relate to objects can be illustrated in terms of Lacan's discourse of the master.

$$\uparrow \frac{S_1}{\$} \xrightarrow{} \frac{S_2}{a} \; /\!/ \; \downarrow$$

One way of thinking about Lacan's discourses are as little machines that propel a certain discourse forward. Here the product of each discourse (the lower right-hand corner of the discourse) has a paradoxical status in that it is simultaneously something produced by the discourse and something that contributes to the continuation of the discourse. In the discourse of the master, associated with discourses of transcendence, the discourse attempts to identify and define objects, yet there is always a remainder, *objet a*, that evades identification. Like a Markov chain, this remainder, in its turn, generates a next round of discourse attempting to capture and integrate the remainder. In short, the discourse of the master treats the remainder not as a constitutive feature of all objects, as the mark of their being as strange strangers, but rather as an accident to be surmounted and overcome. In other words, ontologies of transcendence are governed by a telos, even if impossible, of attaining full presence.

In the case of the graphs of sexuation, we have already seen how masculine sexuation is a structure of semblance whereas feminine sexuation is a structure of truth. Masculine sexuation is a reaction to the fundamental split of being that attempts to surmount this split and cover it over through the enaction of an exception. This carries over into the difference between ontologies of presence and transcendence and ontologies of immanence and withdrawal. However, the seeds of this erasure of withdrawal can already be detected within ontological discourses organized around withdrawal. Within ontological discourses organized around immanence, Φ marks that tendency within ontologies of immanence to erase withdrawal. Φ marks the yearning or desire for full plenitude or actuality that erases the strange stranger. As such, Φ is the seed within immanence upon which the semblance of an exception is constructed. However, as we will recall from the discourse of the master, any exception, S_1, veils $\bar{S}$, the barred subject, in the position of truth. In other words, S_1, whether in the form of a master-signifier, a transcendental subject, God, consciousness or mind is a semblance or masquerade that cloaks and disguises its own withdrawal, parading itself as fully present or actual.

Lacan's graphs of sexuation allow us to make our first pass at what constitutes a flat ontology. In the first approximation, flat ontology consists in the thesis that there are no transcendent terms, no exceptions, no positions "out-of-field", with respect to withdrawal. Here being is flat in the precise sense that all beings are characterized by withdrawal and self-othering. In this regard, all beings that populate the multiple-composition of being are strange strangers. The consequence of this is a democracy of strange strangers. Where there is no hegemon that stands above and outside withdrawal as a full actuality, there is only a flat plane composed of strange strangers. As Morton puts it, "[d]emocracy implies coexistence; coexistence implies encounters between strange strangers".[283]

6.2. The World Does Not Exist

Crucial to the flat ontology proposed by onticology is the thesis that the world does not exist. Alternatively, we could say that the whole does not exist. Here I am deeply indebted to Alain Badiou's *Logics of Worlds* and Timothy Morton's dark ecology proposed in *Ecology Without Nature*. In *Logics of Worlds*, Badiou demonstrates that every concept of the Whole is beset by inconsistency.[284] In *Ecology Without Nature*, Morton argues that we must abandon the concept of nature as a unified whole or milieu within which beings reside and with respect to which humans and culture constitute an outside such that nature is always "over there".[285] To my thinking, Morton's conception of being without nature shares a great deal of affinity to Latour's concept of "collectives". In *Pandora's Hope*, Latour writes that,

> [u]nlike society, which is an artifact imposed by the modernist settlement, [the concept of collectives] refers to associations of humans and nonhumans. While a division between nature and society renders invisible the political process by which the cosmos is collected in one livable whole, the word "collective" makes this process central.[286]

Setting aside Latour's reference to politics, the concept of "society" is, according to Latour, based on a distribution or enclosure of beings where nature and society are treated as two *already* collected wholes that are somehow supposed to relate to one another while remaining entirely distinct. Society is treated as the domain of all that pertains to the human in the form of freedom, agency, meaning, signs, and so on, while nature is treated as the domain of brute causality and mechanism without agency. As a distinction, the concept of society thus encourages us to focus on content and agency, ignoring the role that nonhuman actors or objects play in collectives involving human beings. Within the distinction pertaining to nature, nature is treated as already gathered and unified and we are encouraged to focus on causality and mechanism alone. By contrast, in proposing that we replace the concept of society with the concept of collectives, Latour encourages us to attend to how associations between humans and nonhumans are formed.

In arguing that nature does not exist, Morton challenges the notion that there is an outside to nature or that nature is something other, outside the domain of society. As Deleuze and Guattari put it, [t]here is no such thing as either man or nature now, only a process that produces the one within the other and couples the machines together".[287] Neither nature nor being is an outside that we must stretch to reach or that is encountered when taking a stroll on Black Forest woodland paths, but rather being an immanent field without outside or other. And here, when Deleuze and Guattari refer to machines, I see no reason not to treat these machines as objects. In short, a collective is an entanglement of human and nonhuman actors or objects. However, here it is important to be cautious, for while there are indeed collectives of human and nonhuman objects or actors, we must not conclude that collectives as such are composed of human *and* nonhuman actors. Collectives can just as easily be collectives of tardigrades and other objects, collectives of planets and asteroids, and so on without any human involvement whatsoever. In short, what's important about the concept of collectives is that they mark, like the concept of regimes of attraction, entanglements of objects in a network or mesh. If Morton is so eager to abandon the concept of nature within ecological thought, then this is not, I take it, because he wishes to reduce all of being to culture, but because in order to properly think ecologically we must overcome the notion that nature is a closed whole or totality "over there" or outside of human relations.

If it is so vital for flat ontology to establish that the world does not exist, then this is because the world must not be treated as a milieu in which beings or objects are contained as parts to a whole. In short, if flat ontology is to truly be flat, then it is necessary to establish that the world is not a container within which beings are found. Alternatively, it must be shown that the world is not a super-object composed of all other objects as sub-multiples that form a harmonious whole consisting of beings as complementary and inter-locking parts. As such, following Badiou, there is not *world*, but rather *worlds*. The universe, which is really only a manner of speaking, is a pluriverse or multiplicity of universes. Here, then, it is important to observe the role of the definite article in the thesis that "the world does not exist". Generally when we speak of "the world" we mean this as shorthand for the totality of all that exists. The thesis that the world does not exist is the thesis that no such totality exists nor is it possible for such a totality to be formed. Rather being consists entirely of objects and collectives.

There are two ways of arguing that the world doesn't exist, the first of which has already been hinted at in chapter five in the context of mereology. Within the domain of formal reasoning, Z-F set theory shows the inconsistency of any attempt to form a totality or whole. Set theory provides a variety of resources for contesting the consistency of any totality or whole, however, here I'll focus on the power set axiom. As we've already seen, the power set axiom allows one to take the set of all subsets of an initial set. Thus, if we have a set composed of elements {a, b, c}, the power set of this set would be {{a}, {b}, {c}, {a, b}, {a, c}, {b, c}, {a, b, c}}. At the level of formal reasoning, if the power set axiom spells the ruin of any whole or totality, then this is because it reveals the existence of a bubbling excess within any whole or collection.

This is a variation of Cantor's Paradox. Cantor's paradox demonstrates that there can be no greatest cardinal number precisely because the power set of any cardinal number will necessarily be larger than the cardinal number itself. In a stunning inversion of the ancient thesis that the whole is greater than the sum of its parts, the power set axiom reveals, to the contrary, that the parts are always greater than the whole. As I argued in the last chapter, from a certain perspective each object is a crowd, containing within itself a plurality of other autonomous objects that very likely "know" nothing of the object of which they are parts. Any whole that does manage to establish itself is, as Deleuze has put it, a "One or Whole so special that it results from the parts without altering the fragmentation or disparity of those parts, and, like the dragons of Balbec or Vinteuil's phrase, is itself valid as a part alongside others, adjacent to others".[288] What the power set reveals is the bubbling pluralism of "the" world beneath any unity or totality. Any totality or whole, in its turn, is itself an object or One alongside all sorts of other ones.

At the formal level, the real force of the power set axiom lies in the manner in which it reveals the *possibility* of a multiplicity of relations and objects within any collective. It will be recalled that any exo-relation between objects is potentially itself also an object. If we ask the strange question, "*when* is an object?" we can answer this question with the hypothesis that an object is when exo-relations among other objects manage to attain operational closure such that their aggregate or multiple-composition becomes capable of encountering perturbations as information in terms of their own endo-consistency. On the one hand, the power set axiom reveals the possibility of a plurality of *other* objects within any collective. On the other hand, the power set axiom discloses the possibility of alternative exo-relations among objects, not present in the whole from which the subsets are drawn. Finally, the power set axiom reveals the possibility of withdrawing objects from their relations to collectives so that they might function as autonomous actors, either entering into other collectives, subsystems, or going it alone within the order of being.

If, from the standpoint of formal reasoning, the Whole is not, the One is not, or *the* world does not exist, then this is precisely because these subsets, these other possible objects and relations populating the power set of the Whole or alleged One are neither counted nor countable within the Whole or One. In short, every Whole or One contains an excess within it that is not itself treated as a part of the Whole or One. Put differently, such subsets are included in the set from which they are drawn, without belonging to it. Yet it is precisely this absence of belonging or membership that spells the ruin of the Whole, One, or World.

However, while the formal reasoning of set theory provides us the resources for *thinking* the nonexistence of the world, it does not *establish* the nonexistence of the world. Confronted with the formal demonstration of excess bubbling within any Whole or totality, one can easily respond by pointing out that, as provocative as these formal demonstrations are, the concept of World pertains not to what is *possible*, but to what actually *exists*. In this regard, the demonstration that any collection *could* contain other objects and relations does not establish that the World *does* contain other objects and relations not counted within that totality. Since the concept of World pertains to those relations and objects that do actually exist, the formal demonstration of the inexistence of the World has no purchase on the thesis that the World exists.

If it is to be established that the World does not exist, then what is required is not a demonstration of the *possibility* of the ruin of any Whole, but rather the demonstration that *in fact* the World does not exist. The resources for this second argument have already been developed in my discussion of operational closure in chapter four. There we saw that every object is operationally closed such that it constitutes its own system/environment distinction. The paradox of this distinction is that, while it is a distinction between system and environment, the distinction itself falls on one side of what it distinguishes: the system. In short, the environment/system distinction refers not to two present-at-hand entities, systems and environments, but is rather constituted by systems themselves. This distinction, in its turn, constitutes the entity's openness to its environment, and that openness is always of a selective nature. However, here we must be careful to distinguish between the environment of a system and systems in the environment of a system. While an object does indeed constitute its environment in the sense of constituting those sorts of perturbations to which it is open, objects do not constitute other objects or systems in their environment. At best, working on the premise that an object is open to some other systems in its environment, an object translates perturbations it receives from these other objects.

Two points follow from these observations. First, insofar as environment is constituted by the object "drawing" the distinction between system and environment, it cannot be said that environments are a present-at-hand milieu in which objects exist. As we saw in chapter five in connection with our discussion of developmental systems theory, objects construct their environment even as they are often buffeted by perturbations from systems in their environment. Second, and in a closely related vein, because objects are only selectively open to their environments, it follows that objects are not open to all systems in their environment. The tardigrade does not belong to the environment of a tree, nor does the tree belong to the environment of a tardigrade. Likewise, my three-year-old daughter, *qua* social subject, does not belong to the environment of her toy box. No matter how much my daughter yells at the lid of her toy box when it accidentally falls down upon her head—and she does, indeed, yell and curse, in her own way, the toy box—the toy box does not respond or bow to her will. While she might address her toy box as "little brother" for reasons that thoroughly baffle me, the toy box is indifferent to her designations and scoldings. One might object that certainly the acoustic resonances of her scolding voice perturb the toy box and such an objection would not be mistaken. However, the manner in which the vibrations of this tiny voice affect the polished oak wood of the toy chest do not entail that that oaken toy box transforms these perturbations into information *qua* voice. Sadly, for my daughter, that toy box is as dense as wood.

With Leibniz, perhaps, we can say that there are as many worlds as there are objects. What we cannot say, however, is that the World forms any sort of organic unity or whole in which all objects interrelate with one another as a compossible system. There is no world-system precisely because there is no World. On the one hand, contrary to Whitehead, it simply isn't the case that every entity relates to every other entity. Many entities fall completely outside local collectives such that they are both entirely oblivious to these collectives and such that these collectives are entirely oblivious to them. Put differently, there are a number of instances in which there is absolutely no resonance between entities. Quite literally, they belong to entirely different universes. As in the case of neutrinos that are unable to relate to most other particles due to their neutral charge, scientists have to painstakingly create apparatuses capable of bringing these entities into relation with the entities of our world. On the other hand, even in those instances where entities do relate, each entity relates to other entities on its own terms as a function of the distinctions it draws and its own peculiar organization. As a consequence, there is no whole or totality that can be formed out of the entities that populate the world.

The thesis that the World forms an organic totality where no such totality exists surreptitiously treats the collective as already formed, as already being there, without attending to any of the work and translations required for collectives to come into being. It treats collectives as accomplished, while ignoring the arduous work required for any collective to form itself. As such, it ignores the antagonisms that populate being as well as the lack of resonance between all sorts of objects. While the idea of the World as an organic and harmonious unity might prove comforting and reassuring, providing us with the sense that we belong to a Whole in which each entity has its proper place, such a conception of being does a profound injustice to the entities that populate the multiple-composition of being and ends up recapitulating the discourse of the master and the logic of ontologies of transcendence. Put differently, concepts of World as an organic Whole or totality foreclose the strange stranger. Each entity, the story runs, has its proper place within the organic totality and is defined by its relation to all others. What is thereby abolished is the non-relation of each and every relation and the recognition of that which is entirely non-relational with respect to any particular collective or entity.

If conceptualizations of the World premised on the organic unity of the Whole recapitulate the logic of the discourse of the master and ontologies of transcendence, then this is because such discourses inevitably must have recourse to some entity that perturbs the "natural" order, preventing it from existing harmoniously as ontologies of the World dictate. It is always Man, technology, the foreigner and so on that perturbs the "natural" order. In other words, within the conception of Nature as an organic whole or totality, there is always recourse to some uncanny agency generating disharmony that upsets the harmonic natural order. Such conceptions of being necessarily have recourse to *objet a* as a disruptive agency that upsets the "natural" order. Moreover, this disruptive agency, this trickster, to use Lévi-Strauss's memorable term, is treated as an *accident* that could return the natural order to harmony were it *eradicated*. As such, discourses about the existence of the World and the intrinsic harmony of nature end up repeating the friend/enemy logic analyzed so attentively by Schmitt.

Yet it is not simply that the idea of the World as an organic and harmonic Whole producing *objet a* as a remainder that is problematic. Rather, in declaring that the World exists, that the world forms an organic Whole, all objects are subordinated to the World as parts of the Whole. As such, their only value and being arises from what they contribute to the World or the Whole as elements in this massive machine that swallows them all up in a total system in which they're integrated. The consequence here is that the being of the part is completely effaced, such that the part becomes merely a functional element providing perturbations that the Whole can draw on in producing information in its own ongoing autopoiesis. Objects themselves therefore have no autonomy apart from the Whole and simply are what they are as elements of the Whole. Gaia, it turns out, is either a fascist or a totalitarian.

The point here is *not* that collectives can't be pushed into chaotic basins of attraction that spell their destruction, or, at least, bifurcation, down the road, but rather that these strange strangers are not, to put it in Aristotelian/Scholastic terms, *accidents*. Put more precisely, these strange strangers are not *outside* of worlds, but rather are themselves elements of worlds. The Luddite thesis that Man, technology, and media are unnatural imposters that unbalance the natural order of the World is premised on the existence of a World that never existed to begin with. They treat as ontological what is, in reality, a covert normative judgment. And again, here the point is not that normative judgments shouldn't be made, but that these judgments are made from the standpoint of a particular system or object and do not themselves determine what is or is not. But more fundamentally, from the standpoint of worlds, the harmonic has never existed. It has never been the case that it is merely Man, Technology, or Media that perturbs Nature. The odds are that at this very moment, somewhere in the universe or the multiverse, there is a massive black hole devouring a solar system with a rich and complex ecosystem supporting sentient and intelligent life. The Black Plague swept across Europe and Asia for decades and centuries, wiping out massive populations of humans and other creatures. Precambrian organisms caused the extinction of many of their species by saturating their environment with oxygen, diluting the carbon dioxide they needed to thrive. The dinosaurs very likely became extinct as a result of an asteroid. It is worlds themselves that are out of kilter and lacking in harmony. While we should make the case for certain forms of equilibrium, balance, or harmony, we should refuse to ontologize such claims, treating them as reflective of a "Goddess Earth", and be upfront in the declaration that these are normative judgments made from the standpoint of a particular object or system. From the standpoint of the bubonic plague, sickness is merely a convenient way of replicating itself. In other words, it is not sickness at all.

The thesis that the world does not exist is crucial to flat ontology so as to avoid surreptitiously treating as collected that which is not collected. What the inexistence of the world teaches is that worlds are a work, that meshes must be produced, and that they cannot be said to exist in advance. There is, as Graham Harman has so aptly, beautifully, and poetically put it in *Guerrilla Metaphysics*, a "carpentry" of being. That is to say, collectives must be built by the objects that deign to enter into structural couplings with one another. In this regard, the inexistence of the world draws our attention to what Latour has called the "sociology of associations" as opposed to the "sociology of the social".[289] It seems that if he could, Latour would prefer to abandon the term "sociology" altogether given the manner in which it is thoroughly contaminated by what he calls "the modernist constitution", where nature and society are treated as two entirely distinct domains. Yet if, contends Latour, the term "sociology" should be retained then it ought to be retained not as a theory of that peculiar domain of what is *unique* to the human, but rather as that domain that pertains to associations, relations, or what Harman calls "the carpentry of being". Where the sociology of the social appeals to society, social forces, power, meaning, language, and a host of other nefarious human-related entities to explain why people behave as they do, the sociology of associations instead draws attention to how relations are forged in the creation of assemblages.

The profound difference embodied in Latour's sociology of associations is not only that it draws attention to relations between humans and nonhumans and how these relations are forged and what impact they have, but that we can imagine a sociology of associations that does not involve humans at all. This would not simply be a matter of analyzing bee, ant, and gorilla societies after the fashion of Jane Goodall, but would involve the investigation of collectives involving no sentient beings whatsoever. For example, the sociologist of associations might investigate the impact various storms and winds have on strata and how they manage to maintain such remarkable chaotic consistency. In this regard, the molecular biologist and the chemist are sociologists of association, for they investigate how particular collectives are forged among particular actors. It just happens that these collectives are composed not of humans or animals, but of atoms of oxygen, hydrogen, and heavy metals. What is, above all, important to remember for the purposes of flat ontology is not simply that the World does not exist, but rather that collectives must be forged. Moreover, it must be remembered that not all entities relate to all other entities and that like the floating city of George Lucas's *Empire Strikes Back*, there are collectives that are unassociated with other collectives and that know nothing of other collectives. While the thesis that the World does not exist or that being does not form an organic harmonious totality might appear to be a grim hypothesis, denying us our oneness and unity with everything else, this thesis also embodies the freedom and hope of collectives; for it entails that we can set about the arduous work of building new collectives and welcoming unheard of strange strangers, building what are as of yet unheard of collectives. In other words, the theory that the Whole and World do not exist both promises to free us from a tyrannical collective gone mad and offers the possibility of building other collectives. Rather than critique, which is, in its own way and from its own point of view indispensable, the thesis that the world does not exist offers us the activity of *composition*.

6.3. Being is Flat

The foregoing chapters and sections lead to the conclusion that being is flat. The flatness of being is embodied in two fundamental claims. First, in light of our exploration of the interior of objects in chapter four, it becomes clear that ontologically the bland human-world gap or relationship possesses no metaphysical priority. As Harman puts it, "object-oriented philosophy holds that the relation of humans to pollen, oxygen, eagles, or windmills is no different in kind from the interaction of these objects with each other".[290] Second, onticology and object-oriented philosophy establish what might be called a heteroverse or pluriverse, where entities at all levels of scale, whether natural or cultural, physical or artificial, material or semiotic are on equal ontological footing. As Ian Bogost puts it, "all beings equally exist, *yet they do not exist equally*".[291] Onticology and object-oriented philosophy therefore democratizes being, asserting not one primary gap between subjects and objects, humans and world, mind and reality, but

rather an infinity of gaps or vacuums between objects regardless of whether
humans are involved. Likewise, onticology and object-oriented philosophy
democratize being by defending a plurality of types of objects, ranging from
the semiotic to the natural. Rather than treating one type of object such as
quantum particles as the really real upon which all else is grounded and
to which all else ultimately reduces, flat ontology advocates a pluralism of
types of objects at all levels of scale that are irreducible to one another. In
other words, objects of different types and at different levels of scale are
what Aristotle referred to as genuine primary substances.

As Harman has compellingly argued, philosophy, for the last two
hundred or so years, has been obsessed with a single gap between the
human and the world, treating this gap as metaphysically privileged or
special, unlike all other relations with objects. Within the framework of
onticology and object-oriented philosophy, however, the human-object gap
possesses no privileged status, but is one among many gaps populating a
heteroverse. As Harman remarks,

> [w]hen the things withdraw from presence into their dark
> subterranean reality, they distance themselves not only from
> human beings, but *from each other* as well. If the human
> perception of a house or tree is forever haunted by some
> hidden surplus in the things that never become present, the
> same is true of the sheer causal interaction between rocks or
> raindrops.[292]

From this Harman concludes that, "contrary to the dominant
assumption of philosophy since Kant, the true chasm in ontology lies not
between humans and world, but between *objects and relations*".[293] Far from
the gap between humans and objects constituting a unique form of relation,
withdrawal is a perfectly ubiquitous relation within being characteristic
of *all* relations between objects. All objects are strange strangers with
respect to one another regardless of whether or not humans are involved in
these relations. Moreover, all objects are strange strangers with respect to
themselves.

Within the framework of onticology, the ubiquity of withdrawal
characteristic of all objects is theorized in terms of the operational closure

of objects analyzed in chapter four and the split within objects between virtual proper being and local manifestation analyzed in chapter three. With respect to the operational closure of objects, the relation between objects whether human, social, biological, or inanimate is a non-relation between objects in which objects never directly touch or encounter one another. Like Leibniz's windowless monads, each object is a discrete substance or unit of its own, withdrawn from all other objects without any direct relation or contact. Objects never directly encounter one another, but rather only relate to one another as translations or information. And information is never something transmitted or exchanged by objects, but rather is constituted by each object as a function of its own internal organization and distinctions.

With respect to the split nature of objects embodied in the split between virtual proper being and local manifestation, a similar ubiquity of withdrawal is encountered. The virtual proper being of objects is abyssal and subterranean, such that it itself never comes to presence. Virtual proper being is structured without being qualitative and refers to that domain of powers and attractors presiding over the actualization of qualities or local manifestations. Insofar as virtual proper being is thoroughly withdrawn and never itself becomes present, it can only be inferred through the actual. It is only through tracking local manifestations and their variations that we get any sense of the dark volcanic powers harbored within objects. In other words, through second-order observation or the observation of how an object relates to the world in its non-relation, we form a hypothetical diagram of objects or a map of their attractors or powers. However, insofar as all local manifestations create something new in the form of qualities, this diagram can only ever be partial, hypothetical, and incomplete for, as Spinoza so nicely put it, we don't ever completely know what objects can do.

Nor is the withdrawal of objects ever merely a withdrawal of objects with respect to one another. Withdrawal is a form of non-relation so thorough that objects aren't simply withdrawn from one another, but are withdrawn even from themselves. As we have seen, all objects are akin to Lacanian divided subjects, $\$$. On the one hand, no object ever actualizes the subterranean volcanic core with which its virtual proper being is haunted. This virtual domain is like a reserve or excess that never comes to presence. It is not simply that objects are, in themselves, fully actual and only withdrawn for other objects relating to them, but rather that objects are withdrawn in themselves. On the other hand, the distinctions or organization by which objects produce information for themselves are themselves withdrawn or invisible to the object that deploys them. As we have seen, every distinction necessarily contains two blind spots. Distinctions are blind to the unmarked space produced as a result of the distinction. As Luhmann puts it, objects can only see what they can see and cannot see what they cannot see. Moreover, they do not see that they do not see this. Yet in addition to this, objects are blind to their own operative distinctions. Distinctions can only be observed or used, but never observed *and* used. In making indications or interacting with other objects, the distinctions that render these indications possible become thoroughly invisible.

Insofar as withdrawal is ubiquitous, there is no reason to treat the human-object relation as metaphysically privileged. The human-object relation is not a special relation, not a unique relation, but a subset of a far more pervasive ontological truth that pertains to objects of all types. The point here is not that we should exclude inquiry into human/object relations or social/object relations, but rather that these analyses are analyses for regional ontology, for a particular domain of being, not privileged grounds of ontology as such. The issue here is thus very subtle. It is not a question of excluding the human and the social, but of decentering them from the place of ontological privilege they currently enjoy within contemporary philosophy and theory. Nor does this entail that all objects relate to other objects in exactly the same way. There are as many forms of translation as there are types of objects. Indeed, there are as many forms of translation as there are objects. Moreover, new forms of translation come into being all the time with the emergence of new objects and with the development of objects as analyzed in chapters four and five.

What onticology and, I believe, object-oriented philosophy propose is therefore a subtle shift in the distinctions governing the marked space of what philosophy and theory indicates. Far from seeking to exclude or eradicate phenomenology and bodies of cultural theory in the name of, for example, a naturalism or a scientist materialism, object-oriented ontology aims to *expand* what can be indicated within the domain of philosophy and theory. Onticology and object-oriented philosophy thus find themselves in the position of receiving opposite and opposed objections from all sides. From the culturalists, we receive criticisms declaring that we are rejecting the human, the subject, meaning, signs, and the social. From the naturalists, we are accused of wooly-headed thinking that treats social entities, semiotic entities, texts, films, fictions and so on as real and autonomous entities within being.

In both cases, however, the rejoinder of object-oriented ontology is the same. What is objected to with respect to the culturalists is not the thesis that humans and social entities translate other entities in their own way, nor the thesis that humans and social entities are not genuine entities, but rather the Malkovichism that arises from privileging the human/world or social/world gap. As we saw in 6.1, Malkovichism consists in treating all other objects as blank screens upon which humans project their meanings, intentions, signs, and signifiers. Malkovich, like Narcissus, sees only himself in other objects, denying objects their own autonomy and dignity. The trick of cultural analysis thus lies in demonstrating that what we take to be the object is rather our own alienated image. What object-oriented ontology opposes is not the thesis that humans and society translate other objects, nor the thesis that humans and societies only encounter objects in "distorted" form in their own interior, but rather the culturalist tendency to reduce objects to alienated human reflections. To be sure we can, and should, investigate the manner in which humans and societies translate objects. Put in more technical terms, we should engage in reflexive second-order observations of our own distinctions and how they organize our experience of the world. Yet having made this concession, we must also redraw our distinctions in such a way as to make room for nonhuman objects as autonomous actors in their own right, such that these objects are not treated as merely passive screens for human projections and such that they are treated as perturbing the world in their own way. In other words, the point is to expand the domain of what can be investigated, not to limit it. However, this requires placing objects in the marked space of our distinctions and treating humans and societies as entities *among* other entities.

From the naturalists, by contrast, object-oriented ontologists are accused of treating a variety of psychic and cultural entities as real entities, ignoring the truth that the only real reality is the material and physical world. Put crudely, the naturalist accuses object-oriented ontology of treating as real what is merely an illusion or derivative. To the ears of the naturalist, object-oriented ontology thus looks like a form of arch-culturalism insofar as it treats entities like nations, groups, chairs, films, and so on as genuinely real entities. To make matters worse, the naturalist is appalled by the object-oriented thesis that these entities are irreducible to the physical, material, or natural domain. This ends up getting translated into the thesis that object-oriented ontology rejects neurology, biology, chemistry, physics and a host of other "hard sciences".

However, once again, the point is the same. The aim is not to exclude or reject the entities explored by the "hard sciences", but to refuse a hierarchical conception of being where these entities are treated as the "really real" beings and all the others are treated as derivative illusions or mere effects. Here, again, the aim is not to limit inquiry, but to expand the domain of what can be investigated. With the naturalists, object-oriented ontology agrees that the culturalists or social constructivists have illicitly reduced nonhuman beings to cultural constructs. With the social constructivists or culturalists, however, object-oriented ontology refuses to treat social and cultural entities as mere effects of the material and physical. Rather, object-oriented ontology argues that these entities are genuinely real entities in their own right. What object-oriented ontology thus objects to is the reductivism of many naturalist approaches.

However here we must proceed with care. Object-oriented ontology can readily agree that Supreme Court justices are impossible without brains, even if often it appears that they don't use their brains. The point is that brains are one thing and Supreme Court justices are another thing. Being a Supreme Court justice is irreducible to being a brain. Here we encounter considerations of both mereology and operational closure. In a rather bizarre formulation, we can ask ourselves whether *Antonin Scalia* is a Supreme Court justice. Initially the answer would appear to be an obvious yes, unless, somehow, Scalia is an imposter. However, within the framework of onticology, matters are not so simple. Supreme Court justices are elements within a particular object, namely, the United States. Like all other objects, this object is operationally closed, relating only to itself. As such, Scalia, the individual psychic system, belongs not to that object that contains Justice Scalia as an element, but rather to the *environment* of that object. Put differently, Scalia the individual psychic system belongs to the environment of Justice Scalia the element within a particular larger scale object. Moreover, insofar as the individual psychic system Scalia is itself an operationally closed object, it follows that Scalia's brain belongs to the *environment* of Scalia the individual psychic system. Insofar as Scalia's brain, such as it is, belongs to the environment of the individual psychic system Scalia, and insofar as Scalia belongs to the environment of that object that contains Justice Scalia as a member, it follows that Scalia's brain can only perturb Scalia the individual psychic system, and that Scalia the psychic system can only perturb the social-system or object that contains Justice Scalia as an element. In other words, each of these objects is withdrawn from the other such that each operates in terms of its own operational closure translating perturbations from one another into information.

In this regard, Scalia's brain has little to tell us about Justice Scalia. Put differently, Justice Scalia is irreducible to the individual psychic system Scalia, and the individual psychic system Scalia is irreducible to Scalia's brain. Instead, what we get is something akin to a high voltage Jacob's Ladder where sparks leap from non-communicating object to non-communicating object with each of these objects being irreducible to one another. At this point, I imagine the naturalist protesting that I'm proposing a thoroughly obscurantist universe populated by all sorts of occult substances like so many ghosts. Am I not here suggesting that Scalia is an immaterial soul and, were it not problematic enough to posit immaterial souls for individuals, have I not now multiplied the sorts of souls that exist through the postulation of even stranger objects like groups, societies, roles, and so on? Is not Ockham spinning in his grave in response to my lack of ontological parsimony?

However, I have already developed the resources for responding to this criticism in section 5.3 where I addressed the ontology of structure. While emergent entities are indeed irreducible to smaller scale entities, this does not entail that they violate any laws of physics or material reality. As we saw in 5.3, the defining feature of structure lies in the manner in which relations among elements making up the endo-structure of an entity or system are constrained. Nothing about these constraints violates the laws of physics or the findings of neurology, however the laws of physics and the findings of neurology cannot themselves account for why relations among elements are constrained or structured in this particular way. It is this nature of constraints or structures that accounts for the irreducibility of larger-scale objects. In a fine discussion of causality and emergence, Protevi writes,

> [t]he concept of emergence entails reciprocal or circular causality. Upward causality is the emergence of systematic focused capacities (the parts of a system function in such a way as to provide for capacities of the system that the individual parts do not possess), and downward causality is the constraint on the behavior of component parts that enables systematic-capacities (the whole exerts an influence on the parts that now have a reduced field of action).[294]

With emergence, higher scale objects take on a life of their own that can only be accounted for in terms of their own organization. Such objects begin to constitute their own elements through their own elements. Here upward causality refers to the manner in which elements of the object produce the object, whereas downward causality refers to the manner in which the object constrains and structures its elements. What we get here is a system-specific causality, unique to each object, that while dependent on lower-scale objects is not accounted for by these objects.

With these observations, we now encounter the heteroverse characteristic of the flat ontology advocated by onticology and object-oriented ontology. Rather than one type of object, such as subatomic particles, that constitutes the really real, we instead get a heteroverse of different types of autonomous and irreducible objects ranging from quarks to tardigrades to ecosystems, groups, institutions, societies, humans, burritos and so on. An awl is no less real than a cane toad by virtue of being fabricated by humans, nor is an institution or group any less real than an awl by virtue of being immaterial. It might be argued that an awl is only an awl so long as it exists within the framework of society. Perhaps this is true, but how is this any different from the other regimes of attraction we explore in 5.1 where we saw that the particular form a local manifestation takes is in part dependent on structural couplings and regimes of attraction? When a sadistic scientist places a cane toad within a glass box without oxygen, that cane toad very quickly loses the capacity to locally manifest qualities pertaining to life. When the awl is detached from society, it is no longer able to locally manifest powers of punching holes in wood or leather. In these instances, what has been abolished is not the entity itself, but rather the ability of the entity to locally manifest itself in a particular way. Of course, in the case of the frog, entropy begins to set in rather quickly. Then again, it appears that this particular limitation on local manifestations arising from the absence of particular structural couplings is not necessarily irreversible in that it appears there are many instances where frogs can be brought back to life.

With this heteroverse of varied objects, we begin to see just how much the concept of society and the concept of collectives discussed in 6.2 differ from one another. The distinctions organizing the concept of society draw attention to subjectivity, signs, meanings, narratives, texts, discourses, power, social forces and so on. By contrast, the concept of collectives draws our attention to a variety of very different actors, human and nonhuman, perturbing and translating each other in particular ways within networks or assemblages. No doubt, it is something like this that Guattari was after in *Chaosmosis*. As Guattari writes,

> [s]hould we keep the semiotic productions of the mass media, informatics, telematics and robotics separate from psychological subjectivity? I don't think so. Just as social machines can be grouped under the general title of Collective Equipment, technological machines of information and communication operate at the heart of human subjectivity, not only within its memory and intelligence, but within its sensibility, affects and unconscious fantasms. Recognition of these machinic dimensions of subjectivation leads us to insist, in our attempt at redefinition, on the heterogeneity of the components leading to the production of subjectivity. Thus one finds in it: 1. Signifying semiological components which

appear in the family, education, the environment, religion, art, sport [...]. 2. Elements constructed by the media industry, the cinema, etc., 3. A-signifying semiological dimensions that trigger informational sign machines, and that function in parallel or independent of the fact that they produce and convey significations and denotations, and thus escape from strictly linguistic axiomatics.[295]

Guattari appears to envision the analysis of collectives where a variety of different actors or objects ranging from subjects to signs to technologies and groups and institutions interact with one another in a highly complex fashion. To Guattari's list, of course, we could add the presence or absence of roads, power lines, internet connections, weather patterns, cane toads, ocean-going ships and canoes, H1N1 viruses and a host of other objects. Guattari's ontology is flat in the precise sense that all of these entities are full-blown actors rather than mere screens for human signs and intentions. And, of course, collectives need not involve signs or humans at all, but can be purely inhuman as in the case of the atmosphere of Saturn.

At this point, it is not unusual to hear humanist correlationists cry foul, accusing object-oriented ontologists of technological and environmental determinism. In my view, this is an unfair criticism. Somehow pointing out that it is impossible to fry eggs without a frying pan or some similar cooking surface becomes equivalent to the thesis that frying pans determine people to fry eggs. Somehow pointing out how the inland remoteness of China's abundant coal reserves played a role in China not kicking off the industrial revolution is transformed into the claim that this remoteness determined the form that Chinese culture took. In this regard, any qualification of human freedom, any evocation of actors other than meaning, narratives, signifiers, and discourses is responded to with incredulity at the suggestion that humans are merely among other beings rather than at the center of beings such that nonhuman beings are merely their screen, passive things upon which they impose form through their intentions and techniques, and where the world is merely our own alienated reflection. Such is the height of Malkovichism.

Faced with decades of content-based cultural criticism that implicitly, at least, adheres to Marx's formula that the aim of philosophy is not to represent the world, but rather to change it, it is peculiar that such theory doesn't seem to recognize that such cultural critiques seem to be fairly unsuccessful in producing their desired change. Here one would think that social and political theorists would become aware that this absence of change suggests that perhaps meanings, signifiers, signs, narratives, and discourses are not the entire story. One would think that *in addition* to these semiotic actors that play a role in collectives of humans and nonhumans, greater attention would be directed at the role of nonhuman actors in human collectives and the role they play in constraining the possibilities of existence. Such an attentiveness to these nonhuman actors would provide us with the resources for thinking strategies of composition that might push collectives into new basins of attraction. Whether or not a village has a well, a city has roads that provide access to other cities, and whether people have alternative forms of occupation and transportation can play a dramatic role in the form collectives take. However, in much of contemporary cultural theory, these sorts of actors are almost entirely invisible because the marked space of theory revolves around the semiotic, placing nonhuman actors in the unmarked space of thought and social engagement.

However, setting aside these criticisms, the more basic ontological point is that there can be no question of technological or environmental determinism precisely because objects cannot be determined by other objects. Insofar as all objects are withdrawn from one another, insofar as objects only relate to their environment selectively and through their own distinctions or organization, there can be no question of objects determining one another. This holds for humans as well. The most one object can do to another is perturb it, and even this is not always the case as objects are only selectively related to their environment such that there are many things towards which they are completely blind. In this regard, the manner in which one object responds to another always embodies a high degree of creativity.

In many respects, all of onticology culminates in the four theses of flat ontology. It is flat ontology that constitutes the democracy of objects. However, this democracy of objects does not amount to the thesis that all objects contribute equally to all other objects or to all collectives. Clearly tardigrades contribute little or nothing to collectives involving human beings. Here, then, I return to Ian Bogost's thesis that all objects equally exist, but not all objects exist equally. Entities perturb other objects more and less. Entities play greater and smaller roles in various collectives. Some entities, no doubt, do not perturb other objects at all, and as we saw in the case of Roy Bhasker in the first chapter, other objects are dormant. Flat ontology is not the thesis that all objects contribute equally, but that all objects equally exist. In its ontological egalitarianism, what flat ontology thus refuses is the erasure of any object as the mere construction of another object.

Notes

Introduction

1. Samuel Alexander, *Space, Time and Deity* vol. I (London: Adamant Media Corporation, 2007) p. 7.

2. Richard Dawkins, *The God Delusion* (New York: Houghton and Mifflin, 2008).

3. Bruno Latour, *We Have Never Been Modern*, trans. Catherine Porter (Cambridge, MA: Harvard University Press, 1993.

4. Karen Barad, *Meeting the Universe Halfway: Quantum Physics and the Entanglement of Matter and Meaning* (Durham: Duke University Press, 2007).

5. Claude Lévi-Strauss, *The Savage Mind* (Chicago: University of Chicago Press, 1966) pp. 17 - 18.

6. Marshall and Eric McLuhan, *Laws of Media: The New Science* (Toronto: University of Toronto Press, 1988) p. 42.

7. Latour, *The Pasteurization of France*, trans. Alan Sheridan and John Law (Cambridge, MA: Harvard University Press, 1988) p. 193.

Chapter 1

8. Martin Heidegger, *Being and Time*, trans. John Macquarrie and Edward Robinson (San Francisco: Harper Collins Publishers, 1962).

9. Jacques Lacan, *The Seminar of Jacques Lacan: Book XX, Encore: On Feminine Sexuality*, trans. Bruce Fink (New York: W.W. Norton & Co., 1998) p. 56.

10. Graham Harman, *Tool-Being: Heidegger and the Metaphysics of Objects* (Chicago: Open Court, 2002).

11. Quentin Meillassoux, Aft*er Finitude: An Essay on the Necessity of Contingency* (New York: Continuum, 2008) p. 6.

12. *Ibid.*, p. 5.

13. Michel Foucault, *The Order of Things: An Archaeology of the Human Sciences* (New York: Vintage Books, 1994).

14. Michel Foucault, *The Archaeology of Knowledge & The Discourse on Language*, trans. A.M. Sheridan Smith (New York: Pantheon Books, 1972).

15. Slavoj Žižek, *The Sublime Object of Ideology* (New York: Verso, 1989) pp. 87 - 89.

16. Roy Bhaskar, *A Realist Theory of Science* (New York: Routledge, 1998) p. 21.

17. Thomas S. Kuhn, *The Structure of Scientific Revolutions* (Chicago: University of Chicago Press, 1970).

18. Bhaskar, *A Realist Theory of Science*, p. 23.

19. Cf. Gilles Deleuze, "Immanence: A Life..." trans. Nick Millet, *Theory, Culture & Society – Explorations in Critical Social Science* 14.2 (1995).

20. Roy Bhaskar, *The Possibility of Naturalism: A Philosophical Critique of the Contemporary Human Sciences* (New York: Routledge, 1998) p. 5.

21. Bhaskar, *A Realist Theory of Science*, p. 13.

22. Ibid., p. 22.

23. Ibid., p. 33.

24. Ibid.

25. Ibid.

26. David Hume, *An Enquiry Concerning Human Understanding* (Oxford: Oxford University Press, 1999) p. 114.

27. Bhaskar, *The Possibility of Naturalism*, p. 9.

28. Bhaskar, *A Realist Theory of Science*, p. 46.

29. Ibid., p. 51.

30. Ibid., p. 13.

31. Ibid., p. 34.

32. Ibid., p. 50.

33. Bhaskar, *A Realist Theory of Science*, p. 39.

34. Heidegger, *Being and Time*, p. 34.

35. Bhaskar, *A Realist Theory of Science*, p. 39.

36. Meillassoux, *After Finitude*, p. 55.

37. Ibid., p. 56.

38. Ray Brassier, Iain Hamilton Grant, Graham Harman, Quentin Meillassoux, "Speculative Realism," *Collapse* vol. III (Falmouth: Athenaeum Press, 2007).

39. René Descartes, *Discourse on Method and Meditations on First Philosophy*, trans. Donald A. Cress (Indianapolis: Hackett Publishing Company, 1998) p. 69.

40. Immanuel Kant, *Critique of Pure Reason*, trans. Paul Guyer and Allen W. Wood (Cambridge: Cambridge University Press, 1998).

41. GW.F. Hegel, *Hegel's Phenomenology of Spirit,* trans. A.V. Miller (Oxford: Oxford University Press, 1977). Under Robert Pippin's reading, Kant's transcendental unity of apperception and the manner in which it is necessarily included in all representations is the key to Hegel's absolute idealism. Cf. Robert B. Pippin, *Hegel's Idealism: The Satisfactions of Self-Consciousness* (Cambridge: Cambridge University Press, 1999).

42. Bhaskar, *A Realist Theory of Science*, p. 48.

43. Jean-Paul Sartre, *The Transcendence of the Ego*, trans. Forrest Williams and Robert Kirkpatrick (New York: Hill and Wang, 1990) pp. 40 - 42.

44. Bhaskar, *A Realist Theory of Science*, p. 64.

45. Graham Harman, *Prince of Networks: Bruno Latour and Metaphysics* (Melbourne: Re.Press, 2009) pp. 112 - 116.

46. Bhaskar, *A Realist Theory of Science*, p. 36.

47.   Ibid., p. 16.

Chapter 2

48.   Jane Bennett, *Vibrant Matter: A Political Ecology of Things* (Durham: Duke University Press, 2010) p. 5.

49.   Graham Harman, *The Quadruple Object* (Winchester, UK: Zer0 Books, forthcoming).

50.   Alain Badiou, *Logics of Worlds*, trans. Alberto Toscano (New York: Continuum, 2009) p. 119.

51.   Graham Harman, *Guerrilla Metaphysics: Phenomenology and the Carpentry of Things* (Chicago: Open Court, 2005) p. 76.

52.   Ibid., p. 81.

53.   Aristotle, Metaphysics, in *The Complete Works of Aristotle (Two Volumes)* ed. Jonathan Barnes (Princeton: Princeton University Press, 1984) p. 1028a10 - 30.

54.   Aristotle, Categories, *Complete Works*, p. 2a10 - 15.

55.   Ibid., p. 2b25.

56.   Harman, *Guerrilla Metaphysics*, p. 76.

57.   Ibid., p. 85.

58.   Aristotle, Categories, p. 3a10.

59.   Ibid., p. 3b35.

60.   Ibid., p. 3b25.

61.   Ibid., p. 4a10.

62.   Ibid.

63.   Ibid., 8b25.

64.   Gilles Deleuze, *Difference and Repetition*, trans. Paul Patton (New York: Columbia University Press, 1994) p. 35.

65.   John Locke, *An Essay Concerning Human Understanding* (Oxford: Clarendon Press, 1979) pp. 295 – 296.

66.   Kenneth Burke, *A Grammar of Motives* (Berkeley: University of California Press, 1969) p. 23.

67.   Meillassoux, *After Finitude*, p. 6.

68.   Kant, *Critique of Pure Reason*, p. A176/B219.

69.   Ibid., p. A43/B60.

70.   Ibid., p. A182/B225.

71.   Harman, *The Quadruple Object*, chapter 1.

72.   Kant, *Critique of Pure Reason*, p. A270/B326.

73.   Ibid., A271/B327.

74.   Harman, *The Quadruple Object*.

75.   Gilles Deleuze, *Bergsonism*, trans. Hugh Tomlinson and Barbara Habberjam (New York: Zone Books, 1991) p. 44.

Chapter 3

76.   Timothy Morton, *The Ecological Thought* (Cambridge, MA: Harvard University Press, 2010) p. 7.

77.   Steven Connor, "Topologies: Michel Serres and the Shapes of Thought," *Anglistik* 15 (2004): 106. Quoted in Cary Wolfe, "Bring the Noise: The Parasite and the Multiple Genealogies of Posthumanism", in Michel Serres, *The Parasite*, p. xvii.

78.   Henri Bergson, *Matter and Memory*, trans. Nancy Margaret Paul (New York: Zone Books, 1991) pp. 48 - 49.

79.   Gilbert Simondon, *L'Individuation: à la lumière des notions de forme et d'information* (Millon: PUF, 2005) p. 51.

80.   Pierre Bourdieu, *Pascalian Meditations,* trans. Richard Nice (Stanford: Stanford University Press, 2000).

81.   Manuel DeLanda, *Intensive Science & Virtual Philosophy* (New York: Continuum, 2002) p. 23.

82.   Deleuze, *Difference and Repetition*, pp. 186 - 187. Modified.

83.   Ibid., pp. 208 - 209.

84.   Ibid., p. 209.

85.   Barad, *Meeting the Universe Halfway*, p. 69.

86.   Deleuze, *Difference and Repetition,* p. 228.

87.   Ibid., p. 229.

88.   Ibid., p. 38.

89.   Peter Hallward, *Out of This World: Deleuze and the Philosophy of Creation* (New York: Verso, 2006) p. 2.

90.   John Protevi, "Out of This World: Deleuze and the Philosophy of Creation," *Notre Dame Philosophy Reviews*, August 3, 2007.

91.   Ibid.

92.   Deleuze, *Difference and Repetition*, p. 183.

93.   Deleuze, *Negotiations*, trans. Martin Joughin (New York: Columbia University Press, 1995) p. 136.

94.   Deleuze, *Difference and Repetition*, p. 208.

95.   Ibid., p. 209.

96.   Ibid., p. 210.

97.   Ibid., p. 182.

98.   DeLanda, *Intensive Science and Virtual Philosophy*, pp. 11 - 12.

99. Deleuze, *Difference and Repetition*, p. 182.

100. Ibid., p. 183.

101. Ibid.

102. Ibid., p. 209.

103. Harman, *Tool-Being*, p. 244.

104. Ibid.

105. Ibid., pp. 246 - 247.

106. Deleuze, *Difference and Repetition*, p. 278.

107. Ibid., p. 222.

108. DeLanda, *Intensive Science and Virtual Philosophy*, p. 10.

109. Ibid., p. 47.

110. Aristotle, Metaphysics, p. 1033a25.

111. DeLanda, *Intensive Science and Virtual Philosophy*, p. 15.

112. Ibid.

113. Ibid., p. 31 - 32.

114. Ibid., p. 32.

115. Bruno Latour, "Irreductions," *The Pasteurization of France* trans. Alan Sheridan and John Law (Cambridge, MA: Harvard University Press, 1988) p. 174.

116. Ibid.

117. Harman, *Prince of Networks*, p. 128.

118. Ibid.

119. Steven Shaviro, *Without Criteria: Kant, Whitehead, Deleuze, and Aesthetics* (Cambridge, MA: The MIT Press, 2009) p. 19.

120. Benedict de Spinoza, *Spinoza: Complete Works*, trans. Samuel Shirley (Indianpolis: Hackett Publishing Company, Inc., 2002) p. 278.

121. Harman, "Levi Responds," *Object-Oriented Philosophy*. May 24, 2010. Available at http://doctorzamalek2.wordpress.com/?s=Levi+Responds.

122. Deleuze, *Difference and Repetition*, p. 211.

123. Ibid.

124. Ibid., p. 212.

125. Latour, "Irreductions," p. 158.

126. Harman, *Prince of Networks*, p. 129.

127. Harman, *Guerrilla Metaphysics*, p. 81.

128. Slavoj Žižek, *The Parallax View* (Cambridge, MA: The MIT Press, 2006) p. 17.

129. Ibid.

130. Slavoj Žižek, *For They Know Not What They Do: Enjoyment as a Political Factor* (New York: Verso, 2002) p. xxvii.

131. Ibid., p. xxvii.

132. For an excellent discussion of how Žižek overcomes this deadlock by drawing on Hegel, cf. Adrian Johnston, *Žižek's Ontology: A Transcendental Materialist Theory of Subjectivity* (Evanston: Northwestern University Press, 2008).

133. Slavoj Žižek, *The Sublime Object of Ideology* (New York: Verso, 1989) p. 193.

134. Žižek, *For They Know Not What They Do*, p. 36 - 37.

135. Slavoj Žižek, *Tarrying With the Negative: Kant, Hegel, and the Critique of Ideology* (Durham: Duke University Press, 1993) p. 36 - 37.

136. Ibid., p. 37.

137. Cf. Žižek, *For They Know Not What They Do*, pp. 72 - 80.

138. Ibid., p. 112.

139. Slavoj Žižek, *The Puppet and the Dwarf: The Perverse Core of Christianity* (Cambridge, MA: The MIT Press, 2003) p. 66.

140. Žižek, *The Parallax View*, 26.

141. Ibid.

142. Ibid., p. 18.

143. Lacan, *Encore*, p. 56.

144. Ibid., p. 33.

145. cf. Barad, *Meeting the Universe Halfway*.

146. Ibid., p. 74.

147. Ibid., p. 72.

148. Ibid., p. 58.

Chapter 4

149. Latour, "Irreductions," p. 166.

150. Alfred North Whitehead, *Process and Reality* (New York: The Free Press, 1978) p. 23.

151. Ibid.

152. Humberto R. Maturana and Francisco J. Varela, "Autopoiesis: The Organization of the Living", in *Autopoiesis and Cognition: The Realization of the Living* (Boston: D. Reidel Publishing Company, 1980) pp. 78 - 82.

153. Niklas Luhmann, *Social Systems*, trans. John Bednarz, Jr. (Chicago: University of Chicago Press, 1989) p. 12.

154. Luhman, "Identity—What or How?", in *Theories of Distinction: Redescribing the Descriptions of Modernity*, ed. William Rasch (Stanford: Stanford University Press, 2002) p. 115.

155. Ibid., p. 118.

156. G. Spencer-Brown, *Laws of Form* (New York: E.P. Dutton, 1979) p. 1.

157. Luhmann, *Social Systems*, p. 29.

158. Heinz von Foester, *Understanding Understanding: Essays on Cybernetics and Cognition* (New York: Springer-Verlag, 2003) p. 266.

159. Gotthard Bechmann and Nico Stehr, "The Legacy of Niklas Luhmann," *Society* 39 (2002) p. 70.

160. Maturana and Varela, *The Tree of Knowledge: The Biological Roots of Human Understanding*, trans. Robert Paolucci (Boston: Shambhala, 1992).p. 89.

161. Maturana and Varela, "Autopoiesis: The Organization of the Living", pp. 78 - 79.

162. Luhman, *Social Systems*, pp. 21 - 22.

163. Maturana and Varela, "Autopoiesis: The Organization of the Living", p. 78.

164. Luhmann, *Social Systems*, p. 65.

165. Ibid., pp. 40 - 41.

166. Ibid., p. 17.

167. Ibid., pp. 16 - 17.

168. Ibid., 25.

169. Ibid.

170. Ibid., 20.

171. Ibid., p. 24.

172. Ibid., p. 21.

173. Ibid., p. 25.

174. Ibid., p. 22.

175. Ibid., p. 17.

176. Morton, *The Ecological Thought*, p. 60.

177. Luhmann, *Social Systems*, p. 210.

178. Ibid., p. 212.

179. Luhmann, *Ecological Communication,* trans. John Bednarz, Jr. (Chicago: University of Chicago Press, 1989) p. 29.

180. Ibid., p. 18.

181. Luhmann, "What is Communication?", *Theories of Distinction*, ed. William Rasch (Stanford: Stanford University Press, 2002) p. 156.

182. Luhmann, *Social Systems*, p. 59.

183. Hans-George Moeller, *Luhmann Explained: From Souls to Systems* (Chicago: Open Court, 2006) p. 11.

184. Luhmann, *Social Systems*, p. 36.

185. Luhmann, "The Cognitive Program of Constructivism and the Reality that Remains Unknown", in *Theories of Distinction*, p. 135.

186. Luhmann, "The Autopoisis of Social Systems", in *Essays on Self-Reference* (New York: Columbia University Press, 1990) p. 10.

187. Luhmann, *Social Systems*, p. 40.

188. Ibid., p. 67.

189. Gregory Bateson, "Pathologies of Epistemology", in *Steps to an Ecology of Mind* (Chicago: University of Chicago Press, 2000) p. 490.

190. Bateson, "Form, Substance, and Difference", in *Steps to an Ecology of Mind*, p. 458.

191. Luhmann, *Social Systems*, p. 75.

192. Luhmann, "Meaning as Sociology's Basic Concept", *Essays on Self-Reference*, p. 31.

193. Luhmann, *Social Systems*, p. 67.

194. Luhmann, "Meaning as Sociology's Basic Concept," p. 25.

195. Ibid., p. 27.

196. Luhmann, *Ecological Communication*, p. 22 - 23.

197. Niklas Luhmann, "The Cognitive Program of Constructivism and the Reality That Remains Unknown", in *Theories of Distinction*, p. 145.

198. Cf. Harman, *Prince of Networks*, pp. 188 - 211.

199. Ibid., pp. 189 - 190.

200. Gilbert Gottlieb, "A Developmental Psychobiological System's View: Early Formulation and Current Status", in *Cycles of Contingency: Developmental Systems and Evolution*, eds. Oyama, Susan, Paul E. Griffiths, and Russell D. Gray (Cambridge, MA: The MIT Press, 2001) pp. 41 - 42.

201. Ibid.

202. Lacan, *The Four Fundamental Concepts of Psychoanalysis*, trans. Alan Sheridan (New York: W.W. Norton & Co., 1998) pp. 21 - 23.

203. Ibid., p. 22.

204. Ibid.

205. Ibid., p. 21.

206. For a detailed discussion of Lacan's discourse theory, cf. Levi R. Bryant, "Žižek's New Universe of Discourse: Politics and the Discourse of the Capitalist," *International Journal of Žižek Studies* 2.4 (2008).

207. Lacan, *The Four Fundamental Concepts of Psychoanalysis*, p. 22.

208. Latour, "Irreductions," p. 181.

209. Ibid., p. 162.

210. Latour, *Reassembling the Social: An Introduction to Actor-Network Theory* (Oxford: Oxford University Press, 2005) p. 39.

211. Latour, "An Attempt at Writing a 'Compositionist Manifesto'" Available athttp://www.bruno-latour.fr/articles/article/120-COMPO-MANIFESTO.pdf.

212. Michel Foucault, *Discipline and Punish: The Birth of the Prison*, trans. Alan Sheridan (New York: Vintage Books, 1995) pp. 135 - 169.

213. Ibid., p. 135.

214. Richard Lewontin, "Gene, Organism and Environment: A New Introduction", in *Cycles of Contingency*, pp. 55 - 56.

215. Ibid., p. 55.

216. Susan Oyama, "Terms in Tension: What Do You Do When All the Good Words are Taken?", in *Cycles of Contingency*, pp. 182 - 183.

217. Latour, *Reassembling the Social*, p. 8.

218. Loet Leydesdorff, *A Sociological Theory of Communication: The Self-Organization of the Knowledge-Based Society* (Universal Publishers, 2003) pp. 5 - 6.

219. Lacan, *The Seminar of Jacques Lacan: Book II: The Ego in Freud's Theory and in the Technique of Psychoanalysis*, trans. Sylvana Tomaselli (New York: W.W. Norton & Co., 1988).

220. Lacan, *Écrits: The First Complete Edition in English*, trans. Bruce Fink (New York: W.W. Norton & Co., 2006) p. 223.

221. Lacan, *The Seminar of Jacques Lacan: Seminar X: Anxiety (1962 - 1963)*, trans. Cormac Gallagher (Unpublished) lesson of 14 November 1962.

222. Slavoj Žižek, *The Plague of Fantasies* (New York: Verso, 1997) p. 7.

223. Cf. Žižek, *Tarrying With the Negative*, pp. 9 - 12.

224. Jacques Lacan, *Écrits*, p. 357.

Chapter 5

225. Richard Lewontin, "Gene, Organism and Environment", in *Cycles of Contingency*, p. 62.

226. G.W. Leibniz, "The Principles of Philosophy, or, the Monadology (1714)," in *Discourse on Metaphysics and Other Essays*, p. 78.

227. Cary Wolfe, *Critical Environments: Postmodern Theory and the Pragmatics of the "Outside"* (Minneapolis: University of Minnesota Press, 1998) p. 77.

228. Robert C. Tucker (ed.), *The Marx-Engels Reader* (New York: Norton, 1978) p. 595.

229. Paul Bains, *The Primacy of Semiosis: An Ontology of Relations* (Toronto: University of Toronto Press, 2006) p. 90.

230. Ibid.

231. Deleuze, *Difference and Repetition*, pp. 216 - 217.

232. Oyama, *The Ontogeny of Information: Developmental Systems and Evolution*, p. 16.

233. Oyama et. al., *Cycles of Contingency*, p. 2.

234. Richard C. Lewontin, "Gene, Organism, and Environment", in *Cycles of Contingency*, p. 64.

235. Ibid., p. 64.

236. Jared Diamond, *Guns, Germs, and Steel: The Fates of Human Societies* (New York: W.W. Norton & Co., 2005).

237. Paul E. Griffiths and Russell D. Gray, "Darwinism and Developmental Systems," in *Cycles of Contingency*, p. 198.

238. Karl Marx, *Capital* vol. I, trans. Ben Fowkes (New York: Penguin Books, 1990) pp. 340 – 416.

239. Louis Althusser, *Lenin and Philosophy and Other Essays*, trans. Ben Brewster (New York: Monthly Review Press, 2001) p. 116.

240. Ibid., p. 85.

241. Claude Lévi-Strauss, *Introduction to the Work of Marcel Mauss*, trans. Felicity Baker (New York: Routledge,1987) pp. 55 – 56.

242. Ibid., p. 63.

243. Louis Althussser, *Philosophy of the Encounter: Later Writings, 1978 – 1987*, eds. Oliver Corpet François Matheron, trans. G. M. Goshgarian (London: Verso, 2006).

244. Jacques Rancière, *Disagreement: Politics and Philosophy*, trans. Julie Rose (Minneapolis: University of Minnesota Press, 1999).

245. Alain Badiou, *Being and Event*, trans. Oliver Feltham (New York: Continuum, 2005).

246. For the rat-brained robot of Surrey, England cf. http://www.youtube.com/watch?v=1QPiF4-iu6g.

247. Benedict Anderson, *Imagined Communities* (New York: Verso, 2006).

248. Latour, "Irreductions," p. 159.

249. R. Maturana and Varela, *The Tree of Knowledge*, p. 75.

250. Latour, "Irreductions," p. 197.

251. Peter Sloterdijk, *Critique of Cynical Reason*, trans. Michael Eldred (Minneapolis: University of Minnesota Press, 1987.

252. Žižek, *The Sublime Object of Ideology*, p. 29.

253. Niklas Luhmann, *The Reality of the Mass Media*, trans. Kathleen Cross (Stanford: Stanford University Press, 2000) p. 23.

254. Luhmann, *Social Systems*, p. 282.

255. Henri Bergson, *Matter and Memory*, p. 105.

256. Luhmann, *Social Systems*, p. 283.

257. Ibid.

258. Ibid., p. 287.

259. Ibid., p. 286.

260. Ibid., p. 287.

261. Jean-Paul Sartre, *Being and Nothingness: A Phenomenological Essay on Ontology*, trans. Hazel E.Barnes (New York: Washington Square Press, 1984) pp. 40 - 42.

262. Jared Diamond, *Collapse: How Societies Choose to Fail or Succeed* (New York: Penguin Books, 2005) p. 431.

263. Ibid., p. 430.

Chapter 6

264. Virginia Woolf, *Jacob's Room* (New York: Hartcourt Brace & Company, 1992) p. 9.

265. Bruce Fink, *Lacan to the Letter: Reading Écrits Closely* (Minneapolis: University of Minnesota Press, 2004) p. 158.

266. Ibid., p. 155.

267. Lacan, *Encore*, p. 78.

268. Carl Schmitt, *The Concept of the Political,* trans. George Schwab (Chicago: University of Chicago Press, 1996).

269. Lacan, *Encore*, p. 72.

270. Fink, *Lacan to the Letter*, p. 161.

271. Bruce Fink, *A Clinical Introduction to Lacanian Psychoanalysis: Theory and Technique* (Cambridge, MA: Harvard University Press, 1997) p. 51.

272. Lacan, *Encore*, p. 12.

273. Jacques Lacan, *The Seminar of Jacques Lacan: The Logic of Fantasy (1966 - 1967):Seminar XIV,* trans. Cormac Gallagher (Unpublished) lesson of 16 November 1966.

274. Ibid.

275. Jacques Lacan, *The Seminar of Jacques Lacan: The Other Side of Psychoanalysis: Seminar XVII,* trans. Russell Grigg (New York: W.W. Norton & Company, 2007) p. 23.

276. Žižek, *The Sublime Object of Ideology*, p. 181.

277. Ibid., p. 191.

278. Lacan, *Encore*, p. 74 - 76.

279. Brassier et al., "Speculative Realism," p. 367.

280. Žižek, *Tarrying with the Negative*, chapter 5.

281. Morton, *The Ecological Thought*, p. 42.

282. Lacan, *The Four Fundamental Concepts of Psychoanalysis*, p. 276.

283. Morton, *The Ecological Thought*, p. 81.

284. Badiou, *Logics of Worlds*, pp. 109 - 112.

285. Morton, *Ecology Without Nature: Rethinking Environmental Aesthetics*, pp. 181 - 197.

286. Bruno Latour, *Pandora's Hope: Essays on the Reality of Science Studies* (Cambridge, MA: Harvard University Press, 1999) p. 304.

287. Gilles Deleuze and Félix Guattari, *Anti-Oedipus: Capitalism and Schizophrenia*, trans. Robert Hurley, Mark Seem, and Helen R. Lane (Minneapolis: University of Minnesota Press, 1983) p. 2.

288. Gilles Deleuze, *Proust and Signs: The Complete Text*, trans. Richard Howard (Minneapolis: University of Minnesota Press, 2000) pp. 164 - 165.

289. Latour, *Reassembling the Social*, pp. 8 - 9.

290. Harman, *Guerrilla Metaphysics*, p. 1.

291. Ian Bogost, "Materialisms: The Stuff of Things is Many", at Ian Bogost—Video Game Theory, Criticism, Design, February 21, 2010, http://www.bogost.com/blog/materialisms.shtml.

292. Harman, *Tool-Being*, p. 2.

293. Ibid.

294. John Protevi, *Political Affect: Connecting the Social and the Somatic* (Minneapolis: University of Minnesota Press, 2009) p. 9.

295. Félix Guattari, *Chaosmosis: An Ethico-Aesthetic Paradigm*, trans. Paul Bains and Julian Pefanis (Bloomington: Indiana University Press, 1995) p. 4.

Bibliography

Alexander, Samuel. *Space, Time, and Deity.* Vol 1. London: Adamant Media Corporation, 2007.

Althusser, Louis. *Lenin and Philosophy and Other Essays.* Ben Brewster, trans. New York: Monthly Review Press, 2001.

Althusser, Louis, and Balibar, Étienne. *Reading Capital.* Ben Brewster, trans. New York: Verso, 2009.

Anderson, Benedict. *Imagined Communities.* New York: Verso, 2006.

Aristotle. *The Complete Works of Aristotle.* Vol 1 & 2. Jonathan Barnes, ed. Princeton: Princeton University Press, 1984.

Badiou, Alain. *Being and Event.* Oliver Feltham, trans. New York: Continuum, 2005.

———. *Logics of Worlds: Being and Event II.* Alberto Toscano, trans. New York: Continuum, 2009.

Bains, Paul. *The Primacy of Semiosis: An Ontology of Relations.* Toronto: University of Toronto Press, 2006.

Barad, Karen. *Meeting the Universe Halfway: Quantum Physics and the Engtanglement of Matter and Meaning.* Durham: Duke University Press, 2007.

Bateson, Gregory. *Mind and Nature: A Necessary Unity.* Cresskill, NJ: Hampton Press, Inc., 2002.

———. *Steps to an Ecology of Mind.* Chicago: The University of Chicago Press, 2000.

Bechmann, Gotthard, and Stehr, Nico. "The Legacy of Niklas Luhmann". *Society* (39), 2002.

Bennett, Jane. *Vibrant Matter: A Political Ecology of Things.* Durham: Duke University Press, 2010.

Berger, Peter L. and Luckmann, Thomas. *The Social Construction of Reality: A Treatise in the Sociology of Knowledge.* New York: Anchor Books, 1967.

Bergson, Henri. *Matter and Memory*. Nancy Margaret Paul, trans. New York: Zone Books, 1991.

Bhaskar, Roy. *The Possibility of Naturalism: A Philosophical Critique of Contemporary Human Sciences*. New York: Routledge, 1998.

———. *A Realist Theory of Science*. New York: Routledge, 2008.

———. *Scientific Realism and Human Emancipation*. New York: Routledge, 2009.

Bogost, Ian. "Materialisms: The Stuff of Things is Many". *Ian Bogost—Video Game Theory, Criticism, Design*. February 21, 2010, Available at http://www.bogost.com/blog/materialisms.shtml">http://www.bogost.com/blog/materialisms.shtml

Bogost, Ian. *Persuasive Games: The Expressive Power of Videogames*. Cambridge, MA: The MIT Press, 2007.

———. *Unit Operations: An Approach to Videogame Criticism*. Cambridge, MA: The MIT Press, 2008.

Bonta, Mark, and John Protevi. *Deleuze and Geophilosophy: A Guide and Glossary*. Edinburgh: Edinburgh University Press, 2004.

Bourdieu, Pierre. *Pascalian Meditations*. Richard Nice, trans. Stanford: Stanford University Press, 2000.

Braudel, Fernand. *Civilization and Capitalism; The Structures of Everyday Life: Volume 1*. Siân Reynolds, trans. New York: Harper & Row Publishers, 1981.

———. *Civilization and Capitalism: The Wheels of Commerce: Volume 2*. Siân Reynolds, trans. New York: Harper & Row Publishers, 1982.

———. *Civilization and Capitalism: The Perspective of the World: Volume 3*. Siân Reynolds, trans. New York: Harper & Row Publishers, 1984.

Bryant, Levi R. *Difference and Givenness: Deleuze's Transcendental Empiricism and the Ontology of Immanence*. Evanston: Northwestern University Press, 2008.

———. "Žižek's New Universe of Discourse: Politics and the Discourse of the Capitalist". *International Journal of Žižek Studies* 2.4, 2008.

Burke, Kenneth. *A Grammar of Motives*. Berkeley: University of California Press, 1969.

Conner, Steven. "Topologies: Michel Serres and the Shapes of Thought". *Anglistik* 15, 2004.

Dawkins, *The God Delusion*. New York: Houghton and Mifflin, 2008.

DeLanda, Manuel. *Intensive Science and Virtual Philosophy*. New York: Continuum, 2002.

———. *A New Philosophy of Society: Assemblage Theory and Social Complexity*. New York: Continuum, 2006.

———. *A Thousand Years of Nonlinear History*. New York: Zone Books, 1997.

Deleuze, Gilles. *Bergsonism*. Hugh Tomlinson and Barbara Habberjam, trans. New York: Zone Books, 1991.

———. *Difference and Repetition*. Paul Patton, trans. New York: Columbia University Press, 1994.

———. *Empiricism and Subjectivity*. Constantin V. Boundas, trans. New York: Columbia University Press, 1991.

———. "Immanence: A Life..". Nick Millet, trans. *Theory, Culture & Society – Explorations in Critical Social Science* 14.2 (1995).

———. *Logic of Sense*. Mark Lester and Charles Stivale, trans. New York: Continuum, 2009.

———. *Negotiations*. Martin Joughin, trans. New York: Columbia University Press, 1995.

———. *Nietzsche and Philosophy*. Hugh Tomlinson, trans. New York: Columbia University Press, 2006.

———. *Proust and Signs: The Complete Text*. Richard Howard, trans. Minneapolis: University of Minnesota Press, 2000.

———. *Two Regimes of Madness: Texts and Interviews 1975 - 1995*. Ames Hodges and Mike Taormina, trans. New York: Semiotext(e), 2006.

Deleuze, Gilles and Guattari, Félix. *Anti-Oedipus: Capitalism and Schizophrenia*. Robert Hurley, Mark Seem, and Helen R. Lane, trans. Minneapolis: University of Minnesota Press, 1983.

———. *A Thousand Plateaus: Capitalism and Schizophrenia*. Brian Massumi, trans. Minneapolis: University of Minnesota Press, 1987.

———. *What is Philosophy?* Hugh Tomlinson and Graham Burchell, trans. New York: Columbia University Press, 1994.

Deleuze, Gilles and Parnet, Claire. *Dialogues*. Hugh Tomlinson and Barbara Habberjam, trans. New York: Columbia University Press, 1987.

Descartes, René. *Discourse on Method and Meditations on First Philosophy: Fourth Edition*. Donald A. Cress, trans. Indianapolis: Hackett Publishing Company, 1998.

Diamond, Jared. *Guns, Germs, and Steel: The Fates of Human Societies*. New York: W.W. Norton & Co., 2005.

———. *Collapse: How Societies Choose to Fail or Succeed*. New York: Penguin Books, 2005.

Fink, Bruce. *A Clinical Introduction to Lacanian Psychoanalysis: Theory and Technique*. Cambridge, MA: Harvard University Press, 1997.

———. *Lacan to the Letter*. Minneapolis: University of Minnesota Press, 2004.

Foester, Heinz von. *Understanding Understanding: Essays on Cybernetics and Cognition*. New York: Springer-Verlag, 2003.

Foucault, Michel. *The Archaeology of Knowledge and The Discourse on Language*. A.M. Sheridan Smith, trans. New York: Pantheon Books, 1972.

———. *Discipline and Punish: The Birth of the Prison*. Alan Sheridan, trans. New York: Vintage Books, 1995.

———. *The Order of Things: An Archaeology of the Human Sciences*. New York: Vintage Books, 1994.

Guattari, Félix. *Chaosmosis: An Ethico-Aesthetic Paradigm*. Paul Bains and Julian Pefanis, trans. Bloomington: Indiana University Press, 1995.

Hallward, Peter. *Out of this World: Deleuze and the Philosophy of Creation.* New York: Verso, 2006.

Haraway, Donna J. *Modest_Witness@Second_Millennium.Female-Man©_Meets_OncoMouse^{TM}: Feminism and Technoscience.* New York: Routledge, 1997.

———. *Simians, Cyborgs and Women: The Reinvention of Nature.* New York: Routledge, 1991.

Harman, Graham. "Levi Responds". *Object-Oriented Philosophy.* May 24, 2010. Available at http://doctorzamalek2.wordpress.com/?s=Levi+Responds http://doctorzamalek2.wordpress.com/?s=Levi+Responds.

———. *Guerrilla Metaphysics: Phenomenology and the Carpentry of Things.* Chicago: Open Court, 2005.

———. "Speculative Realism: Ray Brassier, Iain Hamilton Grant, Graham Harman". *Collapse.* Volume III, Falmouth: Athenaeum Press, 2007.

———. *Prince of Networks: Bruno Latour and Metaphysics.* Melbourne: Re.Press, 2009.

———. *Tool-Being: Heidegger and the Metaphysics of Objects.* Chicago: Open Court, 2002.

———. *The Quadruple Object.* Winchester, UK: Zer0 Books, forthcoming.

Hayles, N. Katherine. *How We Became Posthuman: Virtual Bodies in Cybernetics, Literature, and Informatics.* Chicago: University of Chicago Press, 1999.

———. *My Mother Was a Computer: Digital Subjects and Literary Texts.* Chicago: The University of Chicago Press, 2005.

Hegel, G.W.F. *Hegel's Phenomenology of Spirit.* A.V. Miller, trans. Oxford: Oxford University Press, 1977.

———. *Hegel's Science of Logic.* A.V. Miller, trans. Atlantic Highlands: Humanities Press International, Inc., 1989.

Heidegger, Martin. *Being and Time.* John Macquarrie and Edward Robinson, trans. San Francisco: Harper Collins Publishers, 1962.

Hume, David. *An Enquiry Concerning Human Understanding.* Oxford: Oxford University Press, 1999.

———. *A Treatise on Human Nature.* Oxford: Oxford University Press, 2000.

Husserl, Edmund. *Ideas Pertaining to a Pure Pheomenology and to a Phenomenological Philosophy: First Book.* F. Kersten, trans. Martinus Nijhoff Publishers, 1983.

Johnston, Adrian. *Žižek's Ontology: A Transcendental Materialist Theory of Subjectivity.* Evanston: Northwestern University Press, 2008.

Kant, Immanuel. *Critique of Pure Reason.* Paul Guyer and Allen W. Wood, trans. Cambridge: Cambridge University Press, 1998.

Kuhn, Thomas S. *The Structure of Scientific Revolutions.* Chicago: The University of Chicago Press, 1970.

Lacan, Jacques. *Anxiety: Book X.* Cormac Gallagher, trans. Unpublished.

———. *Écrits,* Bruce Fink, trans. New York: W.W. Norton & Co., 2006.

———. *The Ego in Freud's Theory and in the Technique of Psychoanalysis: Book II.* Sylvana Tomaselli, trans. New York: W.W. Norton & Co., 1988.

———. *Encore: On Feminine Sexuality, The Limits of Love and Knowledge: Book XX.* Bruce Fink, trans. New York: W.W. Norton & Co., 1998.

———. *The Four Fundamental Concepts of Psychoanalysis: Book XI.* Alan Sheridan, trans. New York: W.W. Norton & Co., 1998.

———. *The Logic of Fantasy: Book XIV.* Cormac Gallagher, trans. Unpublished.

———. *The Other Side of Psychoanalysis.* Russell Grigg, trans. New York: W.W. Norton & Co., 2007.

Latour, Bruno. "An Attempt at Writing a 'Compositionist Manifesto'",. Available at http://www.bruno-latour.fr/articles/article/120-COMPO-MANIFESTO.pdf, http://www.bruno-latour.fr/articles/article/120-COMPO-MANIFESTO.pdf.

———. *Pandora's Hope: Essays on the Reality of Science Studies.* Cambridge, MA: Harvard University Press, 1999.

———. *The Pasteurization of France*. Alan Sheridan and John Law, trans. Cambridge, MA: Harvard University Press, 1988.

———. *Politics of Nature: How to Bring the Sciences Into Democracy*. Catherine Porter, trans. Cambridge, MA: Harvard University Press, 2004.

———. *Reassembling the Social: An Introduction to Actor-Network-Theory*. Oxford: Oxford University Press, 2005.

———. *We Have Never Been Modern*. Catherine Porter, trans. Cambridge, MA: Harvard University Press, 1993.

Lévi-Strauss, Claude. *The Elementary Structures of Kinship*. James Harle Bell, John Richard von Sturmer, and Rodney Needham, trans. Boston: Beacon Press, 1969.

———. *Introduction to the Work of Marcel Mauss*. Felicity Baker, trans. New York: Routledge, 1987.

———. *The Savage Mind*. Chicago: The University of Chicago Press, 1966.

———. *Structural Anthropology*. Claire Jacobson and Brooke Grundfest Schoepf, trans. San Francisco, Basic Books, 1963.

Leibniz, G.W. *Discourse on Metaphysics and Other Essays*. Daniel Garber and Roger Ariew, trans. Indianapolis: Hackett Publishing Company, 1991.

Leydesdorff, Loet. *A Sociological Theory of Communication: The Self-Organization of the Knowledge-Based Society*. Universal Publishers, 2003.

Locke, John. *An Essay Concerning Human Understanding*. Oxford: Clarendon Press, 1979.

Luhmann, Niklas. *Ecological Communication*. John Bednarz, Jr., trans. Chicago: The University of Chicago Press, 1989.

———. *Essays on Self-Reference*. New York: Columbia University Press, 1990.

———. *Problems of Form*. Michael Irmscher and Leah Edwards, trans. Stanford: Stanford University Press, 1999.

———. *The Reality of the Mass Media*. Kathleen Cross, trans. Stanford: Stanford University Press, 2000.

————. *Social Systems*. John Bednarz, Jr. and Dirk Baecker, trans. Stanford: Stanford University Press, 1995.

————. *Theories of Distinction: Redescribing the Descriptions of Modernity*. William Rasch, ed. Stanford: Stanford University Press, 2002.

Marx, Karl. *Capital*. Vol I. Ben Fowkes, trans. New York: Penguin Books, 1990.

————. *The Marx-Engels Reader*. Robert C. Tucker, ed. New York: W.W. Norton & Co., 1978.

Maturana, Humberto R. and Varela, Francisco J. *Autopoiesis and Cognition: The Realization of the Living*. Boston: D. Reidel Publishing Company, 1980.

————. *The Tree of Knowledge: The Biological Roots of Human Understanding*. Robert Paolucci, trans. Boston: Shambhala, 1992.

McLuhan, Marshall and Eric McLuhan. *Laws of Media: The New Science*. Toronto: University of Toronto Press, 1988.

Meillassoux, Quentin. *After Finitude: An Essay on the Necessity of Contingency*. New York: Continuum, 2008.

————. "Presentation by Quentin Meillassoux". *Collapse*. Vol. III. Falmouth, UK, Athenaeum Press, 2007.

Moeller, Hans-Georg. *Luhmann Explained: From Souls to Systems*. Chicago: Open Court, 2006.

Morton, Timothy. *The Ecological Thought*. Cambridge, MA: Harvard University Press, 2010.

————. *Ecology Without Nature: Rethinking Environmental Aesthetics*. Cambridge, MA: Harvard University Press, 2007.

Oyama, Susan, Paul E. Griffiths, and Russell D. Gray, eds. *Cycles of Contingency: Developmental Systems and Evolution*. Cambridge, MA: The MIT Press, 2001.

Oyama, Susan. *The Ontogeny of Information: Developmental Systems and Evolution*. Durham: Duke University Press, 2000.

Pippin, Robert B. *Hegel's Idealism: The Satisfactions of Self-Consciousness.* Cambridge: Cambridge University Press, 1999.

Protevi, John. "Out of This World: Deleuze and the Philosophy of Creation". *Notre Dame Philosophy Reviews*, August 3, 2007.

————. *Political Affect: Connecting the Social and the Somatic.* Minneapolis: University of Minnesota Press, 2009.

Rancière, Jacques. *Disagreement: Politics and Philosophy.* Julie Rose, trans. Minneapolis: University of Minnesota Press, 1999.

Sartre, Jean-Paul. *Being and Nothingness: A Phenomenological Essay on Ontology.* Hazel E. Barnes, trans. New York: Washington Square Press, 1984.

————. *The Transcendence of the Ego: An Existentialist Theory of Consciousness.* Forrest Williams and Robert Kirkpatrick, trans. New York: Hill and Wang, 1990.

Serres, Michel. *The Parasite.* Lawrence R. Schehr, trans. Minneapolis: University of Minnesota Press, 2007.

Schmitt, Carl. *The Concept of the Political.* George Schwab, trans. Chicago: The University of Chicago Press, 1996.

Shaviro, Steven. *Without Criteria: Kant, Whitehead, Deleuze, and Aesthetics.* Cambridge, MA: The MIT Press, 2009.

Simondon, Gilbert. *L'Individuation à la lumière des notions de forme et d'information.* Millon: PUF, 2005.

Sloterdijk, Peter. *Critique of Cynical Reason.* Michael Eldred, trans. Minneapolis: University of Minnesota Press, 1987.

Spencer-Brown, G. *Laws of Form.* New York: E.P. Dutton, 1979.

Spinoza, Benedict de. *Spinoza: The Complete Works.* Samuel Shirley, trans. Indianpolis: Hackett Publishing Company, Inc., 2002.

Stengers, Isabelle. *Cosmopolitics I.* Robert Bononno, trans. Minneapolis: University of Minnesota Press, 2010.

Toscano, Alberto. *The Theatre of Production: Philosophy and Individuation Between Kant and Deleuze.* New York: Palgrave Macmillan, 2006.

Tucker, Robert, C. *The Marx-Engels Reader*. New York: Norton, 1978.

Whitehead, Alfred North. *Process and Reality*. New York: The Free Press, 1978.

Wolfe, Cary. "Bring the Noise: The Parasite and the Multiple Genealogies of Posthumanism". In Michel Serres, *The Parasite*. Minneapolis: University of Minnesota Press, 2007.

———. *Critical Environments: Postmodern Theory and the Pragmatics of the "Outside"*. Minneapolis: University of Minnesota Press, 1998.

———. *What is Posthumanism?* Minneapolis: University of Minnesota Press, 2010.

Woolf, Virginia. *Jacob's Room*. New York: Harcourt Brace & Company, 1992.

Žižek, Slavoj. *For They Know Not What They Do: Enjoyment as a Political Factor*. New York: Verso, 2002.

———. *Organs Without Bodies: On Deleuze and Consequences*. New York: Routledge, 2004.

———. *The Parallax View*. Cambridge, MA: The MIT Press, 2006.

———. *The Plague of Fantasies*. New York: Verso, 1997.

———. *The Puppet and the Dwarf: The Perverse Core of Christianity*. Cambridge, MA: The MIT Press, 2003.

———. *The Sublime Object of Ideology*. New York: Verso, 1989.

———. *Tarrying With the Negative: Kant, Hegel, and the Critique of Ideology*. Durham: Duke University Press, 1993.

———. *The Ticklish Subject: The Absent Center of Political Ontology*. New York: Verso, 1999.

Zubiri, Xavier. *On Essence*. A. Robert Caponigri, trans. Washington, D.C.: The Catholic University of America Press, 1980.

Made in the USA
Middletown, DE
08 September 2016